COUNSELING DIVERSITY IN CONTEXT

COUNSELING

DIVERSITY

IN CONTEXT

Jason Brown

UNIVERSITY OF TORONTO PRESS

Copyright © University of Toronto Press 2017
Higher Education Division

www.utppublishing.com

Library and Archives Canada Cataloguing in Publication
Brown, Jason, 1968–, author
    Counseling diversity in context / Jason Brown.

Includes bibliographical references and index.
Issued in print and electronic formats.

ISBN 978-1-4426-3530-2 (cloth).—ISBN 978-1-4426-3529-6 (paper).—ISBN 978-1-4426-3531-9 (html).—ISBN 978-1-4426-3532-6 (pdf).

1. Cross-cultural counseling. 2. Community psychology. 3. Social problems—Psychological aspects. 4. Cultural pluralism—Psychological aspects. 5. Social justice. I. Title.

BF636.7.C76B76 2017   361'.06   C2016-905199-4
                                                              C2016-905200-1

We welcome comments and suggestions regarding any aspect of our publications—please feel free to contact us at news@utphighereducation.com or visit our Internet site at www.utppublishing.com.

North America
5201 Dufferin Street
North York, Ontario, Canada, M3H 5T8

2250 Military Road
Tonawanda, New York, USA, 14150

ORDERS PHONE: 1-800-565-9523
ORDERS FAX: 1-800-221-9985
ORDERS E-MAIL: utpbooks@utpress.utoronto.ca

UK, Ireland, and continental Europe
NBN International
Estover Road, Plymouth, PL6 7PY, UK
ORDERS PHONE: 44 (0) 1752 202301

ORDERS FAX: 44 (0) 1752 202333
ORDERS E-MAIL: enquiries@nbninternational.com

Every effort has been made to contact copyright holders; in the event of an error or omission, please notify the publisher.

This book is printed on paper containing 100% post-consumer fibre.

The University of Toronto Press acknowledges the financial support for its publishing activities of the Government of Canada through the Canada Book Fund.

Printed in the United States of America.

To Shelley, Kaylee, Jenna, and Kobe

CONTENTS

PREFACE

As a boring, white, middle-class, heterosexual male, I've had many advantages. I've also been tremendously lucky. I went to university, where I amassed a major amount of debt traveling through sociology, social work, educational psychology, and counseling training. My partner is very supportive, but also pragmatic in response to my idealism and brings me down to earth when I need it most. But it is my three children who helped me realize what I'm supposed to be doing. They remind me every day that my roles as a driver, bank machine, dog walker, playmate, and occasional amateur comedian are more important than most other things in life. It is a wonderful, as well as exhausting, gig!

More to the point of this book, the mixture of influences that led to its development were the different jobs where I met people who had such different life experiences than I, the friends I made working in human service agencies and volunteering on different projects, and the teachers I had in the community and in school who taught me what I needed to know when I needed to know it.

I have been greatly influenced by friends and leaders in Indigenous communities from the Canadian Prairies and Northern Ontario. Working in communities has taught me about healthy skepticism of outsiders, especially do-gooders and researchers who were there to meet their own ends and not those of the collective. Over time, I became more sensitive to a view that sharply contrasted with the privileged, individualistic lens I was raised with: both personal and social problems were a product of severely constrained opportunities and multiple losses across generations.

Applying this understanding in a counseling context posed some difficulty. As a psychologist in corrections, I was conflicted between causes and solutions as being, on the one hand, clearly contextual and, on the other, bad (sometimes devastatingly bad) personal choices. I also struggled with a tension between the Western view of health and treatment dominant in my professional training and the culturally based spiritual healing that Indigenous

Elders provide. I came to believe that these do not need to be *either-or* decisions. They can be *both-and* decisions.

The more I reflected on the cultural differences between people, their families, and their communities and nations, the more I saw each as offering complementary strengths. This became the focus of a course developed for the Counselling Psychology Program where I work. I soon found that this view was consistently undermined by the practical realities of advantage and disadvantage. For me, this unequal playing field became the fundamental and essential content in multicultural counseling.

The idea of social justice and its applications in counseling captured my attention. The first section of this book is a review of what others have said about the topic. Within the literature, it was noted repeatedly that there was less attention to the *how* than the *why* of social justice activities in counseling. This book represents an attempt to craft an argument in support of how context influences mental health, and how professional counselors can address that context in a way that explicitly works to level the unequal playing field.

Goals

This book is written as a primary or supplementary text for helping professionals in graduate multicultural counseling courses in Canada and the United States. It offers a view of counseling practice that includes a range of ways to be involved in social change efforts. While it is recognized that these activities fall outside of the clinical efforts of most professionals, they are known approaches and techniques illustrating how social change happens that counselors, directly or indirectly, either support or challenge.

The book is divided into two sections. The first section presents an argument about how unequal context affects personal mental health. The second section outlines a sequence of steps showing that community-level change can be promoted.

In each chapter, Internet links provide current examples of community change and invite students to discuss how those contextual forces are associated with personal mental health. The discussion questions for each chapter provide a starting point for reflection about how counselors can integrate knowledge of contextual forces into their work with individual clients. The questions also point to ways that counselors may support social change outside of their professional roles and in the role of citizen.

It is hoped that as students progress through the text, they will become more critical and involved in political movements, more deliberate in professional and civic efforts that have social justice implications, attend therapeutically to social disadvantage with clients, and invite clients to utilize or create external resources and supports as appropriate.

INTRODUCTION: A SOCIOPOLITICAL PERSPECTIVE

Outline

Introduction

The past 15 years have witnessed significant and far-reaching developments in counseling about the topic of diversity. Studies on multiculturalism have attended very clearly to ways that diversity exists and interacts within individuals as well as conceptual and practical ways to attend to this diversity. The attention to ethnicity, class, and gender as important contributors to personal identity sensitizes counselors and enables them to recognize and incorporate this awareness into their practice with clients. While culturally sensitive practice has contributed to increased awareness by counselors of their own culture and identity as well as the culture and identities of their clients, the focus has remained on lateral similarities and differences across individuals and cultures.

Within multicultural counseling calls for social justice have been made. These calls necessitate awareness of not only lateral diversity through respect for and attention to cultural difference but also hierarchical diversity through recognition and attention to oppression and liberation. From such a perspective there are different experiences of power associated with membership in and identification with different cultural groups. The ways to attend to and incorporate this understanding into practice require counselors to reconsider how their own and others' social and political experiences factor in to perceived causes and appropriate interventions.

In this chapter, the concept of social justice is presented to reflect calls from within the profession for counselors to develop this understanding and consider approaches to their work that are informed by it. A brief description and history of social justice are followed by an overview of the contents of this book. The chapters that follow include ideas about counseling practice that are not only sensitive to oppression, but that also suggest how oppression may be indirectly and directly challenged by counselors within and outside of their offices.

Social justice has been suggested as the **fifth force** in counseling (Pieterse, Evans, Risner-Butner, Collins, & Mason, 2009). A social justice approach to counseling "refers to using all of the methods of counseling and psychology to confront injustice and inequality in society" (Kiselica & Robinson, 2001, p. 387). However, efforts to address injustice and inequality are not new to the profession. Indeed, the origins of career counseling, a precursor to contemporary counseling, were rooted in vocational guidance. The founder of vocational guidance, Frank Parsons, noted in 1909 that power and money were unevenly distributed in the quickly changing industrial landscape. In addition to his work through the Vocational Bureau in Boston, Parsons advocated for youth and women as well as those without financial means or housing (Hartung & Blustein, 2002).

Counseling has a social justice orientation but its expression was supplanted by the major theoretical developments influencing professional practice. The **first** of these **forces** was psychoanalysis with its emphasis on unconscious and intrapsychic determinates of psychopathology. The **second force** was cognitive with its emphasis on operational and contingent determinates of behavior. The **third force** was humanistic with its emphases on individuals' acceptance and expressions of freedom and responsibility. Attention to the social environment and relationship to intrapsychic processes became more prominent with the **fourth force** of psychotherapy, multicultural counseling.

During the 1970s cultural diversity began to appear as a topic at conferences and in the professional literature, reflecting dissatisfaction with counselors' abilities to address the needs of an increasingly diverse population. The American

Psychological Association formed a task force to develop **multicultural competencies**, which led to the production of the first document by Derald Wing Sue and colleagues in 1982. The most recent version of these competencies was approved in 2002 by the American Psychological Association's Council of Representatives and is known as the *Guidelines on Multicultural Education, Training, Research, Practice, and Organizational Change for Psychologists.*

Feminist and critical views have made major contributions that brought attention to the interrelated social and political conditions that produce disadvantage. There is growing support within counseling for practice that is sensitive and responsive to diversity. However, there has been less attention given to the use and liberating effects of culturally based psychotherapies. Additionally, the recognition of forces outside of the individual as legitimate targets of intervention by counselors has not yet been connected with actionable ideas or strategies. This book provides some ways to reconsider sociopolitical assumptions upon which counseling practice is often based and to apply social justice in counseling.

What Is a Socially Just Psychology?

Contextual factors in culturally competent counseling practice have been attended to. In the US, Sue and Sue's (2003) influential thinking on the subject has attended to individual, professional, organizational, and societal levels of intervention. In Canada, Arthur and Collins (2015) have identified the need for action by counselors to promote change to systems that negatively affect their clients. What is missing is a comprehensive account of the types and nature of sociopolitical forces, their interactions and impact on individuals and communities.

A basic premise of this book is that: (a) sociopolitical forces operate and interact with individuals in ways that (b) produce inequities, which (c) create conditions of oppression based on cultural group membership, and (d) diminish their potential for and experience of well-being. **Social justice** can be considered a deliberate effort through both intrapersonal and community interventions "to minimize oppression and injustice in favor of equality, accessibility, and optimal developmental opportunities for all members of society" (Kennedy & Arthur, 2014, p. 188).

Why Should Social Justice Matter?
Health status varies considerably based on group membership. In health care, life expectancy (Statistics Canada, 2016), self-reported health status (Alang, McCreedy, & McAlpine, 2015), and reporting of health problems (Veenstra & Patterson, 2016) each vary according to cultural group membership.

In relation to mental health, residence in the most economically challenged communities is associated with the highest levels of mental health need, but the lowest access to and utilization of services (Durbin, Moineddin, Lin, Steele, & Glazier, 2015).

Unearned privilege exists and offers several advantages (Muntaner, Ng, Vanroelen, Christ, & Eaton, 2013). The conditions into which we are born have a significant influence on how long we will live, our material circumstances, and our quality of life. Said another way, the playing field of life is unequal. The consequences of this unequal playing field tend to reproduce themselves (Porter, 2015). For example, families with high income and educational status tend to have offspring who enjoy similar advantages in their own adult lives. In order to increase opportunities for those experiencing the most disadvantage, alteration of the field itself offers potential for meaningful change.

Counseling helps individuals cope with their challenging circumstances. It can enhance intrapersonal strength to the levels at which resiliency can be activated. For some, this makes it possible to rise against conditions that oppress and move toward a more favorable set of conditions. Professionals can simultaneously promote wellness among individuals and groups through efforts to challenge oppressive sociopolitical forces. Finally, there is a substantial interest in the concept and application of social justice and **social action** among graduate students and faculty (Ali, Liu, Mahmood, & Arguello, 2008; Baluch, Pieterse, & Bolden, 2004; Beer, Spanierman, Greene, & Todd, 2012; Brown, Collins, & Arthur, 2014; Constantine, Hage, Kindaichi, & Bryant, 2007; Goodman, Liang, Helms, Latta, Sparks, & Weintraub, 2004; Miller & Sendrowitz, 2011; Palmer & Parish, 2008; Pieterse, Evans, Risner-Butner, Collins, & Mason, 2009; Singh, Hofsess, Boyer, Kwong, Lau, McLain, & Haggins, 2010).

Can Social Justice Be Incorporated into Practice?

A significant barrier to the implementation of social justice in counseling is identifying what it is and how to do it. It is important to distinguish social justice conceptually from multicultural counseling. Multicultural counseling attends to notions of inclusion and acceptance of diversity, while social justice focuses on oppression and the marginalization that occurs as a consequence of it (Pieterse, Evans, Risner-Butner, Collins, & Mason, 2009). Relatively little attention has been paid to the conceptual and practical application of social justice for counselors (Winter & Hanley, 2015). It has been noted (Pieterse, Evans, Risner-Butner, Collins, & Mason, 2009) that "if counsellors and counseling psychologists are indeed seeking to accept social justice as a central aspect of their training and identity, current efforts to address social justice at the level of counseling psychology and training may be inadequate or not clearly articulated" (p. 109).

Fortunately, there are models that can be drawn from that include underlying principles, counselor development, and outcomes of social justice. Based on multicultural, feminist, and critical psychology, underlying principles have been identified (Goodman, Liang, Helms, Latta, Sparks, & Weintraub, 2004). These principles include: (a) self-examination, (b) sharing power, (c) giving voice, (d) raising consciousness, (e) using a strengths focus, and (f) providing tools for personal and social change. Requisites for this work are located in (a) self-awareness, (b) awareness of client, (c) integration of this awareness into working alliances, and (d) social action to influence systems (Arthur & Collins, 2015). Finally, specific efforts associated with this awareness by counselors may include: (a) challenging oppression, (b) empowering communities, (c) engaging in political advocacy, as well as (d) promoting a social justice agenda in professional associations (Palmer & Parish, 2008).

Should Social Justice Be Incorporated into Practice?

Some professionals are reluctant to engage in social action, and for good reason (Helms, 2003). First, efforts on behalf of or in partnership with disadvantaged communities are rarely funded. The reality is that many counselors have debt after years of study, and all have bills to pay. Second, community and political action threaten the perception by some of the "value free" status of the profession. However, as will be considered later in this book, counseling and its professional organizations are neither value neutral nor disconnected from the sociopolitical forces in play. Third, those who associate community action with ideas and activists on the political left may reject it as too radical. Fourth, social justice takes a great deal of time and energy with unpredictable results. Such efforts can be tiring and take energy away from pursuits that offer needed balance in a demanding line of work. Finally, such efforts can raise the profile of counselors who may be viewed as critical of colleagues, employers, or funders which could threaten their professional practice.

Taking Up the Challenge

From a social justice perspective, however, the ways counselors view themselves, clients, and communities, as well as their roles and responsibilities in relation to each, may be challenged. For example, who really benefits from our work? Does our work make a difference where a difference really matters (Miller & Sendrowitz, 2011)? This perspective also pressures counselors to recognize themselves as cultural people who experience privilege and oppression and occupy different positions on the unequal playing field. Once counselors have engaged in that work, they can more readily recognize the cultural identities, lives, and experiences of clients as both unique as well as similar and different from their own.

A socially just counseling practice is based in the counselor's abilities to recognize, engage, and connect through similarity and across difference. It also requires service through therapeutic as well as external work. Perhaps the most challenging aspect of a social justice perspective is to consider how interrelated the personal and professional lives of counselors are and how they may contribute to an unjust status quo. In addition, there is a challenge to be politically conscious and deliberate in both social action and inaction.

Ethical and Professional Responsibilities

Conflicting opinions exist about the evidence in support of social justice within the major codes of ethics. However, the American Psychological Association and the Canadian Psychological Association reflect awareness and commitment to social justice, as evidenced by their principles of equity, access, participation, and harmony. There is, however, no commitment to social action (Winter, 2015).

Professionally, the topic of justice has been a focus of attention and Prilleltensky (2013) offers a convincing argument in support of the need for fairness to achieve wellness. While the societies in which we live focus on merit to promote fairness, it is argued that because of the unequal playing field, the principle of need should be favored. Prilleltensky goes on to argue that individuals, communities, and societies can and should have maximum wellness that does not come at another's expense. A worthy ethical and professional pursuit is to learn to practice in a multicultural, multiethnic, multi-faith, multi-sexual, multi-racial, multi-gendered, and multi-abled society (Moodley & Palmer, 2014; Moodley & Kinha, 2015).

In this book, readers are invited to consider their practice with individuals experiencing oppression as well as ways they might engage in external work to target sociopolitical forces that both disadvantage and advantage cultural groups.

Structure and Overview of the Book

This book is divided into two sections: "Understanding the Context" and "Changing the Context." In the first section, an argument in support of a sociopolitical view of mental health and professional counseling practice is made. In the second section, ways that professional counselors can support community level change are offered.

"Understanding the Context," Chapters 1–4, begins with an introduction to sociopolitical forces and their relationship to personal wellness. Attention is then drawn to personal and professional values and beliefs associated with the topics of oppression and liberation. Finally, ways that oppression and liberation may be attended to in counseling practice are considered.

In Chapter 1, the focus is on recognition that the training counselors receive is contextually situated. A focus on intrapersonal change through altering perspective or interpreting present or early life experiences and thoughts or behaviors often does not recognize the sociopolitical context within which it occurs. This sociopolitical context offers great potential for considering forces that contribute to wellness of communities and individuals.

In Chapter 2, the emphasis is on the sociopolitical nature of mental health. Evidence concerning population trends in wellness are juxtaposed against the limitations of institutionalized medicine that narrowly define health as illness to prescribe treatment for symptoms. The range of contributors to wellness offers areas within which change that affects many can be made. Because sociopolitical disadvantage at the population level is associated with psychological effects at the individual level, a psychological perspective on oppression and liberation is offered.

In Chapter 3, attention is turned to the counselor. The values and beliefs that guide the practice of counselors are a mixture of political, professional, and personal. Counselors who are aware of the experiences they have in relation to privilege and oppression, similarity and difference, as well as inclusion and exclusion can take deliberate actions in accordance with their views. Views about society and its citizens, professions and professionals, as well as the roles counselors fill contribute either to sociopolitical change or maintaining the status quo.

In Chapter 4, attention is focused on culturally based psychologies and their contributions to wellness. Counseling practice in a sociopolitical context may itself be oppressive when it reinforces dominant views concerning causes and interventions for mental health on an individual who identifies with and experiences life from a non-dominant cultural worldview. Cultural psychologies are clearly located in specific worldviews that may be appropriate for understanding and working sensitively and effectively with clients who identify with them.

"Changing the Context," Chapters 5–10, begins with a conceptual model that links sociopolitical awareness to community change. Forces that impact communities are considered before a review of major approaches, applications, and tactics of community change. A model for community change is offered as a way for counselors to identify processes and determine their desired level and type of involvement. Specific examples of community change are presented and followed by a distillation of principles that demonstrate their application within organizations and programs. Finally, considerations for evaluation of community change efforts are presented.

In Chapter 5, a conceptual model is presented that incorporates socio-political forces of oppression and liberation with individual psychological experience via cultural identity. The purpose of the model is to link individual, personal psychological well-being with sociopolitical determinates of health. The concept of intersectionality is invoked to explain how cultural identities can be claimed by an individual as well as represent collective experiences of group members. In this model, individual and community wellness share a common basis from which interventions can follow.

In Chapter 6, the focus is on community as a target of intervention. Major sociopolitical forces that affect communities are presented to highlight contributors and detractors from collective empowerment. The concept of social capital is used to characterize interrelationships between members that represent a source of power. Power is suggested to be a force that operates to maintain the status quo as well as create change.

In Chapter 7, the emphasis is conceptual, concerning ways that commu-nity change can be pursued. The efforts of leaders in community change are profiled to illustrate different approaches, such as development, planning, and action. The benefits and drawbacks of each are presented as are the condi-tions under which each is favored. Current models of practice for community change offer a range of possibilities for incorporating one or more approaches for collective benefit. Specific tactics are also presented.

In Chapter 8, the focus is practical and includes steps that could be followed to promote community change. It is emphasized that counselors armed with this understanding about a process of community change can be deliberate in their level of participation at different phases of the process. For each type of participa-tion, the potential benefits and drawbacks are considered. Ethical issues that could be encountered by counselors involved in community work are also identified.

In Chapter 9, examples of community change efforts are presented. The types of change range from a single issue and single approach to multiple related issues and approaches. The application of community change processes and skills can be extended to work within organizations and in program devel-opment. The same principles of community-based, asset-oriented approaches that are grounded in cultural awareness and appropriateness apply to work outside of organizations, organization building, organizational change, as well as the development of new initiatives and group-based services.

In **Chapter 10**, the topic of evaluation is considered. Change at community levels, organizations, and programs, as with change experienced by individuals in counseling, can be similarly assessed. The scope, method, and topic varies according to the purpose, needs, and resources of the evaluator. However, similar principles apply.

Conclusion

Social justice instructs practitioners to attend to the personal effects of social hierarchies produced by inequality. From such a view, counseling contributes to the creation and promotion of equal opportunities for participation by all citizens of a society. It is argued that without social change, limits on personal change for those who are most disadvantaged are neither adequate nor sustainable. As well, without a view to social justice, professional efforts may actually preserve the status quo and reinforce inequitable social positions.

Discussion Questions

1. What is an appropriate basis of a "just society"? Consider the ideas of both merit (benefits based on performance) and need (benefits based on opportunity). In a just society, what is the fairest basis for decision making and outcomes?
2. Social justice has a long history outside of psychology. What do you think of when you read about social justice? Is your reaction to the idea positive, negative, or mixed? Does it have any place in the counseling profession? Why or why not?
3. Are all problems that are brought to the attention of a counselor the result of living in an unjust society? Why or why not?
4. Counselors have a primary ethical and professional responsibility to the clients they work with. What should counselors do when they and their client locate the source of his or her problem as outside of himself or herself?

Web Links

- Counselors for Social Justice (American Counseling Association)
  https://counseling-csj.org
- Counsellors for Social Justice (Canadian Counselling and Psychotherapy Association)
  https://www.ccpa-accp.ca/Chapters/social-justice/
- Women and Psychology Section (Canadian Psychological Association)

http://www.cpa.ca/cpasite/UserFiles/Documents/publications/
guidelines%20for%20psychological%20practice%20women.pdf
- Aboriginal Psychology Section (Canadian Psychological Association)
http://www.cpa.ca/aboutcpa/cpasections/aboriginalpsychology
- The Society for the Psychological Study of Social Issues (American
Psychological Association)
https://www.spssi.org/index.cfm?fuseaction=Page.viewPage&pageId=
483&parentID=479

Key Terms

fifth force

first force

second force

third force

fourth force

multicultural competencies

social justice

social action

PART ONE

Understanding the Context

In Chapter 1 through 4, it is argued that social status is interconnected with personal well-being through culture. Said another way, cultural differences exist within a social hierarchy. The groups each person identifies with reflect not only differences in values, beliefs, and practices, but different levels and means of social and political influence. A sociopolitical perspective illuminates these differences as well as the forces that create and sustain them. In the interest of more substantial and long-term benefit of counseling for mental wellness among clients and communities, this knowledge can be incorporated into professional practice that confronts oppression. For example, poverty is an oppressive force. Those who experience poverty may internalize social messages about one's worth and capacity in ways that become self-oppressing. Counselors, in addition to assisting clients with the recognition of and alteration to internalized judgments, recognize the need for social and political change in ways that produce equal opportunities for the full participation of all citizens. How social and political change is to be undertaken is tied to the personal awareness of a counselor and reflects her or his own experiences of advantage and disadvantage as well as the source and role of assistance outside of self and family. As citizens, counselors have the power to act and the ability to do so responsibly. As professionals, however, counselors make an ethical commitment to the personal well-being of each person in a society. Culturally specific psychologies are professional expressions of power and influence the roles and activities of counselors. They are united in the intention to reduce inequity through the personal and collective liberation of members of historically oppressed groups.

CHAPTER 1

A SOCIOPOLITICAL PERSPECTIVE

Chapter Outline

Counselors are trained in different helping traditions. Each tradition is attentive to power in the therapeutic relationship. However, the sociopolitical forces that exist in the context within which we and our clients live are often not addressed. Counselor education typically focuses on the processes and means to assist clients in changing their experiences through internal work. This is important but not the only way that counselors can help. What is suggested in this chapter is that counselors consider the influence of sociopolitical context with a view to power differentials in the lives of clients. Counselors may enhance their practice through recognition of the importance of environment as a contributor to personal challenges and wellness as well as a worthy and achievable target for change.

The chapter begins with an overview of the intentions for a sociopolitical perspective of counseling practice before moving to an example to illustrate the central ideas within such a view. In subsequent sections, through a brief presentation of several key concepts, the potential for considering this view in counseling practice is offered.

Social and Political Forces in Counseling

Much has been written in counseling about theories of personality and change processes. Theories have focused on the individual as the primary recipient and agent of change. The focus has been, in large part, on the remediation of psychological problems. There has also been great attention to methods created and used within psychology. From such a view diversity reflects difference. However, it is lateral difference. It is assumed that all members of a society have equal opportunities. Taking this view further, there is also an assumption that all approaches to psychological diagnosis and intervention take into equal account a similar range of problems. The environment is relegated to the role of context and reduced to a constant seen to produce similar effects on members of all groups. Fundamental theories that underlie approaches to intervention, albeit with modifications in language and symbols to make them culturally sensitive, apply equally well to members of all cultural groups. The cultures and positions of those who make major contributions to theory and practice are not explicit and potential limitations to applicability with other cultural groups not thoroughly explored.

This emphasis has led to practice that does not specifically attend to the hierarchical relationships that exist between, as well as within, groups in a diverse society. The equal opportunity view locates problems that come to the attention of counselors as deficits residing within the individual. As such, there has been less attention to capacities and strengths or to an approach that holds the promotion of wellness and personal responsibility in the highest regard. Notwithstanding the importance of agency and free will, a sociopolitical perspective widens the level of responsibility to also include the collective. The environment, from such a perspective, is viewed as more than a context for functioning. It is a major determinate of illness and wellness.

What could counseling practice look like if professionals were to attend specifically to sociopolitical forces that create and contribute to the relative advantage and disadvantage of groups and individuals? Sociopolitical forces include both social and political factors. Social factors are those that influence the development, organization, and function of societies. Political factors are those that influence government, decision making, and participation. In a multicultural society diversity represents coexistence of many different cultural groups. However, cultural groups are not equal. Each group has a relative status in relation to each other group. While some may occupy similar levels of social and political influence, others are particularly advantaged or disadvantaged.

Consider race and ethnicity as examples. These statuses are associated with differential economic and political influence. There are significant differences in both Canada and the United States in average income that reflect growing disparity along racial and ethnic lines. There is increasing separation between those at the top of the income distribution and those at the bottom. When one factors in race and ethnicity, groups are differentially represented at levels of the income hierarchy (Shapiro, Meschede, & Osoro, 2013). Such differences reflect political power in relation to participation in local governance (Giger, Rosset, & Bernauer, 2012). Members of more affluent groups have a greater likelihood of involvement and influence in societal affairs.

From a sociopolitical perspective the possibilities beyond typical counseling practice can be explored for their potential value to a client. This perspective also includes the recognition that a valid target for change may exist outside of the client and the counseling office.

Consider the differences between typical counseling practice and a sociopolitical view of practice in the following case example.

Case Example

You are an intern at a university counseling center. You receive a new referral named Mary. The client is a 28-year-old woman who identifies as a First Nations person. She is in her first year of general arts studies and her parents live in a northern fly-in community. Mary lives with her aunt and uncle in the city. Mary worries constantly and is having trouble sleeping. Her studies have suffered, her grades are falling, and she is questioning her decision to attend university.

What comes to mind when you think about your meeting with this woman? What might you want to know and how do you think you can help?

A typical assessment might focus on the possibilities for a diagnosis of a mood or anxiety disorder. Suicide risk and a safety plan would be performed if appropriate. A referral for a medical or psychiatric consultation may be made. Treatment could include assertiveness training, activity scheduling, or an anxiety education group.

From a sociopolitical perspective additional possibilities may be explored. These would be expressed both in terms of getting to know the client and her worldview as well as recognizing the sources of challenges in her environment. In addition, interventions outside of the client and counseling office may be considered.

Personal history would emphasize knowing her as a person, as a member of a family and a community. As well, it would be important to know what experiences led her to university and what it means to her, her family, and her community to be a student. Although culture is embedded throughout, it would be essential to ask about her worldview.

Locating the problem using a sociopolitical perspective would recognize the effects of historical and current experiences originating in the environment but felt internally. It would be important to explore the potential role of historical trauma in her difficulties. It would also be important to locate her cultural strengths. Her experiences as a First Nations person in an institution where the educators and education are not reflective of her experiences and ways of knowing could be turned inward to form negative judgments about herself. Counseling interventions stemming from the recognition of trauma and potential for internalized oppression may be considered. Culturally based healing by someone with the appropriate training and expertise, either in place of or in combination with counseling, may be appropriate.

Interventions outside of the client and the counseling office could attend to the need for membership and participation in a community with the collective strength such affiliation provides. The role of the counselor may follow from recognition of the needs on campus of First Nations students and direct involvement or support for initiatives led by First Nations students for First Nations students. Student organizing for institutional support and change would be viewed as essential to promote healthy development, buffer challenges, and work toward positive change of policies or practices that disadvantage First Nations students.

Concepts related to a sociopolitical perspective for counseling build on and extend research in psychology and other disciplines. The purpose for introducing these concepts here is to provide a basis from which diversity and power can be viewed as interrelated ideas that together vertically extend environmental and ecological perspectives in counseling.

Culture

Culture is a broad and encompassing term. It is also a fundamental idea and essential topic in the consideration of group membership and identity. There are limitations to its use as a basis for comparison, such as the overlap between cultures and among members who simultaneously belong to more than one cultural group and in differing amounts or who change affiliations. However, shared experiences among members of a group identify members in meaningful ways. These ways have been extensively studied. Some significant ways of defining culture are presented in the sections that follow.

Culture (Pedersen & Lonner, 2015) can be understood as five concentric spheres of influence from largest to smallest, including the universal, ecological, national, regional, and racio-ethnic. Universal culture is based on the recognition that as human beings each of us is determined and influenced by the same physiology. Ecological culture stems from the climate, vegetation, animals, and seasonal changes of the places we are born and live. National culture refers to the effects of governments, languages, and institutions. Regional culture is a local culture within the national culture. Racio-ethnic culture is the culture within which individuals outside of the dominant race or ethnic group reside. Each person simultaneously participates in each of these cultures, which are forces over which she or he has little to no control.

Within each of these layers there are values, beliefs, institutions, and artifacts that have meaning for each group's members (Spencer-Oatey, 2012). The **values** include fundamental beliefs about important matters, such as the origin of life and the purpose of existence (Cuddy et al., 2015). Related to this topic, and of importance in this book, is the purpose and meaning of suffering and its remediation. **Norms** refer to standards of conduct that are seen as appropriate and respectable among members of a group (Frese, 2015). Central importance is attached to the morality and immorality of particular kinds of conduct based on notions of what is right and wrong. Some of these are encoded into laws or minimum standards, which are basic, while others are aspirational and held up as worthy of achievement. **Institutions** are the organizations that are meaningful to the group (Grusec & Hastings, 2014). These institutions are formal, such as religious collectives, as well as informal, such as the family. They are of varying significance but importance cannot be determined based on whether the institution is formal or informal. Some informal institutions are more important than those that are formally designated. Finally, **artifacts** are the outcomes that the culture produces, which are tangible evidence of its existence and its creations (Goldstein, 2015). These can be shared or private, sacred or secular, physical or intellectual, but have some significance to the group and are its creation or by-product.

Psychology and counseling reflect culturally embedded concepts and practices. Culture is present in definitions of wellness and illness as well as understandings of why and how each occurs. Historically, culture in psychology was a universalist view of individuals and groups who could be compared based on how much or little of each of the same qualities they possessed or represented. While this view simplified the way that culture was considered, it missed out on important qualities of experience that were part of several cultures or a single culture. Most damaging, however, was the misrepresentation of psychology as culturally neutral when it reflected the cultures of its contributors. Such criticism led to the development of cultural psychologies constructed explicitly from particular cultural perspectives to represent experiences of groups and individuals who are members of that culture.

The relationship between culture and psychology can be viewed in different ways. From one perspective, psychology, with its theories and principles, is universal. In this view the same ideas are thought to reflect the experiences of all individuals though perhaps in different degrees. This field of study is known as cross-cultural psychology. From another perspective, psychology reflects differences across cultural groups within which each member possesses similar qualities. This is one view within the field of cultural psychology. Another view within the field of cultural psychology is that the nature of psychology itself, or its equivalent within a culture, is constructed and understood by that culture for that culture. In the sections that follow examples of each are provided.

Cross-Cultural Psychology

The purpose of cross-cultural psychology is to determine the reach of psychological concepts and constructs into cultures other than those from which they were initially developed (Draguns, 2013). The practice includes the measurement of traits thought to be universal. This is rooted in differential psychology which is the study of ways that individuals differ from one another in relation to common factors. For example, research into the "Big Five" personality traits has produced considerable evidence in support of their existence (Cobb-Clark & Schurer, 2012; Joshanloo & Afshari, 2011; Migliore, 2011). These traits include openness to experience, conscientiousness, extroversion, agreeableness, and neuroticism (Leutner, Ahmetoglu, Akhtar, & Chamorro-Premuzic, 2014). **Openness to experience** refers to curiosity and openness to creativity, while **conscientiousness** speaks to order and logic of conduct. **Extroversion** includes an outgoing and sociable approach to life, while **agreeableness** refers to compassionate understanding of others. **Neuroticism** refers to sensitivity and vulnerability to worries, doubts, and fears. From this perspective, every person functions somewhere on a range from low to high on each of these traits that, together, represent a universal set of experiences. Research has found that these ideas have varying levels of generalizability across cultures. Importantly, their significance and meaning for individuals and groups varies considerably. For example, the extent to which the trait of extroversion is

relevant and meaningful to a Buddhist monk in Tibet would be very different than to a salesperson in New York City.

Some research on national cultures organizes values on continua. A well-
known model is Hofstede's cultural dimensions, which has its origins in
the 1960s comparing IBM employees in different countries. The dimensions in this model include experience and expression in relation to
individualism-collectivism, high-low power distance, short-long term orientation, and indulgence-restraint (Minkov & Hofstede, 2011). **Individualism
and collectivism** refer to orientations to others and the reference points
for major decisions in life. Individualist cultures focus on the individual as
the main unit of society while collectivist cultures focus on the group as the
main unit of society, leading to decisions with reference to the experience
of one versus decisions with reference to the experience of many. **High and
low power difference** refers to the degree of perceived difference within a
culture between those at the top and those at the bottom of the social hierarchy. For cultures with low power difference, a hierarchy does not exist, while
for cultures with high power difference, the differences between levels of a
hierarchy are significant and have implications for the people at each level
as well as interactions between individuals at different levels. **Short- and
long-term orientation** refers to the scope with which members of that
culture view the future. Short-term orientation takes a narrow scope focusing on the lifetime of the viewer, while a long-term orientation takes a broad
scope to view the effects across another generation or more. **Indulgence
and restraint** refer to the extent to which cultures speak to the relationship
between thought and action. Members of high indulgence cultures are more
action oriented and members of high restraint cultures are more thought
oriented. While these dimensions have some limitations in their generalizability, the more significant challenge to their use is the lack of attention to
cultural variation within nations.

Cultural Psychologies

A major criticism of cross-cultural approaches to psychology has been the
extent to which constructs and mechanisms developed by one cultural group
have been uncritically applied to others. For example, both the "Big Five"
and "Cultural Dimensions" were developed in the United States using a
natural science approach to research. In contrast to cross-cultural psychology,
cultural psychology (Ratner, 2012) focuses on qualities and characteristics of
phenomena that characterize members of a cultural group (Wyer, Chiu, &
Hong, 2013). The purpose is not to compare cultures, but rather to represent the psychology of a particular culture (Mohatt, Fok, Burket, Henry, &
Allen, 2011).

Different psychologies have been developed by different groups to represent central ideas and functions. The examples that follow represent major culturally based contributions to psychology and counseling. A more detailed discussion of each appears in Chapter 4. The introduction here is to illustrate and situate these approaches within different relationships between culture and psychology. **Feminist psychology** is a cultural psychology that conceptualizes gender issues as a fundamental basis for all ideas stemming from the study of mind (Eagly, Eaton, Rose, Riger, & McHugh, 2012). A basis of feminist psychology is the study of what is typical and problematic from women's perspectives. The notion of patriarchy as a social force and source of oppression makes important contributions to the nature of all other psychological phenomena, such as power and control (Cole, Rothblum, & Chesler, 2014).

Indigenous psychology refers to the psychology that a particular culture, within a particular geographic area, defines by itself for itself. It is distinguished by the use of methods of study that are culturally meaningful. For example, not only are specific cultural experiences represented as core concepts, but they are also identified as using approaches that are appropriate, such as storytelling as opposed to surveys or focus groups (Yang, 2012). Indigenous psychology has focused on the concept of the mind and its relationship to daily life, as well as strengths, problems, and solutions (Hwang, 2011). Aboriginal psychology is an Indigenous psychology insofar as its meaning and use was developed by the Aboriginal community for the Aboriginal community. As an Indigenous psychology, Aboriginal psychology uses knowledge that is culturally based and culturally obtained. A more detailed description of Aboriginal psychology as a culturally based psychology is presented in Chapter 4.

Diversity

Diversity refers to extent of difference between individuals and groups along cultural dimensions (Diller, 2014). Identity is the sense of self and degree of attribution that one places in various contributors to that sense of self (Paniagua, 2013). These contributors can be based in gender, race, class, sexual orientation, disability, and religion. They also co-act and interact. Most people identify with several cultures and associate with others on the basis of similarities and differences. From this view, all human interactions occur across cultures.

Consider the example of Linda, a new office employee. She has a hearing impairment. From a cross-cultural perspective, diversity occurs in relation to the importance or frequency of a set of common qualities or characteristics of interest. For example, the study of disability from this perspective could focus on the type and extent of hearing impairment relative to not having a hearing impairment. From a cultural psychology view, diversity has a particular meaning and importance within a particular context. The study of disability from this perspective could focus on the experience of having a hearing impairment in a highly verbal workplace. From an Indigenous perspective, in addition to meaning within a particular context, the methods by which the information is obtained are rooted in the culture. The focus on having a hearing impairment in a highly verbal workplace may necessitate the use of American Sign Language (ASL), if acceptable to the participant, through which to interact with and represent others.

It is essential to recognize that knowledge and extent of identification within different cultures varies as well. Four statuses that have been described as processes and outcomes when one is exposed to a new culture include assimilation, separation, integration, and marginalization (Ward & Kus, 2012). **Assimilation** refers to the absorption of the new culture and withdrawal from existing affiliations and identifications. **Separation** is the experience of maintaining boundaries between the previous and the new. **Integration** refers to the inclusion of new experiences within one's sense of self and a merging of the new into the old. **Marginalization** is a complete withdrawal from both the new and existing affiliations and identifications into a state of non-identification, which is the most isolating state. To continue with the example of an individual with a hearing impairment in a highly verbal workplace, Linda could choose to assimilate by participating verbally through training and support or equipment if appropriate (e.g. cochlear implant), by learning to lip read, or by improving her hearing and oral communication abilities. She could separate by maintaining a distinction for herself between her workplace, where she uses speech-to-text technology (e.g. Ava app), and her family and community, where she does not use that equipment or those skills. Integration could include incorporating both equipment and skills for improved hearing and oral communication with her family and at the same time using ASL at work. The most concerning possibility is that Linda decides that because of the differences at work and home, she cannot separate or blend them and chooses instead to withdraw from both settings.

When faced with a new culture, represented through interaction with an individual, group, or entire community, the novelty or differences may become apparent. The differences can be subtle or overt and may include the feeling that one is being carefully watched and scrutinized, or being told that there are "ways that things are done around here." The choices of responding to difference vary considerably between individuals and groups, but possible ways they are interpreted may include distancing, denial, defensiveness, devaluing, or discovery (Sue, 2013). **Distancing** refers to the desire to use psychological or physical boundaries to separate oneself from others, while **denial** refers to the focus on sameness that overrides evidence of difference. **Defensiveness** refers to the need to protect oneself from the potential influence of the other, and **devaluing** is to consider one's own perspective as more appropriate or correct than the one held by another. **Discovery** refers to the curiosity about the difference and the other as well as receptivity to what can be learned from the encounter. Continuing with the workplace example, staff members could choose to distance by avoiding interactions with Linda or denying the difference by greeting her like any other new employee despite her difficulty hearing the greeting. A defensive position may be to consider reasons why this new employee did not fit in that "have nothing to do with her hearing impairment." A devaluing response might be to "feel sorry" for her, despite her lack of such feelings toward herself, and believe that she is not like the other staff. Discovery may lead one to seek out from her and knowledgeable others appropriate ways to interact with her across the difference and then together find ways that work effectively for communication.

It is a challenge to recognize these ways of responding to difference within ourselves, and to be brutally honest with ourselves about what we believe and how we choose to act. A framework that can be used to explore our reactions and develop awareness is the **Johari window**. It was developed in 1955 by Joseph Luft and Harry Ingham as a means to improve communication in the workplace. The window includes four statuses that refer to layers of awareness that are represented by known or not known to self or others (Gibson, 2012). The statuses of Arena and Façade refer to the self-awareness that is shown (Arena) or hidden (Façade) from others. The statuses of **Blind Spot** and Unknown refer to the absence of self-awareness that is apparent (Blind Spot) or absent (Unknown) to others. Using the example of employee reactions to difference in the workplace, the Arena is what is apparent to others. Avoidance (distancing), overfriendliness (denial), scheming (defensiveness), or devaluing (pity) may be apparent to self in the workplace. One could also have these reactions and work to hide them from others using the Façade. When one in the workplace recognizes the reactions that are apparent to others (i.e., pretending it is business as usual, but avoiding the area around the office where the new staff person is located), they are in the blind spot. When one's reactions are hidden from both others and self, they are unknown. An example of this might be evident in a staff person putting effort into planning an "excuse" for not wanting to take basic ASL training. What is important about this concept is that over time and experience, the Unknown category can diminish in size and as it does, leads to further development of Façade or Blind Spot. Over time through feedback, the Arena is strengthened to eventually become the largest area (Slaby, 2014).

Competence

Cultural competence has become an important concept in psychology and counseling. It has been developed as a series of stages, competencies, and relationships (Diller, 2014; Trompenaars, 2012). In terms of stages, cultural competence is represented by **cultural destructiveness** (e.g., get rid of difference), **cultural incapacity** (e.g., difference is wrong), **cultural blindness** (e.g., there are no differences), **cultural pre-competence** (e.g., notice difference but act inappropriately), **cultural competence** (e.g., notice and value difference), as well as **cultural proficiency** (e.g., adapt to difference) (Cross, 2008). Cultural competence includes self-awareness as well as awareness of the other and sensitivity of interventions to the other as delivered by a self-aware practitioner (Kirmayer et al., 2012). As a quality of relationships, cultural competence has its basis in trust and respect as well as agreement on goals and tasks.

There is a danger in perceiving self, therapies, or organizations as culturally competent. This designation implies that an outcome has been achieved. The achievement of cultural competence has been challenged by the notion of **cultural humility** in counseling (Hook, Davis, Owen, Worthington, & Utsey, 2013). Cultural humility is other-oriented rather than self-oriented (Kirmayer, 2012). It is a commitment to continuous learning, explicit recognition of the power imbalances between counselors and their clients, as well as advocacy for their clients through partnerships with agencies and organizations that represent their interests (Waters & Asbill, 2013). It is a process and not an outcome (Gallardo, 2013). Extending the workplace example further, a counselor working with a staff member who struggled with the potential of changing his practice to accommodate the needs of his new co-worker with a hearing impairment may start at cultural incapacity. Recognition that difference is neither wrong nor right but rather the new reality of his workplace could become a focus for his ability to cope. If he was able to recognize that the new co-worker could teach him about her experience, from which he could learn to be more aware and empathetic, he would reflect a culturally humble attitude.

Power

From a sociopolitical perspective, power has been defined several ways. It may refer to the capacity to move people in a desired direction to accomplish some end (Homan, 2015). Power can also be the ability to realize one's values in the world (Robinson & Hanna, 1994). It could be the ability to accomplish one's will with and without opposition (Rubin & Rubin, 2008). Power has been defined as the capacity of some persons to produce intended and fore-seen effects on others (Wrong, 1968) as well as the ability to prevent someone from doing something she or he wants to do (Bradshaw, Soifer, & Gutierrez, 1994). In counseling, power is assumed to exist and, to varying extents and in varying directionalities, is a necessary ingredient in the helping and change processes (Kirschenbaum, 2015). However, there are significant power dynamics that also operate between and within cultural groups outside of the coun-seling office (Porter, 2015). These dynamics affect the nature of the challenge encountered and reinforce differences and hierarchies in the community and society within which a client lives.

For the purposes of this book, power is something a person or orga-nization possesses and is willing to use. It involves a sense of purpose or intention to meet a need or achieve a benefit. It is neither good nor bad but it is a requisite for action. The judgment of power can be made based on the intended use and benefit but not on its existence or utility. Power is situ-ational. It is not just what one has or represents personally or collectively, but what is represented by other parties at a particular time for a particular purpose. It can be used equally to dominate, manipulate, coerce, collaborate, share, and cooperate.

Power can take different forms. These forms reflect ways that individu-als experience and use it. What makes it an essential topic for social justice in counseling is that the power differences counselors are attentive to in the counseling room are equally present within the relationships clients have with people outside of the counseling room. From this perspective, power is an important component of the counseling relationship that should be explic-itly addressed. It is also a force that can be identified within all relationships and strengthened to bring about both personal and sociopolitical change. For example, consider the experience of a 20-year-old father named Liam who chooses to raise his infant child after his relationship with the mother ended. He may feel discouraged, unsupported, and criticized for his choice to be a stay-at-home dad. When Liam listens to and believes those messages, his abil-ity to combat them is diminished. When he recognizes his own potential to influence those messages around him, he is more capable of doing what he believes is best for his child.

Personal bases of power include awareness, values, skills, information, and purpose (Beetham, 2013). **Awareness** is what one brings of self into the situ-ation: the awareness of one's own strengths and weaknesses as well as of how her or his presence is likely to be, and indeed is, experienced by others. In the above example, Liam recognizes that messages about his choice to stay at home reflect what some others think, and his choice and success make their own message to others he comes into contact with. **Values** refer to those beliefs about morality and what is right and wrong that are expressed in what is important and valued as well as what is unimportant and devalued. From the same example, Liam is valuing what his child needs and, although it is not what others of his gender and age are doing, showing that it is "the right thing" to do. **Skills** are the knowledge and techniques that are developed through personal experiences as well as professional education and training. From the example, Liam is developing his skills to be a responsive and caring parent. **Information** is what one knows about an area that is relevant to the issue at hand, and purpose is both formally stated and informally enacted reasons for being involved and participating in the actions taken. Finally, Liam is developing knowledge about what is needed and available to men in his community who decide to be the primary caregivers for their children.

Group-Based Power

While personal bases of power can be recognized and enhanced, the power to influence sociopolitical conditions requires collective efforts. Groups hold considerable power. Continuing with the example of the 20-year-old father, as he develops his knowledge about what is needed and available to men in his community who are parenting he will be better positioned to bring people together on this issue. It would be important for him to examine the groups-based power sources they would be facing and could develop. In a group there may be several different types of power including reward, coercive, legitimate, referent, expert, and informational (Pierro, Raven, Amato, & Bélanger, 2013). **Coercion** is effort to gain compliance through force. This may be recognized in the absence of services for young men who are parenting. Although not a clear example of force, the absence of support would be experienced as isolating and exerting pressure to conform. **Reward** power is the ability to provide something tangible or to withdraw it. Recognition of the need to acknowledge young men who are single parents would be an example of reward power. **Legitimate** power is what is delivered through a socially sanctioned process. In this example, the presence of community support and social services that were sensitive and helpful would be sources of legitimate power. **Referent** power refers to the effort that one's associations have collectively. In this example, the potential to develop alliances with professional, community, or political groups could help to bring awareness and support to his and other men's experiences. **Expert** power is based on the knowledge or skills that are possessed. Continuing the same example, the ability to have experienced caregiving in the absence of support or social recognition and his development of an awareness of what was needed and how it could be achieved would provide him with this kind of power.

Informational power is based in the means to guard or share information needed or desired by others. From the same sources as his expertise, his ability to have and share information with others could be very powerful (Naples, 2012).

Professional Power

While the locations and types of individual- and group-based power are important to recognize and develop in the interests of change that benefits clients, professionals also have access to several types and forms of power. Counselors have legitimate power through professional memberships, expert power because of their training, and informational power as gatekeepers of important information. These types of power are manifested in prestige, income, and occupation. They can also be used to bring awareness of issues to their professional groups and draw attention to the issues through professional communications. The ability to draw expert attention to an issue can also lend some credibility to it in the eyes of others. A professional counselor could exercise informational power by writing a newspaper piece on the plight of young single fathers to bring awareness to the issue. It is essential though that counselors recognize the importance of acting *with* their clients so as not to take or slow the development of personal power to change conditions. An example of this might be the counselor who takes it upon himself to approach a local agency on behalf of a client without first being clear with the client and himself about the purpose, need, and benefits for the client and the community. It is essential to remain aware of the power that clients can access or bring based on their own group memberships. Families, networks, and constituencies can be equally important sources of power. Finally, personal sources of power exist within all clients.

Privilege

Privilege based on the nature and degree of power experienced as counseling professionals is located in the circumstances within which one is born and lives as well as the opportunities one receives as a professional. While it takes a great deal of self-reflection and honesty to critically explore what opportunities and outcomes one has had based on cultural identity, cultural membership, and cultural status, it is essential to recognize this to be able to recognize cultural experiences and positions experienced by clients. Some professionals, when challenged about their privilege feel guilt, while others feel responsibility. Having privilege is not itself problematic. Rather, it is what one does with privilege that matters.

The process of discovering privilege may begin with the recognition of one's self as a cultural person. Culture, as with the air we breathe, is within us and all around us. One challenging but important way to develop this recognition is with personal or professional immersion experiences where we put ourselves in an unfamiliar setting. These experiences make the "culture" that surrounds us evident (Barden & Cashwell, 2013). It may be shocking (and overwhelming) or awakening (and inspiring). It can also teach us how what we take for granted or assume about the who, what, where, when, why, and how of a person or place are both similar to and different from what is already known. The ability to take the chance on being somewhere or doing something unfamiliar reflects a degree of risk-taking and openness to new experience, which is what counselors often expect of clients. The ability to learn about difference and similarity provides experience from which counselors can learn about their own values, beliefs, and preferences as well as judgments that come into play when encountering another person or setting.

The recognition of self and environment as a cultural person in a cultural environment affords awareness of what it may be like for a client. For example, it can awaken an appreciation of the experience of a client who has physically or socially relocated into a new setting or group (Gone & Calf Looking, 2011). The relationship between the timing, both developmental (i.e., person) and sociopolitical (i.e., context), as well as the purpose (i.e., moving toward or moving away) and the effect (i.e., adapt, immerse, persist, resist) of the change are all worthy of cultural exploration. In addition, perceptions of difference play out in counseling work through the concept of transference and countertransference with culturally influenced pre-transference (i.e., the client's expectations about her counselor) and culturally influenced pre-countertransference (i.e., the counselor's expectations about her client) (Hipolito-Delgado, Cook, Avrus, & Bonham, 2011).

Activism

Another often neglected but important way to use knowledge about cultural difference and power is to locate them in the environment. A tendency for counselors is to look at how an individual experiences the world and to focus on what that person can do to change herself or himself. From a sociopolitical perspective culture and power are intertwined and differences reflect hierarchical relationships. When it is clear that the client's disadvantage is rooted in her or his cultural identity, group, or affiliation, is it helpful to encourage adaptation (Collins, Arthur, Brown, & Kennedy, 2013)? By doing so, are counselors suggesting to clients that they accept those circumstances? From a sociopolitical perspective such a goal reinforces the status quo. Disadvantage is maintained and those who experience it improve their mental health only by adjusting or conforming to it.

When I was a graduate student, I was involved in a research project on the experiences of women living in poverty. My role was to conduct focus groups that had been arranged by the project coordinators at particular locations and times. I traveled across a city and was involved with over a dozen focus groups, but remember one experience vividly. I was meeting with a group of women living in a public housing complex. There were about nine or ten of us together. As we went through the topics, the participants began to add more detail to their answers. When the group was nearly complete, one of the participants mentioned that her doctor put her on medication to treat depression and it seemed to be helping. After she offered this information, each of the participants offered a similar story of medication treatment for depression and anxiety, which were costs covered by social services. While they viewed the medication as making a positive difference in how they coped with living in poverty, it did nothing to change those circumstances.

As counselors we can choose to change circumstances in different ways. Change can be promoted by assisting a client in taking action on her or his own behalf to change circumstances through empowerment. Change can be promoted by taking action as a counselor on behalf of client interests. Counselors can also think more broadly about the groups that are affected and, in the role of professional, become involved in research or service work that supports the interests of a group or organization that is making a positive difference. Finally, each of us as citizens of our communities and nations can become active in political and social efforts that promote positive change in the lives of disadvantaged groups.

A Sociopolitical Perspective

A sociopolitical perspective is the recognition of the social and political forces associated with the issues clients bring to counseling (Ratts & Pedersen, 2014). It requires sensitivity to what lies underneath the challenges faced as well as strengths held. It explicitly attends to the ways clients are judged by others and experience diminished opportunities to realize full social and political participation. Such a perspective extends a typical approach taken by counselors, by requiring a social and political consciousness of conditions that are intolerable and need to be changed as a direct result of professional and public efforts. The purpose of this change is to reallocate power from those locations and expressions that govern social and political forces to those locations and expressions that are within the means of those who are disadvantaged by them. This perspective is both a personal and professional blessing as well as a curse because any change to the status quo threatens the implicit and explicit hierarchies that counselors depend on for our own comfort and security as professionals. It is also more work because it requires sensitivity to those forces both within and outside of individuals that are amenable to change and because it adds responsibility to choose to be either part of the problem or part of the solution in relation to those external forces.

Person in Environment and Ecological Theories

Theories that attend to the "fit" between individuals and their physical and social contexts have been developed. These offer the closest theoretical approach from within counseling to draw upon. It is important to keep in mind that while both person in environment and ecological theories offer explicit attention to the environment, they do not offer explanations of social and political forces associated with cultural diversity nor do they propose ways to intervene.

Walsh, Price, and Craik offer important and interesting possibilities in two editions of their edited book *Person-Environment Psychology* (1992, 2000), including a focus on life domains, personality types, interactional goals, individual interactions, environmental interpretation, interpersonal relationships, and transactional approaches to interpersonal relationships. The second edition of their work continued to develop these concepts into models and explored the topics of socioanalysis, systems, organizational environment, ecology of well-being, evaluating place, matching clients with treatments, and working life in context (Walsh, 2003). From this model, the experiences of women in the poverty focus group would be situated in their relationships with the service systems, such as health and perhaps, social, justice, and education, with which they interact. An intervention could be to promote more effective relationships between the participants and relevant service providers. There are three limitations of a person in environment conceptualization: (a) while this perspective recognizes the social environment as a fluid entity, its influence is represented as a context within which individuals function; (b) in this perspective the target of change is the person for the most part and to some extent the "fit" between person and environment, with little attention to change in the environment; and (c) there is no apparent attention in this perspective to power differentials that charge the social and political environment.

According to ecological theory, the environment (Bronfenbrenner, 2009) consists of interacting layers. Bronfenbrenner positioned the theory as one of reciprocal relationships between the individual and the layers, which exert a powerful influence on the development of that individual. The microsystem, mesosystem, exosystem, macrosystem, and chronosystem provide influence, through interaction with the individual, on her or his life trajectory (Lau & Ng, 2014). **Microsystems** are the groups and institutions in the social and physical environment that most directly influence an individual, such as peers, schools, religious institutions, and families. The **mesosystem** is the interaction between the microsystem influences and the individual. The **exosystem** refers to the influences on an individual from environments that indirectly affect her or him, but do directly influence the groups and institutions in the immediate social environment, such as a change in schools or parental employment, grandparent relocation, or the loss of a friend. The **macrosystem** is the social context that includes the influence of the culture, such as traditions and values that are embedded within the cultural groups of which one is a part. The **chronosystem** is the context at a point in time, allowing for change over time to view present circumstances in the environment and the individual as impermanent and transitional. From this theory, the experiences of women in the poverty focus group could be understood in relation to the systems, as represented in person–environment, as well as the cultures with which the women identify as potential sources of strength, connection, and meaning. An intervention could be to promote more effective connections between the women through their cultural experiences and affiliations.

Bronfenbrenner's is the most comprehensive view available within the psychological literature concerning the social environment and its influence on an individual. While it allows for person and environment interaction, as well as explicitly recognizing cultural and temporal factors, it is less sensitive to the interpersonal experiences of such factors by individuals over their lifespan and is silent on both power differentials at each level and processes of change to the environment. While the model helps to view environmental factors in operation, it does not offer a route for change.

Fortunately, the recognition of power and the complementary concept of empowerment offer a means to understand the hierarchical relationships that occur and interact between and within sociopolitical environments. Culturally based psychologies have emerged in response to recognized power differences in the sociopolitical environment. Not only do they recognize negative forces in the environment that disproportionately affect members of their communities, but they also define for themselves what is most important for promoting personal and community-level change. These perspectives are presented in Chapter 4.

Conclusion

Counselors are trained to focus on internal change and, to a lesser extent, on change in their clients' closest relationships. However, the social and political environment within which both counselors and clients live is a major contributor to mental health and therefore, a worthy target for change. While practice concerning cultural differences often attends well to the ways that practices between groups and individuals vary, it also tends to minimize the power differentials that exist. While cultures vary in norms and values, processes and outcomes, the context within which they operate is deeply hierarchical with growing disparity between those at the extremes. A sociopolitical perspective offers both new opportunities for change and challenges for clients, professionals, and the environments within which we live.

Discussion Questions

1. What social privileges do you experience, and where do you experience them? How do you notice and view those without the privilege you experience in that context? What do you do with that knowledge? At the time? Later?

2. What social disadvantages do you experience, and where do you experience them? How do you notice and view others without that privilege? What do you do with that knowledge? At the time? Later?

3. What is cultural awareness? Where is this learned? How did you learn it? Is it about difference or rank? How do you view yourself in relation to those with a perceived higher social rank? How do you view yourself in relation to those with a perceived lower social rank?

4. What is cultural sensitivity? What experiences have challenged you to explore your own cultural identity? In what social contexts do you feel "different" and the "same" as others? In what ways do you feel "different" and the "same"? Is it primarily an intellectual experience? Or does it extend into emotion, spirit, and behavior?

5. What types and levels of influence do you believe the environment exerts on the individual, and the individual exerts on the environment? What makes it possible for individuals who experience disadvantage to alter the context where they experience it? How can counselors work to alter those contexts? Where have you experienced the benefits of another person's or group's efforts at social change?

Web Links

- National Center for Cultural Competence
  http://nccc.georgetown.edu
- Indigenous Cultural Safety Training Program
  http://www.culturalcompetency.ca
- Power in Psychotherapy and Counseling
  http://www.zurinstitute.com/power_in_therapy.html
- A World of Activism: How You Can Get Involved
  http://culturesofresistance.org/get-involved
- The Center for Artistic Activism
  http://artisticactivism.org/get-involved/
- Inkspire: Inspiring Ideas into Action
  https://inkspire.org/
- Famous Activists
  http://www.biography.com/people/groups/activists

Key Terms

values (culture)
norms (culture)
institutions (culture)
artifacts (culture)
openness to experience
conscientiousness
extroversion
agreeableness
neuroticism
individualism and collectivism
high and low power difference
short- and long-term orientation
indulgence and restraint
feminist psychology
Indigenous psychology
assimilation
separation
integration
marginalization
distancing
denial

defensiveness
devaluing
discovery
Johari window
Blind Spot
cultural destructiveness
cultural incapacity
cultural blindness
cultural pre-competence
cultural competence
cultural proficiency
cultural humility
awareness (power)
values (power)
skills (power)
information (power)
coercion
reward
legitimate
referent
expert

informational   exosystem
microsystems   macrosystem
mesosystem   chronosystem

CHAPTER 2

DETERMINANTS OF MENTAL HEALTH

Chapter Outline

In this chapter factors that operate at community and societal levels associated with mental health as well as their manifestation in differences between cultural groups are identified. An approach that specifically attends to power disparities is offered as a way of enhancing the personal wellness, strength, and influence of individuals in counseling.

Mental health has been defined as "a state of well-being in which every individual realizes his or her own potential, can cope with the normal stresses of life, can work productively and fruitfully, and is able to make a contribution to her or his community" (World Health Organization, 2014). Mental health is concerned with the wholeness of a person and her or his energies directed toward optimal functioning and wellness. The purpose of this chapter is to highlight the range of social contributors to mental health, focusing in depth on the nature and effects of poverty on optimal functioning. The force of social disadvantage and its expression through symptoms of class difference manifest internally as a personal experience of oppression. A psychological approach to oppression is presented as a means to orient the work of counselors toward psychological liberation. To this end, psychologies of oppression and liberation, grounded in works reflecting both historical and contemporary contributions to the existence of a colonial mentality as well as social liberation, are offered.

Sociopolitical Factors in Health

Both sociopolitical advantage and **disadvantage** can be identified through the study of population level group differences relative to particular outcomes. The greater the variation in a particular outcome between groups, the greater the relative advantage and disadvantage experienced by members of those groups. From a sociopolitical perspective, as presented in Chapter 1, personal problems that clients bring to counseling are inseparable from the environments within which they live. That environment is not experienced the same way by each person. It is experienced relative to cultural location and the status it affords relative to other groups. This status is reflected in outcomes evident at a population level. These outcomes illustrate the experiences of most members of a particular group. Many outcomes have been studied such as educational attainment, income level, and employment status. However, there are also differences in relation to political participation at community and government levels. In addition, a range of health and illness indicators as well as life expectancies have been calculated for different groups. The purpose for presenting these here is to reinforce the notion that cultural group membership is associated with intergroup variation in social and political outcomes. Of particular concern is the experience of sociopolitical disadvantage and its salience in the lives of counseling clients.

Consider the example of a 30-year-old female client with three children, including a newborn, starting trade school after leaving a violent relationship with her male partner. Emily tells her counselor that obtaining the needed childcare from her mother means returning to the town where her ex lives. When asked about the violence, she informs you that everyone in town knew and no one said or did anything to help because "it happens a lot in [X]." As her counselor the disadvantages resulting from her physical and psychological injuries, as well as from her parenting responsibilities, are evident to you. You also recognize that the environment where Emily lived contributed to her present and anticipated challenges. While her emotional recovery and educational success may be achieved through counseling, the fact remains that all women are unsafe in that community.

Disadvantage exists because of **inequity**. Inequity is the recognition that large-scale efforts to equalize sociopolitical location and status are needed to increase the opportunity and influence of members of disadvantaged groups. **Social justice**, as presented in Chapter 1, is an orientation to counseling practice that is based in the notion of justice so that equal life chances are realized by all members of a society. To continue the present example, the life chances for women around the world as well as in that particular community are not the same as they are for men. As long as women experience fewer opportunities and less influence in their communities than men, the disadvantage and problems it produces for counseling will persist.

Social Determinates of Health

There has been a great deal of attention to the concept of social determinates of health, which although tied most explicitly to physical health, applies to mental health as well (Allen, Balfour, Bell, & Marmot, 2014; Bährer-Kohler, 2012). These determinates have been identified at national levels and invite international comparisons. For example, a report by the World Health Organization (2013) on violence against women found that of women who have been in an intimate relationship worldwide, 30 per cent have experienced violence by a partner. The rate was 36.6 per cent in Africa, 29.8 per cent in the Americas, 37.0 per cent in the Eastern Mediterranean, 25.4 per cent in Europe, 37.7 per cent in Southeast Asia, and 24.6 per cent in the Western Pacific. Women who have experienced violence at the hands of an intimate partner were also more likely to have a baby with low birth weight, have an abortion, be HIV positive, and experience depression.

According to the World Health Organization (2015), social determinates of health are "the conditions in which people are born, grow, work, live and age, and the wider set of forces and systems shaping the conditions of daily life. These forces and systems include economic policies and systems, development agendas, social norms, social policies and political systems." They are forces in the environment over which *individuals* have little or no control, but because they are social, *can be changed in response to collective efforts.* Social determinates of health have also been used to study their utility in mental health, and more specifically, mental disorders

(Allen, Balfour, Bell, & Marmot, 2014). For example, low socioeconomic status is strongly associated with frequency of mental disorder, as are low educational attainment, material disadvantage, unemployment, and social isolation (Thornicroft & Maingay, 2002).

In the United States, social determinates are defined by the Centers for Disease Control and Prevention (2015) as "life-enhancing resources." They include food and its supply, housing conditions, economic and social relationships, transportation, health care, and education (Marmot & Wilkinson, 2005). As an example, the cluster of disadvantage represented by low socioeconomic status is highly predictive of increased mortality among young adults (Denton & Walters, 1999). An important contribution of this conceptualization are the qualities that influence whether or not a resource to improve health status is used. These qualities include the **availability** (does the resource exist?), **accessibility** (can individuals obtain it?), and **appropriateness** (is the resource the right kind of resource for members of that group at that time?) of the resource. To continue the example from the beginning of this chapter, given her unemployment and social isolation, as well as her gender, Emily is in a socially disadvantaged position in relation to both mental health and physical health. Resources in her environment, if they are to have the effect of improving her situation, need to exist (e.g., a safe residence for women and children in her community), but also be obtainable (e.g., the residence has space) and the right kind of opportunity (e.g., is long-term) to be useful. However, a valid criticism of this approach to addressing disadvantage is that it does not go far enough. For example, the safety of women while they reside at the residence may be protected, but the existence of the residence in and of itself does not address the problem of violence against women in that community.

The Ottawa Charter is an international agreement that was signed at the First National Conference on Health Promotion in 1986, organized by the World Health Organization. In Canada, social determinates have been identified in the Charter and developed as a series of operationalized and measurable qualities associated with relative disadvantage. Specific determinates (Raphael, 2009) include income, education, unemployment and job security, employment and working conditions, early childhood development, food insecurity, housing, social exclusion, social safety network, health services, Aboriginal status, gender, race, and disability. However, the Ottawa Charter goes farther than the Centers for Disease Control model to include both population level targets and actions to address disadvantage. Targets for intervention include adequate and affordable shelter, education, and food as well as sufficient income and sustainable resources (Raphael, 2006). Action areas of the Charter included healthy public policy, supportive environments, community action, personal skill development, and health care service reorientation to the prevention of illness and promotion of wellness (Nutbeam, 2008; Potvin & Jones, 2011). From this perspective, an extension of the example that began this chapter could include recognition of Emily's income situation, unemployment and job security issues in her community, as well as social safety, inclusion, race, and disability. The environmental determinates are more broadly recognized and actions via policy change and community action are offered as is personal skill development. From the same example, one possibility could be to have employers in the community implement family violence policies in their workplaces. Another possibility may be for women to organize an effort to put pressure on the local law enforcement to develop a family violence protocol. Skills development could be pursued through targeted upgrading programs for women interested in making a career change.

Theories of Disadvantage

It is important to consider ways that disadvantage affects individuals. There are two major groups of theories that explain the influence of social disadvantage on health (Lynch, Smith, Kaplan, & House, 2000). **Cultural/behavioral theories** focus on the individual and her or his choices as the main predictor, while **materialist/structuralist theories** focus on the resources and context of one's life. From a cultural/behavioral perspective, individual choices are the strongest influence on health (Lantz et al., 2001). From this perspective, each person makes decisions that influence her or his own health status. Decisions that lead to poorer health when aggregated across groups of people are more highly present in some groups than others (Marmot & Wilkinson, 2001). Based on the example at the beginning of this chapter and a cultural/behavioral perspective, given the social determinates associated with lower income and isolation among women in her community, Emily's own choices and behavior are understood to be placing her at risk for violence by her partner. From this perspective, it is her responsibility to change or leave. Such a view discounts the force of the environment and factors within it, such as men's attitudes about women, which are both powerful and outside of her control.

Materialist/structuralist theories refer to the nature of resources and access to those resources in the context within which one lives (Lynch & Smith, 2002). In this perspective two streams can be identified (Coburn, 2004), including the materialist and neo-materialist views, which are that living conditions directly or indirectly influence health, and the psychosocial comparison view, which is that perceptions of self are rooted in comparisons made to others. From a materialist view low income and social isolation for women at a community level, where there are also attitudes that support violence against women, make it difficult to engage with other women while also putting them in a vulnerable position. From a neo-materialist view, the same income and social isolation not only make it difficult to engage with others, but also over time and repetition become more influential, the attitudes more engrained, further increasing dependence, deepening both vulnerability and risk. From the psycho-social comparison view, Emily would recognize her situation relative to other women outside the community, and based on the comparison would recognize differences in her income and isolation as well as community attitudes about violence against women. This view recognizes the role of environment and its effect on the individual to produce conditions that predispose her and others in her situation to the same outcome.

The problem with these perspectives is that the culturists locate all responsibility in the individual and the materialists locate all responsibility in the environment. Neither is complete by itself. Taken together, however, the theories offer a way to understand both individual and environmental contributions to disadvantage. A combined approach may be possible, such as the social environment creates disadvantage and individuals operate within it, but can, through collective effort, change it.

Poverty

Poverty represents a cluster of social disadvantage (Dean & Platt, 2016). The Human Poverty Index is a value calculated by the World Health Organization (2008) to make international comparisons. Of the 19 countries highest on the Human Development Index in 2008, relative to the proportion of the population below 50 per cent of the median, Canada ranks twelfth and the United States ranks last at nineteenth.

Different perspectives on poverty center on responses to the focal issues of "what is enough" and "who makes that decision" (Blackorby & Donaldson, 1980). **Absolute** definitions of poverty refer to a lack of basic necessities (e.g., either one does or does not have clean drinking water in her or his home). **Relative** definitions of poverty center on the inadequacy of what one has or does not have in relation to what others have (e.g., one does not have clean drinking water in her or his home but others in the community do). There are two main types of poverty lines (Duclos & Grégoire, 2002). **Restrictive** poverty lines refer to the essentials necessary to sustain physical life with the purpose of ensuring survival (e.g., access to clean drinking water, basic shelter, and sufficient calories to survive). **Inclusive** poverty lines refer to essentials for physical as well as social, emotional, and spiritual life with the purpose of ensuring participation in community life (e.g., a home that is comfortable and appropriate for the conditions in which one lives and a healthy balanced diet).

Several measures of poverty exist. They fall into one of three categories including consumption basket, equity-based, and mixed consumption/equity (Jitsuchon, 2001). A **consumption basket** measure is based on the cost of necessary goods. The decisions about these goods are arbitrary but generally restrictive or inclusive in amount and type for a particular geographic location and family composition (e.g., income that does not rise to the level to afford the cost of needed goods at the local grocery store). An **equity-based** approach is calculated on the basis of a fraction of average income for a particular group relative to a comparison group in a particular location (e.g., if the average income in a community is $30,000 per year, an income lower than $15,000 would be considered living in poverty). A **mixed** approach refers to the proportion of household income that is spent on necessary goods (e.g., if more than 70 per cent of income is spent on food, clothing, and shelter, it would be considered poverty).

Each definition is rooted in values and beliefs about the meaning of poverty. Each definition also has a particular purpose (Audet et al., 2014). Often, governments favor restrictive equity-based lines because they are inexpensive and simple to measure. Anti-poverty advocacy groups tend to favor inclusive consumption basket lines because of their pursuit of social inclusion and recognition of relative cost based on location. Counselors who are aware of their own beliefs and the beliefs of their clients can recognize the efforts made, barriers encountered, and limits reached by clients in recent financial difficulty due to an unexpected change, clients with multigenerational experiences of poverty, and clients residing in high-poverty neighborhoods or communities (Goodman et al., 2015). Each of these possibilities describes a different experience and reflects varied interpretations of causes and effects of poverty (Reed & Smith, 2014).

Case Example

Consider your own beliefs about poverty in relation to a client's experience in the following example. Dave and Melissa, parents of two school-aged daughters, are referred to you because of relationship problems. Your practice is in a large urban center and they rent an apartment a distance away where housing is more affordable. You have a sliding fee for service based on gross annual household income and find out when you are making arrangements to meet that, between Dave's full-time and Melissa's casual employment, they earned less than $50,000 last year. You figure that with deductions, this is about $40,000 in take-home pay.

Would you consider a family of four living on $40,000 in this area to be living in poverty?

Where would you draw the after-tax poverty line for a family with similar structure? Why?

- 0 to $9,999
- $10,000 to $19,999
- $20,000 to $29,999
- $30,000 to $39,999
- $40,000 to $49,999
- $50,000 to $59,999
- $60,000 to $69,000
- $70,000 to $79,000
- $80,000 to $89,000
- $90,000 +

Compare what you thought to the following list of poverty lines that are in use in Canada (Table 2.1). These include the line drawn by the Fraser Institute, another from the Social Planning Council of Toronto, and two unofficial poverty lines calculated by Statistics Canada including the Low Income Measure and the Low Income Cut Off.

How does this information about their financial situation factor into your expectations about the relationship issues they are experiencing? Do you see the potential for money to be a prominent concern in this relationship? If it

TABLE 2.1 Poverty Lines

Consumption Basket Measures	
Restrictive—Sarlo (2009) Food, Shelter, Clothing, and Other	$24,323
Inclusive—SPC of Toronto (2013) Food, Shelter, Clothing, and Other	$44,668
Equity-based Measures	
Restrictive—Statistics Canada LIM (2009) 50% of median adjusted family income	$37,592
Inclusive—CCSD LIM (2012) 50% of average adjusted family income	$38,920
Mixed Consumption/Equity	
Statistics Canada LICO (2012) Proportion of food, clothing, and shelter expenses relative to total income	$49,942

is not a pressing issue for the couple, could it remain so for you as an underlying concern?

If you or they see it as a concern, your beliefs will influence both your interpretations and efforts with the couple. It is also important to recognize social disadvantage, its effects on individuals and families, as well as ways that it can be altered.

Correlates of Poverty

There are a variety of beliefs that counselors bring to the session as well as those that our clients hold about their situations and attributions. Attitudes about causes and consequences of poverty have been explored in research with postsecondary students (Stacey, Singer, & Ritchie, 1989). In one study, students were asked to rate each "cause" and "consequence" on a scale from 1 to 7, where 1 is very important, and 7 is very unimportant. Check your ratings against theirs.

In Table 2.2, there are 16 "causes" of poverty. Please rate each on a scale from 1 (very important) to 7 (very unimportant).

In Table 2.3, there are 12 "effects" of poverty. Please rate each on a scale from 1 (very important) to 7 (very unimportant).

More recent data from a sample of nursing students in a Canadian university revealed that structural understandings versus behavioral understandings of poverty were most strongly supported as contributors to poor health (Reutter, Sword, Meagher-Stewart, & Rideout, 2004). Comparing the two sets of attitudes about poverty, the first study found that students viewed family and social factors as significant causes of poverty, with economic and family effects as the most significant. The second study found that students viewed health problems among those living in poverty as a result of circumstances, not of behavior. Behavioral adaptation to living circumstances was favored as the theory. The reason this matters in counseling is because the beliefs counselors hold determine how they hear and understand clients and how one approaches the counselor role. Students in these studies, as future helping professionals, viewed poverty as the product of forces outside of individuals in their family and social environments with individual behavior in the context of poverty as limited and adaptive. While such a view is clearly cognizant of the limited choices available, the best choices within those limitations are pursued.

Case Example

A female client named Rachel comes to see you as a counselor. The public welfare organization in your area funds your agency to see their clients to support their search for employment. You know that she will be cut off welfare

TABLE 2.2 *Causes* **of Poverty**

1. Lack of effort and laziness	1/2/3/4/5/6/7
2. Poor money management	1/2/3/4/5/6/7
3. Lack of intelligence	1/2/3/4/5/6/7
4. Lack of physical attractiveness	1/2/3/4/5/6/7
5. Economic and taxation systems at fault	1/2/3/4/5/6/7
6. Salaries and wages are too low	1/2/3/4/5/6/7
7. Economic system does not create enough jobs	1/2/3/4/5/6/7
8. Financial system is prejudiced	1/2/3/4/5/6/7
9. Little money in the family	1/2/3/4/5/6/7
10. Little emphasis on success in the family	1/2/3/4/5/6/7
11. Family is unable to provide opportunities	1/2/3/4/5/6/7
12. Strain in family life	1/2/3/4/5/6/7
13. Bad luck	1/2/3/4/5/6/7
14. Factors beyond their control	1/2/3/4/5/6/7
15. Some persons are doomed to be poor	1/2/3/4/5/6/7
16. Unlucky in gambling and taking chances	1/2/3/4/5/6/7

n = 200 university students in New Zealand

	Average Rating
Internal Factors (1–4)	4.7
Societal Factors (5–8)	3.6
Family Factors (9–12)	3.4
Luck Factors (13–16)	4.8

if she does not attend appointments with you or does not make progress toward a job. You learn that Rachel is under a great deal of pressure to look after her two children, aged six and seven years, that her husband has been laid off from his job as a landscaper, that she has chronic pain, and that the family

TABLE 2.3 *Effects* of poverty

1. Have little money to pay for things	1/2/3/4/5/6/7
2. Cannot provide financial help to others	1/2/3/4/5/6/7
3. Cannot do the things you want to do	1/2/3/4/5/6/7
4. Do not like yourself very much	1/2/3/4/5/6/7
5. Are bored	1/2/3/4/5/6/7
6. Afraid of the future	1/2/3/4/5/6/7
7. Other people look down on you	1/2/3/4/5/6/7
8. Become a burden to society	1/2/3/4/5/6/7
9. Low social status	1/2/3/4/5/6/7
10. Life is difficult in their families	1/2/3/4/5/6/7
11. Have many family worries	1/2/3/4/5/6/7
12. Family morale is low	1/2/3/4/5/6/7

n = 200 university students in New Zealand

	Average Rating
Economic (1–3)	3.0
Social (4–6)	4.2
Familial (7–9)	3.8
Psychological (10–12)	4.7

has borrowed all they can from friends and family to make ends meet. Her last paid work experience was before her children were born. Rachel is reporting symptoms of anxiety and discloses that she has been having thoughts about suicide but assures you that her intent to overdose on her husband's prescription painkillers is low.

Considering the larger systemic context of her anxiety and suicidal ideation you begin to explore the chain of events that lead you through the cycles of disadvantage that perpetuate poverty, including the links between mental health, housing, crime, employment, and education.

- Why is Rachel suicidal?
  o Because she is anxious
- Why is she anxious?
  o Because she worries constantly about her children's safety
- Why does she worry so much?
  o Because they live in a public housing unit where there is a lot of crime
- Why does the family live in housing where crime is a problem?
  o Because she and her husband cannot afford to live anywhere else
- Why can't they afford somewhere else?
  o Because her husband has difficulty keeping a job and,
  o Because she has been raising the children
- Why has she been raising the children?
  o Because she does not trust her husband to do it
- Why doesn't she trust her husband?
  o Because he has a substance abuse problem
- Why does he have a substance abuse problem?
  o Because he has chronic pain
- Why does he have chronic pain?
  o Because he was doing manual labor for many years
- Why was he doing manual labor for years?
  o Because he has a Grade 6 education
- Why does he have a Grade 6 education?
  o Because he left school once he was placed in foster care
- Why was he in foster care?

Your obligations as a counselor would likely include the consideration of risk and management of suicidal ideation, as well as intervention for her anxiety within a context of understanding the positive and negative effects of her employment status on the family. You may also note that in addition to the urgent concerns of suicide and anxiety, there are broader factors at play where positive change may make a difference, such as broadening opportunities in the areas of housing, nutrition, education, and employment. The risk of focusing only on the suicide and anxiety leaves unaddressed the conditions that provide her with the small range of options that poverty creates for Rachel to work within.

Mechanisms of Action
Earlier in this chapter two major types of theories that explained the relationship between disadvantage and individual behavior were considered. Cultural/behavioral theories focus on the individual and her or his choices as the main

predictor of disadvantage, while materialist/structuralist theories focus on the environmental contributions to disadvantage. In relation to poverty, as reflected in this section, the relationship between disadvantaged conditions and individual behavior is clearly more complex. The nature of the interplay has been a subject of theoretical development. Pathways through which external conditions of poverty affect one's psychology to create internal conditions have been proposed. These offer theories about how external disadvantage becomes internalized.

These pathways include **developmental**, **psychobiological**, and **social comparative approaches**. From a developmental perspective, childhood experiences of poverty are carried into adulthood (Holzer, Schanzenbach, Duncan, & Ludwig, 2007). For example, the food choices made by a parent with limited access to fresh food and no appropriate storage are limited to highly processed, convenience foods that have little nutritional value. Such foods are associated with short bursts of attention, compromising children's learning ability at home and in school. School difficulties early in life challenge later achievement in school, particularly in highly sequential subjects such as mathematics and sciences. The persistence of achievement problems into adolescence leads to a perceived lack of ability at school and a search for other sources of reinforcement and esteem, gravitating into groups of others facing similar challenges and possibly resulting in leaving school early. Adulthood without formal education severely limits employment opportunities, potentially perpetuating a cycle of limited accessibility to meet basic needs.

From a psychobiological perspective the demands and opportunities present in one's life, when in significant and chronic imbalance (i.e., demands exceeding capacities) have a significant biological effect. A chronic stress response affects neuroendocrine function, altering cortisol levels, ACTH, catecholamine, endorphin, hormone, and insulin production. There are also autonomic metabolic effects including cardiovascular, respiratory, renal, gastrointestinal, metabolic, and homeostatic. Finally, the immune system is compromised through effects on immunoglobulins, white cell count, lymphocytes, and cytokines (Marmot & Wilkinson, 2005). The biological functioning associated with chronic poverty takes a toll on one's physical health. Some effects are transient and others permanent, but both contribute to a range of health conditions that are more highly represented among individuals living in poverty, such as obesity (Lee, Andrew, Gebremariam, Lumeng, & Lee, 2014).

In a social comparative approach, the perceived disadvantage relative to others provides a strong force on psychological experience and change over time. The deprivation that is felt, relative to others in one's neighborhood, community, or nation, impedes hardiness and resilience. For example, one's perception of her or his dress, style of communication, and means of transportation may vary within the same school during childhood. The social position one acquires by wearing second-hand or unclean clothing, using slang, mispronouncing words, and relying on pedestrian and public transportation, relative to those who wear new clothing, use clear formal language, and have private transportation, erodes self-esteem and confidence through feelings of inferiority, potentially building into resentment (Raphael, 2006).

Oppression

Oppression is the feeling of being weighed down (Gill, 2014). It is experienced as external force against one's efforts. Cultural diversity is interconnected with oppression in that every cultural group has a relative sociopolitical position to every other cultural group. This position dictates the strength and nature of the oppressive forces working against its members. This is a critical concept for counselors because oppression is both very powerful and influential and likely to be unrecognized. Consider the possibility that, as a counseling professional, you represent, based on this identification only, a class status that advantages you relative to those of a lower socioeconomic status. Imagine walking into a car dealership and asking for a test drive as a middle-class woman versus a woman pushing a stroller with two small children who are eating potato chips because they were the only thing she could find for them that morning. What would you expect the reaction to be? While the woman with children would likely not get the attention of a salesperson the other woman most certainly would. Such differential treatment reflects prejudicial attitudes. Together, social advantage, prejudice, and power produce oppression. Clients who have the experience of being treated as if they were inferior, have been judged critically by others, and have a low level of influence over their circumstances are living in an oppressive environment. While experiences of oppression are located in the environment, one's interpretations of such experiences may become part of a view of self and the world we live in.

Multiple theoretical explanations for the existence of oppression at a societal level have been offered, with conflict and critical theory as the most influential to the ideas represented in this book (Rubington & Weinberg, 2010). From a **conflict** perspective, oppression is the product of conflict over limited resources. These resources are connected to the capital to purchase some desired or needed good or service or the means of producing that capital. This interpretation is linked closely to a Marxist model representing oppression as a historical invention, not a natural state (Peffer, 2014). Marxists are critical of capitalism, its differentiation and maintenance of the population within social classes that are unalterable without revolutionary social change (Barker, 2013).

A key idea from this perspective is that oppression limits the possibilities that individuals, as members of disadvantaged cultural groups, can recognize and actions that they can take to claim their own means of production (Gough, McFadden, & McDonald, 2013). In the example of the women in the car dealership, the mother would be likely perceived as having limited financial means and greater limitations on her potential to earn. Her value to the salesperson would be lower than someone without the same limitations. She may also have come to expect that she will be viewed that way. Over time and through the accumulation of experiences, she may even come to believe that her feelings of inferiority are unalterable, deserved, or necessary.

From a **critical theory** perspective, oppression exists because social structures favor some groups and disadvantage others. These social structures exist at institutional and societal levels. Like conflict, the major forces that exert influence on individuals operate at the highest levels. For conflict, the core from which these originate is capitalism and the effect is class divisions. However, for critical theory, any system that favors some groups over other groups is oppressive. Examples of oppressive forces encountered in North America at a societal or national level include the official observance of only Christian holidays, the norm of a nuclear family, the use of English, and dual emphasis on individualism and personal responsibility (Goodman et al., 2015). Institutionally, cultural groups, whether they be race-based, class-based, gender-based, disability-based, sexuality-based, or religiously based, have differential access to and representation in health, education, justice, and social services. There are significant differentiations in representation at the highest levels of political office and business leadership positions (Maillé, 2015). Stereotypes, which are represented in the media, portray members of particular groups in disparaging ways (Scharrer & Ramasubramanian, 2015). A key idea from the critical theory perspective is that any effort that increases equality at the expense of hierarchy creates positive change (Mirowsky, 2013). Through collective efforts, oppressive institutional forces can be challenged and, with time and large-scale efforts, transformed. Following the example of the woman with children in a car dealership, her perceived value to the salesperson for a sale may initially be low. However, if she held and communicated her affiliations as both the secretary of the parent teacher association at a local school and president of the board of directors at the out-of-school care center attached to that school, her standing would very likely change.

If we recognize that mental health is significantly affected by social conditions that result from differences in power and opportunities between cultural groups, our efforts to intervene should attend to those differences (Gill, 2014). As the example here reflects, the experience of an oppressive environment can be both internalized and externalized. In practical terms, counselors are most often asked to help individuals and families, and not communities and societies where major contributors to individual problems exist. Counselors are also most familiar with, knowledgeable about, and skilled in addressing internal psychological processes. This is of great importance because, as suggested in the example where a judgment of inferiority was accepted, the internal barriers that form as a result of repeated experience of external barriers are essential to address. Without such change, it would be difficult to experience sufficient capacity and agency to participate and take social action.

Psychology of Oppression

The psychology of oppression is both "the psychological effects of social oppression and the psychological requirements that sustain it . . . social oppression includes a psychological component in the victim that contributes to his subjugation" (Ratner, 2014, p. 1289). In other words, one's belief that "facts" exist within the oppressive environment makes those same "facts" apparent in her or his own psyche. For example, the experience of being unfavorably received as a potential customer at a car dealership, if internalized as inferiority and accepted as such, has the consequence of developing a view of the self as less important than other customers. Assuming that these experiences occur more than once and in different circumstances, the belief in one's inferiority strengthens, becomes less open to challenge, and, over time, even becomes imperceptible. Such is the process of **internalized oppression** (David, 2013).

It can be helpful to consider social forces as part of the problem for which clients seek counseling services. When working with any individual or family, counselors may recognize these social forces and conceptualize the internalization of negative messages from the context that become part of a client's psyche as problematic. This psychology of oppression is based in the recognition that harmful messages about self from the social environment become incorporated into one's belief system (Ratner, 2014). The messages are engrained to such an extent that they are unchallenged, acted upon, and used to justify experience (Matthews & Adams, 2009). They can be subtle or overt as well as limiting. They form the psychological context within which individuals experiencing oppression operate (Enns & Green, 2013). Such a context is impoverished insofar as the affected individual does not entertain the possibility of moving beyond or rising above these self-imposed limits (Mays, Cochran, & Barnes, 2007) and uses these beliefs to judge others in similarly oppressed circumstances.

Movement beyond these self-imposed limits can be a terrifying prospect. The security they provide offers **psychological safety**. For example, the belief that "I deserve a good job" for an individual who has been on long-term social assistance raises the possibility that he is not only capable, but entitled to earn a decent income. This belief itself creates tension between what is and what can be (Greenleaf & Bryant, 2012). While it seems possible, the series of steps involved and progression through them may be daunting. Retreat from this belief can be psychologically safer as well as socially reinforced (e.g., "people on social assistance don't want to look for work") despite it being inaccurate, judgmental, and constraining.

Another consideration is the estimated probability of change. How do counselors estimate the probability of change? Training may teach that the possibilities for relief from anxiety symptoms are often very good if one follows through with talk therapy and possibly medication (Barlow, 2014). However, little is known about the potential for change in the social environment, which creates the conditions that allow for restriction and containment of opportunities experienced by individuals facing anxiety, such as stereotypes.

Case Example

In Canada, colonial effects on Indigenous peoples stemmed from first contact more than a century ago. There was large-scale loss of life from exposure to disease from which the original peoples had no immunity. Targeted efforts followed that controlled territories and movements. Cultural practices were banned (Tamburro & Tamburro, 2014). In **residential schools**, children were forcibly separated from their families and communities, taught that their ways of life were inferior, punished for speaking their languages, neglected, and both physically and sexually abused (MacDonald & Hudson, 2012). These efforts were codified into colonial law through the Indian Act. Apprehensions of Indigenous children from their communities and families were undertaken in the mid-twentieth century during a period known as the **60s Scoop**, during which the children were adopted out into non-Indigenous homes (Blackstock, 2011).

A great deal of cultural strength remained active throughout this time and into the present. There is also a strong group of national and regional Indigenous organizations. There is formal recognition through the **Royal Commission on Aboriginal Peoples** (1996), the Federal Government's Apology for the Residential Schools (2008), and the **Truth and Reconciliation Commission** (2015) that colonial efforts occurred and were an abuse of power. However, there remain great inequities between the life chances for Indigenous and non-Indigenous peoples in Canada. If the United Nations Health Index were applied to Indigenous peoples in Canada, they would rank thirty-second, while Canada ranks seventh (Loppie Reading & Wien, 2009).

The legacy of colonial efforts and effects continue to be felt and have been identified as **historical trauma** (Gone, 2013a). Historical trauma refers to large-scale losses. The losses included life, and many felt a loss of relationship to the land, traditional practices, and opportunity accumulating across generations. These losses are felt by each generation and cause pain and instability within and between individuals, families, and communities (Evans-Campbell, 2008; Wesley-Esquimaux, 2007). The depth of trauma is often beyond what mainstream counseling can address and often fits within the realm of traditional healing. However, counselors can recognize the depth and extent of historical trauma and symptoms, such as substance misuse and relationship problems in a context of poverty. While the experiences of Indigenous peoples in Canada reflect social disadvantage occurring across generations, an internal representation of disadvantage is reflected in the concept of colonial mentality.

Colonial Mentality

Colonial mentality represents feelings of personal inferiority in relation to a cultural ideal that is represented by a dominant group and based in an individual's membership in a less dominant group (Ferrera, 2011). Its origins are tied to imperialist expansion of territory across the globe and forced impositions on original inhabitants. This is an important concept because it recognizes externally imposed systems of control and subjugation on an independent and self-governing people through the use of force. Like internalized oppression, it too includes the development and maintenance of perceptions of self and judgments about self that constrain an individual. This process occurs outside of one's conscious awareness. The oppressive forces in the sociopolitical context function undetected and without any efforts to enforce them. Messages about relative worth and influence of members of cultural groups are evident both explicitly and implicitly.

A colonial mentality can refer to belief in any social message that confers low social rank within a hierarchy and is limiting to an individual (Verkuyten, 2004). Acceptance of such negative messages can be defined as the presenting issue for counseling. Consider, for example, the challenges facing a client named Anthony who indicates that he is struggling with substance misuse. He is an immigrant to Canada who left Eastern Europe with his mother as a young child because of the family's poverty and lack of opportunity, as well as the violence in her relationship to his father and her fear for her life. Anthony recalls his mother's stories about his grandparents who hid her from the police as a child, but then forced her to marry at the age of 18. Following the loss of his mother, he was alone. His dream of a wife and children, home and stable job have not materialized. His sense of self is rooted in his belief that despite his efforts to be a white middle-class man in a white middle-class neighborhood, if people really knew him, they would reject him as a criminal, spy, or addict. The beliefs he has for himself and about himself are at odds with how he believes others perceive him. These are more than perceptions, because as a child his accent separated him from the other kids and the families in his neighborhood stayed clear of him and his mother. When he was growing up in the 1980s, there was widespread suspicion in North America about Russia. It is important to recognize that internalization of these messages can be on the surface and easily accessed, or subsumed within other messages and beliefs that are more fundamental core beliefs about self. While Anthony is able to recognize his problem with alcohol, the core beliefs he holds about himself, as well as the source of these beliefs, took time to uncover in counseling. The common base of a colonial mentality is that the individual holds and believes in her or his inferiority based on messages about her or his culture received from members of the dominant culture. As a 50-year-old man, he believes that he should have more to show for his life.

There can be a major impact of this mentality on one's sense of **identity** and personhood (Sutphen & Andrews, 2003). The effects may include lack of connection to heritage culture and subscription to the dominant culture. In this example, Anthony's separation from his culture began early and he placed great effort into shedding his accent and hiding his traditional mother from his friends. Not only was Anthony trying to hide from his culture, but he also became convinced that it was inferior to the dominant culture. A high colonial mentality reflects high levels of internalized oppression. It indicates lower acceptance of heritage culture and higher acceptance of dominant culture, lower cultural identity development and lower psychological well-being. Because self-concept is based on both personal and collective self-esteem, ignoring one's cultural self devalues that part of self (Hammack, 2008).

The opposite reaction to pressure to adopt a colonial mentality is **colonial mistrust**. This is how he characterized his mother's reaction to their new life in Canada. She said that if it wasn't for him, she never would have moved, that she did it for him and only him in spite of how difficult it was for her. Colonial mistrust is a steadfast blanket rejection of the messages contained in oppressive forces and a general level of distrust of members of the dominant culture by members of the heritage culture (Moane, 1994). Recognition of oppression within social structures such as the legal system, political system, government agencies, educational system, and health care settings, as well as other entities staffed by dominant culture members, can be important for mental health (David, 2013). Because of Anthony's mother's experience in a country where individual freedoms were curtailed, her suspicion of the government and its agencies continued in Canada. In extreme forms, the effort expended to rigid adherence of heritage and dominant as "good" and "bad," respectively, can lead to difficulties seeing potential opportunities. In this example, the client's mother avoided every interaction that she could and viewed each with mistrust.

Overt colonial mentality may manifest as **discrimination** by members of a heritage cultural group against other members of the same cultural group based on their adherence to traditional norms (Bailey, Williams, & Favors, 2014).

While the efforts to **assimilate** into the majority culture exist on the surface, such as clothing choices, dominant language use, and public interactions with members of the dominant culture, when accompanied by pride in heritage culture it forms a protective factor against **acculturation** stress (Sirikantraporn, 2013). While there is less personally focused opposition and possibly pressure to assimilate if one looks like a member of the dominant culture, there is a risk of internalizing negative judgments made about others of the heritage culture. Covert colonial mentality, where there is also an internalized shame or embarrassment of heritage culture, has been associated with negative self-image and challenges with identity development as well as self-esteem. In this example, Anthony felt rejected by his host culture and did not connect with others from his heritage culture. He made every effort to assimilate and over time developed negative perceptions of European immigrants which he began to apply to himself.

The notion of responsibility is challenging, but essential. A major contributor to therapeutic success is a client's ability to externalize the negative contributors to her or his identity, self-image, and self-esteem, but success also requires an internalization of the responsibility to take action against those who make negative judgments about her or him to protect her or his own psyche (Cote & Levine, 2014). There can be reluctance to challenging self-defeating values, beliefs, and behaviors that have developed over time in response to oppressive social forces. Anthony has developed a strong interest in the notion of family, home, and career, which feel like important goals, but at a deeper level, the underlying systems of experience tied with emotion and spirit can provide a very sophisticated system of thought that he is inferior to others who have achieved these goals.

The major contributions to such a **transformation** are internal and external (Wong, Wong, & Scott, 2006). Internal methods focus on the critical examination of the ways that one allows oppressive messages to be acceptable to one's self. In this example, Anthony may begin to locate his core cultural self as a mixture of Russian and British. Exploring the sociopolitical messages about his national affiliations in Canada can be discussed with the counselor, searched for online, and uncovered through some library research. Learning about the histories and realities of other members of the same group can be engaged internally through informal or formal education, as well as externally, through peer support, activity participation, and organization membership. Anthony's exploration of community groups and organizations, as well as efforts to participate in peer support, activities, and organizations, may allow him to begin to access more clearly what resonates for him, who he is, how that is viewed by others, and how he can combat the judgments he is placing on himself. A counselor's contribution can be in the processing of the new information and assisting with its **integration** into a client's belief system (Hofer & Pintrich, 2004).

Specific strategies for personal change center on the confrontation of oppressive social messages and conditions. One way this could be achieved is by locating sources of information or messages that are particularly harmful and objectively consider their legitimacy with a counselor. Breaking down and neutralizing messages is important, but of equal importance is learning the process of critiquing them, which can be accomplished through practice over time. Another possibility is to seek out helpful messages and find ways to connect with the messengers. Naming the oppression is key, as is knowing the history of the oppression and its effects on self and community. Although such internal work is not a prerequisite for a client's or counselor's actions to challenge sociopolitical forces, such awareness can strengthen recognition of what needs to change and the direction of that change.

Psychology of Liberation

A **liberation psychology** first emerged in Latin America. Its roots lie in 1960s' political and intellectual movements to reorient disciplinary knowledge so that it reflected the needs of the majority of the population who lived in poverty (Martín-Baró, Aron, & Corne, 1994). In addition to philosophy, sociology, theology, and education, the psychology of liberation embraced a need for social change that was informed by the perspective of the oppressed. This psychology was developed in solidarity and partnership *with* the oppressed. This is in contrast to the development of psychology *for* the oppressed, which was how mainstream European and North American approaches to psychology were viewed. Liberation psychology was explicitly political, practical, and conceptual. The focus was on action and reflection (Watts & Serrano-García, 2003).

The main figure with whom the written development of liberation psychology is credited was Ignacio Martín-Baró (1942–89), a Jesuit priest. His writing focused on the role of environment in human suffering and resilience, specifically the effects of and potential to change an oppressive sociopolitical context. From Martín-Baró's perspective, psychological problems could be a normal reaction to abnormal circumstances (Aron & Corne, 1994). His writings from 1966 to his death were prolific and many have not yet been translated from Spanish. Martín-Baró was murdered in 1989 by the Salvadorian army for documenting the realities of Salvadorian society during the revolution and civil war.

Central concepts of liberation psychology include conscientization, realismo-critico, de-ideologized reality, a social orientation, and referential option (Burton & Kagan, 2005). These concepts do not have particular techniques associated with them or a theoretical framework around them. They do, however, offer central tenets of the system of values and beliefs that reflect an orientation to counseling practice. **Conscientization** (Austin, 2014) refers to the individual's experience as fundamentally tied to the sociopolitical structure and to a process of consciousness-raising, which is an awareness of the oppressive forces that exist and influence one's life, through which she or he becomes more deliberate about decisions and actions. One way this could be applied with Anthony is for the counselor to identify the sources of constraint that existed or exist for him. One possibility may be to recognize the anti-Russian rhetoric that was prominent during the Cold War era and how it affected him as a youth. **Realismo-critico** (Afuape, 2015) refers to the notion that theories do not define the problems. Rather, the problems define the theories. One way this may be applied by the counselor with Anthony is by considering the way in which the problem's definition as substance misuse is associated with practical (e.g., legal, employment difficulties) as well as cultural and historical issues (e.g., for a time alcohol was cheaper than water). A **de-ideologized reality** (Tate, Rivera, & Edwards, 2015) is a recognition of the needs of those at the top of the social hierarchy and a reformulation of these needs to the needs and interests of the oppressed. A way this may be applied by the counselor is for her or him to identify with Anthony how alcohol sales and use benefit those in political power. The **social orientation** (Tate, Rivera, & Edwards, 2015) refers to the perception that the nature of psychological problems among oppressed people are the result of an alienating environment. A way this may be considered by a counselor in the example is that the absence of clarity about Anthony's sense of self and affiliation with others and his bombardment with media messages about culture and multiculturalism create the condition of not knowing. The **referential option** (Tate, Rivera, & Edwards, 2015) is an explicit focus on the needs and interests of oppressed groups. For example, Anthony's connections to others with whom he shares some cultural similarities can offer affiliation, security, and contribute to a sense of self.

Key features of this orientation to counseling practice recognize that distress, rather than being psychologized and individualized, is best located in the oppressive context that creates it (Duran, Firehammer, & Gonzalez, 2008). Because distress is caused by the oppression, the steps out of a distressing situation include recognition of one's relationship to the power structures in play and her or his participation in them. It is recognized that personal change and social change can be simultaneous—one does not necessarily have to precede the other.

Conclusion

Mental health is influenced by social and political forces, both those that are internalized by an individual and those that are present within each aspect of her or his environment. Social disadvantage is produced by differentiated status, with those on the lower end of the hierarchy experiencing oppression. Poverty as a relative condition, created by unequal life chances of members of a population, is experienced at a higher rate by some cultural groups than by others. It manifests as a lack of physical resources and is associated with relatively less economic power, lower social status, and political influence. A particularly problematic effect of poverty is its internalization, among those who are oppressed, as "natural" or "deserved." In such cases, not only is internal change needed to see the self as equally worthy and human as all others, but also to recognize the potential for development of political, economic, and social power.

Discussion Questions

1. In what contexts do you notice social disadvantage operating? How do you become aware of it in your personal and professional life? What social determinates of health do you identify with and how does this analysis compare to the lives of others you interact with?
2. The highly controversial notion of a "culture of poverty" contends that there are values and beliefs that individuals living in impoverished circumstances share which militate against changes to economic status. Do you share this notion? If not, how would you defend against it in your professional life?
3. There were several theories of oppression presented in this chapter, including (a) internalization of "character flaws," (b) inability to keep up with the pace of changes to economy, (c) conflict between the haves and the have-nots, (d) not having what others do, (e) being the recipient of a pejorative label, (f) being born into a society where people like you are favored over others, or (g) being a part of the social leadership who decides which interests to advance. Which do you favor? Which do you disfavor? What actions follow from the theory you favor?
4. Internalized oppression is a belief that one, based on a social attribute, is inferior to others with a superior attribute. In what contexts do you feel lesser than? What contributes to that feeling? In what contexts do you feel superior? What contributes to that feeling?
5. Liberation may feel like pressure that one feels is lessening. Can you think of a time when you felt a weight lifted in your life? Can you

describe the experience of having it reduced or removed? What was that like? Are there some "weights" that you would not want altered? How can we respect that decision when made by a client?

Web Links

- Mental Health Evidence and Research: World Health Organization
  http://www.who.int/mental_health/evidence/en/
- Equity in Mental Health Service: Canadian Mental Health Association
  http://ontario.cmha.ca/public-policy/cmha-public-policy/
  current-issues/equity/
- Social Determinates of Mental Health: Adler University (video link)
  https://www.adler.edu/page/institutes/institute-on-social-exclusion/
  projects/mhia/social-determinants-of-mental-health
- Causes of Poverty (International): Global Issues
  http://www.globalissues.org/issue/2/causes-of-poverty
- "'Culture of Poverty' Makes a Comeback": *New York Times*
  http://www.nytimes.com/2010/10/18/us/18poverty.html?_r=0
- Working with Families in the Context of Economic Recession
  http://www.familycentre.org.nz/Publications/PDF's/
  TCXEconomicRecessionWorkingwithFamilies2012.pdf
- Truth and Reconciliation Commission of Canada
  http://www.trc.ca/websites/trcinstitution/index.php?p=3
- The Psychology of Culture: *Monthly Review*
  http://monthlyreview.org/2013/01/01/the-psychology-of-culture/
- Historical Trauma: Sharing Culture
  http://www.sharingculture.info/what-is-historical-trauma.html
- Putting Social Justice into Practice in Psychology Courses: Association for Psychological Science
  http://www.psychologicalscience.org/index.php/publications/
  observer/2007/october-07/putting-social-justice-into-practice-in-
  psychology-courses.html

Key Terms

disadvantage	accessibility
inequity	appropriateness
social justice	cultural/behavioral theories
availability	materialist/structuralist theories

absolute
relative
restrictive
inclusive
consumption basket
equity-based
mixed
developmental
psychobiological
social comparative
conflict
critical theory
internalized oppression
psychological safety
residential schools
60s Scoop
Royal Commission on Aboriginal
    Peoples

Truth and Reconciliation
    Commission
historical trauma
colonial mentality
identity
colonial mistrust
discrimination
assimilate
acculturation
transformation
integration
liberation psychology
conscientization
realismo-critico
de-ideologized reality
social orientation
referential option

CHAPTER 3

VALUES AND BELIEFS

Chapter Outline

Personal
    Culture Orientation Scale
    Self
    Thinking
    Behavior
    Relationships
Political
    Case Example
    Ideology
    Political Spectrum
    Social Policy
    Policy Formation
    Ideology and Personality
    Case Example
Professional
    Traditional Healing
    Ethical Codes
    Case Example
Conclusion
Discussion Questions
Web Links
Key Terms

Values and beliefs underlie all decisions counselors make. They reflect how one views themselves as a cultural person as well as what is both similar to and different from others. These values and beliefs also reflect ideological and political similarities and differences. In addition, these personal and political views interact with the ethical standards of the profession. Understanding self as a cultural person within a sociopolitical environment and in relationship to counseling as a profession is associated with views about social change. It can be helpful for counselors to recognize themselves as political citizens and professionals whose actions align with a social purpose and desired outcome.

When faced with friction between personal, political, and professional ideals, as well as what is actually happening around us and in the lives of our clients, a critical consciousness develops over time and through experience. The purpose of this chapter is to identify values and beliefs associated with cultural differences in personal, political, and professional areas, highlight contributors to the subtle and overt reactions counselors may have to clients, and reflect on civic life and counseling as a profession. At a personal level, values and beliefs can be universal, culturally specific, and unique. Similarly, political values and beliefs are located in ideologies, implicit in the formation and acceptance of policies as well as connected to personality. Professionally, counseling approaches represent underlying values and beliefs about "what works" and ethical standards identify values and beliefs that are to be promoted in practice.

Personal

An important distinction can be made between **etic** and **emic** perspectives (Lee, 1984). An emic perspective, also known as an insider perspective, is from the viewpoint of one who participates in the cultural group. An etic perspective, also known as an outsider perspective, is from the viewpoint of someone who does not participate in the cultural group. Consider your classmates as an example. As students in a course, you share an experience of being a member of the same group. After class, however, many students go their separate ways to interact with other people in other settings as part of other groups. The same can be said of cultural group participation and membership. Despite being students, those who are older and younger, transgendered, male and female, may participate in different cultural groups. Each of us simultaneously holds both perspectives as a member of some groups but not others (Cheshire, 2012).

An important comment about culture included in the definition provided in Chapter 2 bears repeating: cultural groups are layered. Some cultural groups are larger than others, representing more people's values and beliefs. Within larger groups there are smaller groups. This is a key message because the notion of diversity has a distancing effect by emphasizing what makes people different from one another. These differences can be large or small, magnified or minimized. It is equally important to identify similarities. From the most inclusive view possible, the **human family** comprises universal experiences that everyone can relate to (Vontress, 1988). For example, the needs for food, clothing, and shelter are basic and fundamental for each person, family, and community. Cultures develop specific patterns depending on the ways that these needs are most appropriately met for each depending on their histories, current realities, and future aspirations. What a family does to meet basic needs in a large southern urban neighborhood may be quite different from what a family does in a northern, remote community. The routines and rituals, however, have developed in response to shared needs for basic necessities of life (Chantler & Smailes, 2004).

There has been some attention to the structure of a base level of understanding that applies equally across cultures. One approach has been described as a philosophical orientation to counseling practice that has potential to be a unifying basis (Ibrahim, 1984). The basic concepts include the qualities of **human nature**, how **relationships** are defined, the connection between **people and nature**, the **orientation to time**, and tendencies in **expression**. According to this model, differences begin to emerge in response to questions about each concept. Are human beings, by nature, good, bad, or good and bad? Are human relationships linear and hierarchical, collateral and mutual, or individualistic? That is, are they based collectively on the best judgment of the few or the welfare of all, or individually on what is best for each? Do nature and people exist in a harmonious relationship, or is one based on the primacy and control of nature over people, or people over nature? Do human beings focus on the past, present, or future? How do human beings express themselves? How is the expression best described—as being in the present or the future?

Consider the situation of Kevin, a 55-year-old male who is married with two young adult children. He describes himself as a Canadian whose parents emigrated with him and his siblings from Sri Lanka when they were children. Kevin recently lost his job in a factory due to corporate restructuring and at 55 does not have the means to retire. The goal he has is to raise his confidence to a level where he can begin to look for work. To what extent do his values and beliefs about people, relationships, timing, and expression really matter? His beliefs about the world around him are negative, persecutory, and are based in the past and on his value as a laborer.

As his counselor, it may be helpful to connect with him about these areas and consider the possibility of alternative interpretations (i.e., there are good people, there are opportunities, and there are employers who care about employees). There may also be a way to connect with Kevin about the possibility that his future includes opportunity or about relevant ways he could move forward (i.e., there are always people who need others to do things for them, he has beaten the odds before by taking risks, and employers have a need to make themselves wealthy by hiring employees such as himself).

From a more specialist (emic) position, there may be recognition of who is providing a perspective on whom. A critique often offered about psychological approaches is that they are based on Western values and beliefs that may or may not resonate well with individuals from other cultures (Marsella, 2012). A thorough account of values that represent significant differences in worldview has been presented (Baskin, 2011). These distinctions focus on 16 dimensions, from an insider perspective (etic) on Indigenous values and perceptions of difference (emic) from living and working within a Western-dominated values context. These differences exist in the following areas: **permissive** versus **coercive**, **extended family** versus **nuclear family**, **interdependence** versus **independence**, **cooperation** versus **competition**, **nonmaterialistic** versus **materialistic**, **nonaggressive** versus **aggressive**, **humility** versus **confidence**, and **noninterference** versus **interference**. Additional differences include: respect for **elders** versus respect for **youthfulness**, children are gifts versus children are owned, **communal living** versus **isolation**, silence versus noise, emphasis on the group/clan versus emphasis on the individual, time based on nature versus time based on clock, emphasis on **giving** versus emphasis on **acquiring**, and **harmony** with nature versus **control** of nature.

Kevin's cultural experience may be similar in some respects to the counselor's but very different in other ways. What is important is that the recognition of these similarities and differences is in the awareness of the counselor who can choose to work within these values and beliefs to be helpful in a way that is culturally consistent with what the client is accustomed to. It is also essential that the counselor not consider such differences to be targets of change, but rather ways of experiencing that are assets. For example, if he has a more permissive orientation, Kevin may be more inclined to adapt to change than to resist it (i.e., coercive). His reliance on extended family may include efforts to reach out to older, more experienced family members who could provide him with advice and support, in contrast to relying on few or no other family members (i.e., nuclear). An interdependent orientation could be evident in Kevin's tendency to seek help from others in his life rather than trying to find solutions that are the result of only his efforts (i.e., independent). A cooperative orientation might make it more acceptable for him to seek employment in a way that does not infringe on others' efforts rather than in a way that elevates him above others also seeking the same jobs (i.e., competition). A nonmaterialistic orientation could be evident in Kevin's view of employment as a means of meeting basic needs rather than as a way to obtain possessions that others have (i.e., materialistic). A nonaggressive approach could be apparent in the desire to pursue jobs when the time is right as opposed to making "cold calls" asking for work (i.e., aggressive). A humble approach could be evident in a modest accounting of his activities in his resume in contrast to a highly detailed and comprehensive resume (i.e., confidence).

One cultural dimension that has been the subject of considerable attention, and is strongly aligned with values and beliefs, is **individualism-collectivism**. Research on these concepts has led to the development of many instruments used to clarify perceptions of individuals on these dimensions. Recent reviews of these instruments with meta-analyses of scores at the individual, group, and national levels indicate that at an individual level, individualism and collectivism are independent concepts (Oyserman, Coon, & Kemmelmeier, 2002; Realo & Beilmann, 2012; Yang et al., 2012). That is, each person can be high or low in either or both individualism and collectivism (Vargas & Kemmelmeier, 2013).

Culture Orientation Scale

The following is a series of items from an instrument known as the Culture Orientation Scale (Triandis & Gelfland, 1998). The measure is brief and highlights preferences in the areas of collectivism and individualism. In addition, each is classified into horizontal and vertical dimensions. Individuals high in **vertical collectivism** accept the hierarchy and inequality of a collective orientation, while individuals high in **horizontal collectivism** view members of the collective as equals. Those who rate highly on their preference for **vertical individualism** accept inequality among autonomous individuals, while those who indicate a strong preference for **horizontal individualism** focus on equality between all individuals (Triandis & Gelfland, 1998). The following items should be ranked from 1 to 9, with 1 as "never" or "definitely no," and 9 "always" or "definitely yes."

TABLE 3.1 Individualism-Collectivism Questions

It is my duty to take care of my family, even when I have to sacrifice what I want. (VC)

I'd rather depend on myself than others. (HI)

When another person does better than I do, I get tense and aroused. (VI)

The well-being of my coworkers is important to me. (HC)

My personal identity, independent of others, is very important to me. (HI)

It is important that I do my job better than others. (VI)

Parents and children must stay together as much as possible. (VC)

I feel good when I cooperate with others. (HC)

I rely on myself most of the time; I rarely rely on others. (HI)

Winning is everything. (VI)

Family members should stick together, no matter what sacrifices are required. (VC)

Competition is the law of nature. (VI)

If a co-worker got a prize, I would feel proud. (HC)

I often do "my own thing." (HI)

To me, pleasure is spending time with others. (HC)

It is important to me that I respect the decisions made by my groups. (VC)

To find your score, combine individual scores for the four items in each category and then rank the totals from highest to lowest to identify your preference:

Horizontal Collectivism	/36
Vertical Collectivism	/36
Horizontal Individualism	/36
Vertical Individualism	/36

The concepts of individualism and collectivism have been expressed in values and beliefs about the self, thinking, behavior, and relationships. In the following summary of Gorodnichenko and Roland's (2012) analysis, notice yourself in relation to these ideas based on your scores on the Cultural Orientation Scale and how they may be similar to or different from those of a client. Consider the experience of cultural adjustment for a first-generation traditional Muslim woman named Ester from Iran in contrast to a mainstream Western view through the lens of individualism and collectivism. For the purposes of this comparison, consider that Ester's orientation is high in vertical collectivism indicating that she accepts the hierarchy and inequality of a collective orientation. She is low in horizontal collectivism and does not view members of the collective as equal. She has a moderate preference for vertical individualism, within which she accepts inequality among autonomous individuals, and low horizontal individualism, also indicating her acceptance of inequality between individuals.

Self

Research concerning **adjustability**, **self-promotion**, control, and **emotional benefit** has been conducted (Vargas & Kemmelmeier, 2013). An individualist orientation would view the self as independent while a collectivist orientation would see the self as interdependent. In the last example, the client may view herself as interrelated within her community and family. The main modes of learning about self from an individualist orientation would be based in personal reflection, while from a collectivist orientation, others would do the evaluating. Ester would likely have received feedback from others as a way of learning about self. Adjustability from an individualist orientation is very consistent, with the potential to be rigid, while from a collectivist view one would be adaptable as well as inconsistent. Given her adaptability, Ester may be open to change. Control from an individualist orientation is for the individual to shape the world around her or him, while from a collectivist orientation, control is enacted through adjustment and conformity (Marcus & Le, 2013). Ester's efforts may be more consistent with helping family members instead of herself. From an individualist orientation, emotional benefit arises from helping an individual stand out among peers, and from a collectivist orientation this benefit comes from getting along with others (Billing et al., 2013). She may value her children's, husband's, and community's well-being as fundamentally important.

Thinking

From an individualist orientation, thinking is an **analytic** endeavor while from a collectivist orientation, thinking is more holistic in nature (Owe et al., 2013). More specifically, focus from an individualist orientation is on the thing itself while from a collectivist orientation the object and context are equally important. For Ester, her consideration of factors in her decisions may be multiple and interrelated, such as the well-being of her children and husband, as well as other family members and her community. Thinking style from an individualist orientation is abstract and based in logic while from a collectivist orientation, the style is more functional and based in the relationship (He, Sebanz, Sui, & Humphreys, 2014). Ester's relationships and maintaining positive relations may be fundamentally important. There is a risk of fundamental attribution error as a bias in thinking from an individualist orientation, while bias from a collectivist orientation is the service of the needs of the collective. A challenge for Ester may be to accept the need she has to take care of herself and others. Understanding from an individualist orientation is based in the explicit meaning of words while from a collectivist orientation, the **implicit meaning**, tone, and body language are equally important for understanding. She may "read" her family to know how each is coping.

Behavior

The interpretation of meaning of behavior can be differentiated between an individualist and a collectivist orientation. Ability is the hallmark of behavior from an individualist perspective, while effort is the focus from a collectivist perspective. For Ester, attention she puts into her home, children, and husband may be fundamentally important. The response to failure from an individualist perspective is to reorganize and from a collectivist perspective is to try harder. She may be working harder but struggling to keep up with the demands of caring for family members who are struggling themselves. Individualists stand out with their behavior, while collectivists fit in with their behavior. Choice is personal from an individualist orientation and from a collectivist orientation the group influences it. Collective action from an individualist orientation needs to include an incentive while it is naturally strong from a collectivist orientation (Bhullar et al., 2012). **Family ties** from an individualist orientation are weak, but they are strong from a collectivist orientation. Ester may be unrecognized in her efforts, but views them as her duty and may not consider altering them.

Relationships

Relationships also vary between an individualist orientation, with its focus on equality, and a collectivist orientation, with its emphasis on insider versus outsider status (LeFebvre & Franke, 2013). Ester may be very clear about who her family and community are and puts primary emphasis on those interests to the possible exclusion of others. Impositions from an individualist perspective are disliked, and from a collectivist perspective are more likely to be recognized if an insider instigates them (Arpaci & Baloğlu, 2016). However, Ester may take on additional responsibilities if they are needed by a family member. Trust is equally spread with others from an individualist perspective while it is only high within the in-group from a collectivist orientation. Geographic and social mobility are strong from an individualist orientation but weak from a collectivist orientation. She may put great trust in her family but have suspicion of those outside her community.

Political

Personal values and beliefs operate at interpersonal and small group levels as well as extend to the societal level. Although all values and beliefs are political to the extent that they reflect preferred ways for people and groups to operate, there have been studies of attitudes that are explicitly political in their connection to economic and decision making associated with government structure and function. These are critical to social justice in counseling because of their explicit interconnections with sociopolitical factors and mental health.

Cultural diversity is not only an interpersonal phenomenon, but a public and political attitude as well as an agenda that describes how societies recognize and address difference. As is evident from the foregoing chapters, cultural diversity is a societal strength that comes with challenges. One major challenge that needs to be addressed is the hierarchical arrangement of cultural groups with corresponding advantages and opportunities for some over others. Governmental approaches concerning diversity are reflected in their stance on multiculturalism. This stance is based on dominant cultural values and beliefs and is enacted in social policy.

Cultural Mosaic and **Melting Pot** (Smith, 2013) are terms used to describe orientations to multiculturalism in Canada and the United States respectively. While both nations have a diverse ethnic population, each has developed formal policy in a different way relative to immigration and cultural difference. As the labels imply, the idea of a cultural mosaic reflects a particular emphasis on diversity and a recognition of diversity, while a melting pot reflects a particular emphasis on and recognition of commonality. The direction of each reflects different desired outcomes of political efforts. It is arguable whether these approaches actually produce different outcomes, but they do offer contrasting means (Hurn & Tomalin, 2013).

Case Example
A current issue that is explicitly political and personal is the phenomenon of **Islamophobia**. The term was coined by Runneymeade Trust (1997) in the UK. The Centre for Race & Gender (2016) defines it as "a contrived fear or prejudice fomented by the existing Eurocentric and Orientalist global power

structure. It is directed at a perceived or real Muslim threat through the main-tenance and extension of existing disparities in economic, political, social and cultural relations, while rationalizing the necessity to deploy violence as a tool to achieve 'civilizational rehab' of the target communities (Muslim or other-wise). Islamophobia reintroduces and reaffirms a global racial structure through which resource distribution disparities are maintained and extended." The causes of such fear have been theorized as an outgrowth from the increase in the Muslim population worldwide, Western migration, and the September 11 World Trade Center attacks (Gada, 2015).

Islamophobia has been characterized as "a 'phobia' of multiculturalism and the transruptive effect that Islam can have in Europe and the West through transcultural processes" (Marranci, 2004, p. 107). Right-wing political inter-ests in Europe have characterized the cultural differences between Muslims and non-Muslims as insurmountable in order to promote hostility (Betz & Meret, 2009). In the United States, President-elect Donald Trump has called for the "total and complete shutdown of Muslims entering the United States" (Justice & Stanley, 2016).

Fear of Muslims and the religion of Islam have been recognized in psychol-ogy as problematic (Lee et al., 2013). The counseling profession has recognized the challenges facing Muslims in the West: "The overwhelming pressures faced by this group, including surveillance, hate crimes, and institutional discrimina-tion, stimulate an urgent need for psychologists to better understand and ensure the well-being of this population" (Amer & Bagasra, 2013). It has been found that Muslims who perceive high levels of Islamophobia are likely to strug-gle with their identification with a national cultural identity (Kunst, Tajamal, Sam, & Ulleberg, 2012) as well as face significant psychological distress (Kunst, Sam, & Ulleberg, 2013). There is a clear connection between political senti-ment and mental health, as well as the values and beliefs explicit in political efforts of exclusion rooted in irrational fear.

Ideology

Although the term **ideology** refers in its strictest sense to the ideal way to live, it has been widely used in relation to political values and beliefs (Larrain, 2013). **Political ideology** is about social action and social order (Feldman & Johnston, 2014). It can be used for nation building, social movement, revolu-tion, or to frame the orientation of a political party to distinguish its purpose and message from those of other competing groups. It has also come to be used to define government and economic systems, which is the purpose for its use in this book. Many of the earliest ideologies were religions; now many are secular, but some retain religion as a source (Jost & Amodio, 2012).

Ideologies represent assumptions about change, individual and group rights, as well as social inequality (Bajaj, 2011). For example, is the purpose of government and economic systems to protect or reject the status quo? Does the need of the group outweigh the needs of an individual? How much social inequality can be accepted? Political ideologies can exist at higher levels of abstraction, referring to values and beliefs that are shared but within them differences also exist. Can these differences be tolerated? In an orthodoxy, only one ideology is accepted and unity comes about because of **conformity**, while in pluralism there is more than one ideology within a political system and unity comes about through the **toleration of differences** (Hirst, 2014). There is a great deal of complexity within a pluralist system. For example, can all ideologies coexist peacefully? Is reconciliation or compromise always possible?

A classic approach for organizing political ideologies can be created on the basis of two dimensions. Assumptions about goals and methods, referring to forms of governance and economic systems, create four ideological perspectives (Heywood, 2012). These classic ideologies include **conservatism**, **fascism**, **socialism**, and **liberalism** (Alexander, 2014). A classic conservative ideology is a government with leadership by moral right and a centrally controlled economy, while a classic liberal ideology is a government with an elected leader and an unregulated economy (Feldman & Johnston, 2014). Fascism (Passmore, 2014) and socialism (Crosland, 2014), respectively, refer to an imposed leadership and an unregulated economy, and an elected leadership with a controlled economy. Contemporary examples of conservative governance include Liechtenstein with its constitutional monarchy and free market economy and the neo-fascist stance of the totalitarian British National Party with its emphasis on nationalist economics. Contemporary socialism with an emphasis on a one-party state with a centralized, public economy is exemplified by Cuba. Liberalism with its free market economy and elected governance is evident in the United States and Canada.

Political Spectrum

A contemporary political spectrum organizes ideologies from right to left (Lasswell & Kaplan, 2013). On the right side is conservatism with its purpose to preserve the status quo and oppose change, **reactionaries** with its purpose to throw back forces of change and restore old order, and fascism with its focus on mobilizing for war and suppressing pluralism to achieve unity through orthodoxy (Hall, 2015). On the left is **radicalism** (Bonnett, 2013) with its focus on the roots of problems and the need to change societal foundations, socialism with its focus on advancing the interests of the society against those of the elites, and **communism** with its emphasis on public and shared ownership to suppress difference and achieve unity through orthodoxy (Almond, 2015). In the center is liberalism with its emphasis on freedom, social change, individual rights, a market economy, and the use of ideas from the political right and left (Joshi & O'Dell, 2013). Politics in Canada and the United States fall into the center of the spectrum with the different parties varying on their degree of government involvement in economic affairs, which is higher on the left and lower on the right. This is an important awareness to hold as a counselor involved in social justice as the "solutions" to disadvantage vary considerably. In a free market economy assistance via private charity is favored, while a more left-leaning view would hold that government is responsible for making engagement in the economy possible for all citizens.

Social Policy

Social policy is the portion of public policy that combines economic, social, and political forces with a focus on human well-being, social relations, and the systems that produce it. Social policy existed as a field of study following the development of the modern welfare state after World War II. The **Beveridge Report**, as it came to be known, focused on public measures and expenditures to address poverty, illness, housing, education, and employment for citizens (Whiteside, 2014). This direction had a great deal more support in Canada than the United States, but each country has developed a set of national, state or provincial and territorial, and local social programs to address related issues. According to Morel, Palier, and Palme (2012) there are three types of welfare states, including those rooted in **social democracy**, **Christian democracy**, and **liberal ideologies**. From a social democratic approach, universalism underlies the state's provision of service and support, with low need for reliance on the family or the market. A Christian democratic approach focuses on locally delivered, entitlement-based services. Finally, in a liberal approach, which is where the United States and Canada most clearly align, the market and family provide the primary level of support with the state addressing only the most basic needs with services that are usually means-tested. Based on this approach, only those who need the support most are provided with it, and there are tight controls and assessments to determine eligibility for the services. As an example of this, consider your views about the costs of professional service. As a counselor in a public agency, what criteria are used to determine eligibility for services? Are some individuals eligible and others ineligible? What is the rationale for the distinction? In private practice, is any work pro bono? Is a sliding scale used? How are those decisions made?

Consider your views at a societal level. Are there services that should be available to all citizens? Why and why not? Consider the example of the client at the beginning of this chapter who was out of work. Should there be government support for him to make decisions about his career, determine his strengths, or train to develop new skills if necessary? Regarding the example of the woman earlier in the chapter, should there be income or training support for her to be able to remain close to her home and operate a home-based business or local community service that is directly related to the needs of families in her neighborhood? Consider the policy implications for the Islamophobia example, such as the need for more targeted hate crime legislation.

Policy Formation

Although social policies come into being through enacted priorities of governments at different levels, the process by which they are created varies. Several models have been proposed to characterize the ways that policies are constructed, including **traditional**, **rational**, **incremental**, and **public choice** models (Buse, Mays, & Walt, 2012). A traditional model is based on the belief that there is a best solution to a particular problem that is clearly identified and studied before options are generated, alternatives considered, and a decision is made. A rational model is based on a comparison between what is ideal and what is real, with a measure put in place to create a good-enough solution to the identified problem. An incremental model is the outcome of decision makers taking action on their beliefs about the type and likelihood of consequences from a failure to take action against a particular negative outcome. Public choice theory is rooted in the liberal economic theory insofar as the decision is a rational one based in self-interest. The need to create policy that specifically addresses hate crime and strengthens potential sentencing options for convictions may make a difference in threats and violence expressed, but whether it can address public attitudes is questionable. Public spending on media advertisements promoting diversity and recognizing the contributions of all citizens may be a preferred alternative policy development area. An incremental model depends to some extent on the government's values and beliefs about punishment and reward as motivators of behavior, the means to obtain political support to have it passed, and the public reception to such an effort.

Ideology and Personality

How members of the public receive government efforts in economic and social affairs, including potential policy change, can be related back to personal preferences and style. There is merit to the notion that ideas and people select each other (Jost, Federico, & Napier, 2013). While it may be possible to quickly identify the types of political ideas and processes that resonate most clearly, there has been formal research linking personal preferences to ideological commitments. Based on the political spectrum ideas advanced earlier in this chapter, the factors that underlie preferences for particular ideologies focus on two continua: advocating versus resisting **social change** and accepting or rejecting **inequality**. Those with a preference for ideologies at the ends of the spectrum have a greater concern over social change and those in the center are more open to change. Clarity and structure are also preferences more likely held by those at the ends of the spectrum, with relatively less preference for them among those in the center. However, those in the center are among the most likely to tolerate a great range of inequality including economic and social stratification. Consider the following example as illustrative of personal experiences contributing to professional efforts within an explicitly political frame of reference.

Case Example

Frantz Fanon died of leukemia at the age of 36 years but not before having a significant impact on the fields of mental health and social activism. Fanon was born in 1925 in Martinique, which was a French colony, to a middle-class family. His mother was mixed-race and his father was black. The French language and history he learned in school was presented to and accepted by Fanon as his own. Despite his middle-class upbringing, Fanon became sensitive to the racial inequalities most notable through his witnessing of French Navy mistreatment of black citizens.

At the age of 18 years, Fanon left Martinique to join the Allied troops in British-controlled Dominica. From there, he traveled to Free French bases in Morocco and Algeria, and ultimately to France, where he participated in the battles of Alsace. Once the Germans were defeated he and other black soldiers were transferred out of Germany while photos were taken of victorious white allied troops crossing the Rhine River. Fanon became disillusioned. While he was willing to die for his country, he saw how other African and Indian Allied soldiers were treated after the war and began to question his French identity (Bulhan, 2004).

Fanon found his way back to Martinique and completed his undergraduate education. During this time he met the poet Aime Césaire and learned about **negritude** (Césaire, 2001). This understanding fit well with his developing resentment of French colonialism and offered the notion of black racial identity for all Africans worldwide. During his medical training and certification as a psychiatrist in France, Fanon developed a strong interest in the role of culture, mental illness, and health (Alessandrini, 2005).

It was his first attempt at a doctoral dissertation in 1951 that was published in English as *Black Skin, White Masks* in 1952, which reflected on his experience of racism. His experiences in France were of a black-white divide, while his Caribbean experience included lighter and darker skin-based racism. The metaphor that is central to the work is that black citizens have to wear white masks if they are to get by in a white world. Fanon saw **negrification** to have negative effects on blacks and Africans because it normalized negative attitudes toward them and positive attitudes toward whites and Europeans. This dichotomy was so consuming that there were no alternatives (Cherki & Benabid, 2006). The labeling as inferior with an imposed racial identity was traumatizing. Mental illness and discrimination based on race were alienating, took away people's humanity, and were triggered by **colonization**. However, he clearly noted that self-judgments do not have to be filtered through white norms and values (Gibson, 2003).

In 1953 Fanon was head of psychiatry for a hospital in another French colony, Algeria. He was treating French soldiers who were fighting against the indigenous revolutionaries he supported, while also treating Algerian torture victims, so he felt that he had no choice but to quit. He joined the indigenous revolutionary cause and continued his writing (Rabaka, 2010). In *The Wretched of the Earth*, which was published just before his death in 1961, Fanon wrote about race, class, national culture, and violence. He also wrote about the right to use violence to combat oppression. *The Wretched of the Earth* was written by a developing world author for a developing world audience.

Fanon's contributions have been noted in several areas such as cultural psychology, race and ethnic studies, and political science. While his personal experiences contributed a great deal to the values and beliefs represented in his political views, he remained both a psychiatrist and advocate for decolonization. The social changes he pursued were in his activities at work, which were novel for the time in a psychiatric unit. For example, he included Muslim references in place of Christian ones for Muslim patients, encouraged patients to have a choice in their treatment, and started a day treatment or outpatient unit. When his political conscience about treating colonial soldiers who were fighting against the indigenous forces grew, he felt that he had to leave that position. His subsequent political writings focused on not simply replacing white oppression with black oppression, but about being equally human.

Professional

Personal and political values and beliefs are also embedded within approaches applied by counselors. For example, the well-known model used as a basis for understanding mental health from a Western medical perspective is the **biopsychosocial** model. It is a clinical philosophy and guide to viewing the individual as a product of biological, social, and psychological forces. George Engel (1981), its creator, at the time it was offered was responding to a reductionist tendency of medical practice to focus only on the body of the mind–body dichotomy, the scientifically (biologically) observable, and the person as object of study. In its place, he argued for an integration of the mind-body dualism, more complex and interactive explanations of causality including the client's own attributions, and attention to the relationship and interactions between professional and client (Álvarez, Pagani, & Meucci, 2012).

Western talk therapies, the dominant form of intervention by counselors in mental health, emphasize the individual; focus on discrete parts of self; value autonomy, separateness, and individuality; and have a low emphasis on social-contextual forces (Fitzgerald, 2013). Common assumptions underlying these approaches include **verbal communication**, **individual centered**, **expressiveness**, openness and intimacy, **cause–effect orientation**, distinction between physical and emotional wellness, a nuclear family, adherence to time, long-range goals, and clarity without ambiguity (Loewenthal, 2013).

Hurley (2010) offered an analysis of differences between four major approaches to counseling practice including **humanism**, **existentialism**, **behaviorism**, and **psychoanalysis**. These approaches to talk therapy can be arranged according to two dimensions: free will versus determinism and overt versus covert focus. Humanism, based on symbolic interactionism, focuses on meaning created through interpersonal interaction (Dryden, 2012). The needs of the individual are placed slightly higher than the needs of society. The approach is rooted in free will and is overt in focus. Existentialism, based on existential philosophies, focuses on authenticity through the exercise of personal choice and reflection on the meaning of existence. The needs of the individual are elevated above the needs of society. The approach is rooted in free will and is covert in focus (Sharf, 2015). Behaviorism, based on positivism, focuses on stimulus or behavior and response. The needs of society are most important. The approach is rooted in determinism and is overt in focus. Psychoanalysis, based in structural determinism, focuses on unconscious forces (McLeod, 2013). The needs of the client are more important than the needs of society. The approach is rooted in determinism and is covert in focus.

From each perspective, a critique of the other perspectives can be offered (Hurley, 2010). Humanism critiques behaviorism for focusing only on the mechanics, existentialism for missing the importance of being together, and psychoanalysis for being cynical and limiting. Existentialism critiques behaviorism for viewing people as robots, humanism for missing the importance of personal responsibility, and psychoanalysis for not seeing the authentic souls of people. A behavioral critique of humanism is that the approach had no basis in science, of existentialism is that it is mystical nonsense, and of psychodynamic practitioners is that they fail to notice what is obvious. A psychoanalytic criticism of behaviorism is that it is much too surface-oriented, of humanism is that it is too naive about people, and of existentialism is that it misses out on the important issues.

Traditional Healing

Even more broadly beyond the dualistic tendency of Western scientific approaches to counseling, there are **cultural models** of illness and healing (Tseng, Bartocci, Rovera, Infante, & De Luca, 2014). For example, cultural causes of problems may include **supernatural**, **natural**, **somato-medical**, and **psychological**. Supernatural causes are located within powers beyond human understanding and control. These include object intrusion (e.g., contaminating object), soul loss (e.g., person's soul leaves body and is unable to return), spirit intrusion or possession (e.g., evil spirits in body), breach of taboo (e.g., punishment for religious wrongdoing), and sorcery (e.g., malicious intent of others with spiritual powers). Natural causes refer to universal principles that govern all of creation including behavior and health, such as disharmony of natural elements, imbalance, and fate (Moodley, Stewart, & Choudhury, 2011). There are also somato-medical causes of sickness that are considered as undesirable conditions within one's own body, such as distress or problems in an internal organ, too much exercise, work, or food, vitality not maintained, or an inborn illness. Finally, psychological causes refer to undesirable mental affect which results in sickness such as fright, overburdening, and excessive emotion.

Important questions that follow from a cultural perspective may include: What do you call your problem? What do you think caused it? Why do you think it started when it did? What does it do to you? How severe, short, or long? What do you fear most about it? What problems has it caused for you? What kind of treatment should you receive? What are the results you want? The qualities of healers vary considerably depending on the culture and expertise required to treat particular sicknesses and the type of healing undertaken (Shalukoma et al., 2016). Not all healers are trained equally and, even from a particular culture and issue, approaches taken are not necessarily the same (Lor, Xiong, Park, Schwei, & Jacobs, 2016). There are some counselors who have both Western and cultural training and expertise (Nortje, Oladeji, Gureje, & Seedat, 2016). However, those who do not are best served by knowing the local community and making referrals when needed.

Ethical Codes

In the Canadian Code of Ethics for Psychologists (Canadian Psychological Association, 2000) members undertaking activities that the code applies to are required to "place the welfare of the society and individual members of that society above the welfare of the discipline and its own members." Counselors are therefore expected to operate at a level of ethical consciousness beyond what would be expected of those outside the profession. The principles ranked in order of importance to decision making include: (I) **respect for dignity**, (II) **responsible caring**, (III) **integrity in relationships**, and

(IV) **responsibility to society** (Canadian Psychological Association, 2000). These principles are absolute and focus on individual rights. While the most important consideration is the individual client's rights above the rights of others, in cases where there is potential for serious harm, counselors are required to take action to prevent that harm from occurring. Principles I and II reflect exclusive emphasis on the individual client's dignity and welfare, while principle III reflects relationships with clients as well as others. In principle IV, the potential for community-level change is warranted when "structures or policies seriously ignore or oppose the principles of respect for the dignity of persons, responsible caring, integrity in relationships, or responsibility to society" (Canadian Psychological Association, 2000, p. 28). Indeed, under such circumstances, counselors have "a responsibility to speak out in a manner consistent with the principles of this *Code*, and advocate for appropriate change to occur as quickly as possible" (Canadian Psychological Association, 2000, p. 28).

The American Psychological Association's Code of Ethics for Psychologists (2010) has five general principles. These principles are: (A) **beneficence** and **nonmaleficence**, (B) **fidelity** and **responsibility**, (C) **integrity**, (D) **justice**, and (E) **respect** for people's **rights** and **dignity**. These principles are similarly absolute and heavily emphasize the rights of individuals (Ramser, 1996). Similar to the CPA Code, these principles focus on the client and the counselor's relationships with the client and others. However, a difference in relation to diversity is explicitly recognized in the principle E. While it is the final principle to apply in the resolution of an ethical dilemma, counselors are encouraged to be "aware of and respect cultural, individual and role differences, including those based on age, gender, gender identity, race, ethnicity, culture, national origin, religion, sexual orientation, disability, language and socioeconomic status and consider these factors when working with members of such groups" (American Psychological Association, 2010, p. 4). While there is no specific attention to the need for advocacy of leadership in social change, they are encouraged not to "knowingly participate in or condone activities of others based upon such prejudices" (American Psychological Association, p. 4).

The codes under which counselors often operate are not specific to advocacy efforts or community change activities and do center on absolute rights for individual clients. However, both codes offer opportunities for counselors to consider diversity and equity in the dealings with people and not to support prejudiced practices. In the case of the Canadian code, counselors also work toward change at a broader level that benefits individuals and groups facing sociopolitical disadvantage. Consider the ways that citizens and professionals through their political efforts can promote social justice through the following case example of the Canadian Museum for Human Rights.

Case Example

The **Canadian Museum for Human Rights** (CMHR) opened its doors in the fall of 2014. The museum's mandate is "to explore the subject of human rights with special but not exclusive reference to Canada in order to enhance the public's understanding of human rights, to promote respect for others and to encourage reflection and dialogue" (CMHR, 2015). It is situated on First Nations Treaty 1 lands and on the homeland of Métis peoples. The city of Winnipeg has a history of social change from the General Strike of 1919 to Nellie McClung and women's voting rights, and also has the largest urban Aboriginal population in Canada, the largest French-speaking community in Western Canada, and a growing immigrant population.

There are several themes represented throughout the exhibits such as Indigenous perspectives, human rights injustices of the past in Canada, laws and protective mechanisms in place, and a substantial display about the Holocaust and genocides across the world. Fundamental issues include the existence of human rights, what they are and where they came from, what we recognize now as violations, and what we can do about them, as well as a vision for the future and a plan for how to get there. The real influence of this museum is its ability to mark progress on human rights. There are tensions between absolute rights for everyone and relative rights for those who are at risk or in need of protection. There are also tensions between individual rights for each person relative to the group, and group rights, which can be exercised at a cost to the autonomy of individuals, evident throughout the stories and displays.

Conclusion

The values and attitudes of counselors are also subject to the messages of prominent sociopolitical forces that place responsibility for everything on the individual. As citizens of a community, city, or country, each of us recognizes and operates based on a particular view of reality as well as understandings of the social world and of the forces that create and sustain it. An understanding of both social problems and potential solutions follows from this awareness. The role and functionality of government is often considered and criticized in relation to personal welfare and public policy. However, it is rarely considered that political power exists outside of government and that such power, when expressed collectively, can be highly influential on public policy. Within such policy, the professions hold a considerable amount of power. This power is exercised as either support of the political status quo or of progressive social change.

Discussion Questions

1. How have you experienced being both an insider and outsider in relation to other social groups? An emic perspective as an insider on one's own cultural group can be very different than an etic or outsider perspective on the same group. Are there groups with which you carry both insider and outsider status? How can this be a help and a hindrance as a citizen and as a professional?

2. To what extent do you agree with universalist positions about people, their nature, and the challenges they face? What makes people different from one another? And what makes each of us unique? How possible is it to operate from a collectivist belief and value system in a society where individualism is so dominant?

3. Where on the political spectrum do you locate yourself? What are the primary values and beliefs about social change, personal and collective rights, and social inequality represented by your position? Does this position shift? How? Consider the possibility that public health care would include counseling services. Would you support this? Should counseling services remain largely private? Why?

4. Social policy orients the work of public institutions to a particular purpose and population. What social policies do you see as having the most positive effects on the clients you work with? What policies do you see as having the most negative effects on the clients you see? What changes should be made?

5. When you consider the types of activities that counselors engage in, including the schools of thought they represent in their work and their use of talk therapy, to what extent do you see value in traditional healing? Should traditional healing be included in counseling practice? What are the benefits and drawbacks of such a position?

6. From your reading of this chapter, what would you say are absolutely fundamental and universal human rights that all individuals should have? To what extent are these rights protected in the nation, region, and organization or community in which you practice?

Web Links

- Continuum of Individualistic and Collectivistic Values
  http://www.ncset.org/publications/essentialtools/diversity/partIII.asp
- Instruments to Measure Identity and Acculturation
  http://www.ncbi.nlm.nih.gov/books/NBK248425/

- Political Parties of Canada
  http://www.thecanadaguide.com/political-parties
- Negritude Movement
  http://www.blackpast.org/gah/negritude-movement
- The Biopsychosocial Revolution
  http://www.ncbi.nlm.nih.gov/pmc/articles/PMC1495036/
- First Nations Health Authority: Traditional Healing
  http://www.fnha.ca/what-we-do/traditional-healing
- Canadian Museum for Human Rights
  https://humanrights.ca

Key Terms

etic	isolation
emic	giving
human family	acquiring
human nature	harmony
relationships	control
people and nature	individualism-collectivism
orientation to time	vertical collectivism
expression	horizontal collectivism
permissive	vertical individualism
coercive	horizontal individualism
extended family	adjustability
nuclear family	self-promotion
interdependence	emotional benefit
independence	analytic
cooperation	implicit meaning
competition	family ties
nonmaterialistic	cultural mosaic
materialistic	melting pot
nonaggressive	Islamophobia
aggressive	ideology
humility	political ideology
confidence	conformity
noninterference	toleration of differences
interference	conservatism
elders	fascism
youthfulness	socialism
communal living	liberalism

reactionaries
radicalism
communism
Beveridge Report
social democracy
Christian democracy
liberal ideologies
traditional
rational
incremental
public choice
social change
inequality
negritude
negrification
colonization
biopsychosocial
verbal communication
individual centered
expressiveness
cause-effect orientation
humanism

existentialism
behaviorism
psychoanalysis
cultural models
supernatural
natural
somato-medical
psychological
respect for dignity
responsible caring
integrity in relationships
responsibility to society
beneficence
nonmaleficence
fidelity
responsibility
integrity
justice
respect
rights
dignity
Canadian Museum for Human Rights

Discussion Questions
Web Links
Key Terms

Cultural psychologies focus on qualities and processes identified by members of a cultural group for that cultural group. While the origins of some existed before the development of Western counseling theories and practices such as Afrocentric and Aboriginal psychologies, others, such as feminist, LGBTQ, and Latina/o psychologies have developed explicitly in response to the limitations of mainstream approaches. Cultural psychologies are united in the view that mainstream psychology and counseling best align with the sociopolitical context and experiences of white, male, middle class, heterosexual clients.

Diverse perspectives on counseling have been offered by theorists and researchers that attend to both intrapersonal and sociopolitical influences as well as contemporary methods and traditional healing. In this chapter, major concepts from different cultural psychologies are offered as well as profiles of major contributors to professional practice from within each. For each a combination of socioeconomic, political, and historical forces created the need for a culturally based psychology that was sensitive and responsive to the needs and strengths of each group. These psychologies reflect a considerable degree of diversity in relation to their attention to alternative views of well-being and healing, their use of blended approaches that combine mainstream and cultural concepts and practices, or how mainstream practices can be effectively employed with members of particular cultural groups. However, central throughout the perspectives is the need for recognition of oppressive forces and liberation from them through individual and collective social change.

Feminist Psychology

Feminist psychology developed within the women's movement in North America during the 1960s (Cole, Rothblum, & Chesler, 2014). At the time psychology was a male-dominated discipline with theories and approaches to development and counseling based on men's experiences. A major focus for feminist psychology was and is gender and power (Gergen & Davis, 2013).

Origins
While feminist psychology started as a critique of male-dominated theory, practice, and research, which was particularly critical of psychoanalytic theory, it developed into a rich tradition of scholarship and practice (Eagly, Eaton, Rose, Riger, & McHugh, 2012). Women's contributions and work were not

reflected in the counseling methods employed, and it was necessary to describe women's experiences from women's perspectives. In addition, counseling practices and mental health standards were harmful to women who were put down in both obvious and subtle ways (Ball et al., 2013). For example, when non-compliant with **stereotypes**, such as a display of aggressiveness in contrast to the expectation of passivity, the behavior and individual were both **pathologized** (Brennan, 2002).

The development of theory occurred in three phases, which included the use of techniques from other counseling approaches in ways that were empowering for women, the inclusion of feminism in other approaches to remove outdated and sexist content, and the development of a complete theory of diversity and oppression (Donovan, 2012). There are four major perspectives in contemporary feminist counseling, which are liberal, cultural, radical, and socialist (Tong, 2013). In **liberal feminism** (Jasper, 2015) the goal is to help individual women overcome the constraints of their socialization and achieve equality with men through empowerment, dignity, and fulfillment via power analysis and personal expression. In **cultural feminism** (Naples, 2012) oppression is the result of the societal devaluation of women's strengths, and the efforts of this approach center on the feminization of society. Within this perspective, counseling efforts may be geared toward equalization in the therapeutic relationship through self-disclosure. In **radical feminism** (Gunew, 2013) the oppression of women is understood to be embedded in patriarchy and counseling is to be transformative about gender relationships. This may be promoted in counseling through assertiveness building, making changes in daily lives, and using an interpersonal definition of the problem rather than an intrapersonal definition. Finally, in **socialist feminism** (Stewart, 2015) there is a recognition that multiple oppressions exist and societal change is necessary. Within counseling, examples of related activities include refocusing from a negative view to a positive one, turning anger outward where it belongs instead of inward, and dealing with guilt for focusing on self instead of others (Naples & Bojar, 2013).

Concepts

Counseling in feminist psychology may focus on symptom removal, self-esteem, interpersonal relationships, personal empowerment, body image, diversity, political awareness, and social action (Barrett, 2014). Major principles of feminist therapy are that the **personal is political** and that an egalitarian counseling relationship is needed to counter the hierarchical relationships outside of therapy that are oppressive (Hill & Ballou, 2013). Definitions and expressions of distress and illness are reworked and reinterpreted to be understood as political and **socially prescribed** labels that disadvantage women (Rothblum & Hill, 2016).

Oppression is integrated throughout the consciousness-raising within counseling (Hill & Ballou, 2013).

Concepts in the counseling process center on recognition of the sociopolitical context. The problems that women bring into counseling are rooted in the context and cannot be understood apart from that context (Root & Brown, 2014). Women, through consciousness-raising and recognition of personal influence via expertise and understanding of the counseling process itself, make changes in their lives and thereby their context through social action (Enns & Williams, 2012). Major goals of counseling include awareness of **gender socialization**, one's own internalized image of role and replacement of the troubling beliefs associated with it with more functional beliefs (Root & Brown, 2014). Finally, counseling can also attend to skills necessary to change the oppressive environment (Hill, 2013).

Sandra Bem was a major contributor to feminist psychology and counseling practice. Not only did she live her values of gender equality in her private life, but she also did so in her public life as a researcher and clinician. She made significant contributions by her challenges to stereotypical gender roles and norms by being an example herself as well as an expert witness in court. Her contributions to theories of gender development and sexual behavior remain influential.

Key Figure: Sandra Bem (1944-2014)

Sandra Bem had a modest childhood, growing up in a working-class neighborhood. Her mother was a secretary and the family lived in subsidized housing. During university she met her husband, a social psychology professor. Their agreement with marriage was that they would share household duties and decisions (Liben & Bigler, 2015). This was a novel concept at the time as the term **sexism** did not yet exist and traditional gender roles were commonplace (Stewart & Dottolo, 2014). She completed her doctorate in 1968 at Cornell University in developmental psychology where she did specific work in the areas of gender schema, sexuality, and clinical psychology. She went back to school in the 1990s to obtain training in counseling.

Bem's contributions to psychology and social justice were evident in her lifestyle with her **egalitarian** marriage and relationship with her husband who traveled and lectured with her on **sex role stereotypes** (Rahilly, 2015). She was an expert witness in sexual discrimination cases. Her research data challenged assumptions that sex roles were opposite, bipolar, or mutually exclusive. Indeed, individuals could identify with **feminine** and **masculine** qualities, be high in one or the other, low in both (**undifferentiated**) or high in both (**androgynous**) (Jahanbakhsh, Jomehri, & Mujembari, 2015). The conclusion that sex roles were culturally based, started young, and created an uneven playing field for women and men made a mark in psychology and counseling practice (Carr, Hagai, & Zurbriggen, 2015). In *An Unconventional Family*, Bem shared the private details of her life and child rearing, and this awareness greatly influenced her psychotherapy practice for which she was licensed in New York in 2000 (Bowman, 2015). Consider the role of a counselor in the following example and how efforts to help a client cope with his oppressive environment could be supplemented by efforts to change attitudes and provide group support.

Case Example

You are a counselor working in a secondary school. Josh, a 16-year-old, is referred to you because he is struggling with low mood and having difficulty concentrating. His teacher is concerned about his lack of attention to schoolwork. He is attending but not participating, and looking sad and withdrawn in class. This represents a shift in his behavior and there have been no sudden changes in his living or school situation. He recently turned a story in to his English teacher in which the protagonist, a bisexual man, kills himself. The teacher contacted his mother who was supportive of the referral and happy that he would get some help.

Through meeting with this young man you learn that he is indeed struggling. His mood is low, he has trouble sleeping and difficulty concentrating. He is drinking more than usual on the weekends, partying with friends and "other people" he goes out with after his friends go home for the evening. He is having thoughts about suicide and wishes he "wasn't here anymore." Josh has a father of European decent and a mother of Caribbean decent. His mother moved from Jamaica when she was a child. Josh's parents divorced three years ago after his father had an affair with another man. His father lives with his partner in another part of the country. Josh lives with his mom, who is single.

Josh had several girlfriends with whom he had sexual relationships. His first sexual relationship with a male partner was recent, when he was intoxicated and partying on the weekend. He is wondering if he is gay or straight or both. His stress level is increasing, and he is particularly worried about his mother and her family. He knows that they would have a lot of trouble handling the news that he was gay and would not understand bisexuality at all. He's not sure that he does himself. He is reluctant to tell his mother, who is a conservative Christian. There are three interrelated issues surrounding educational performance, mental health challenges, and identity issues.

Counseling Interventions

Regarding educational performance, as a counselor in a school you may consider his challenges to be learning problems caused by stress. Does he need an educational assessment, learning strategies help, classroom accommodations, or homework support?

Regarding mental health challenges, you also know that there are symptoms of depression and potential suicide risk. Does he need a psychiatric assessment for depression, anxiety, or other potential psychiatric issues?

However, there are also issues around identity, family, religion, and peer relationships. Josh is questioning his sexual orientation. He worries that if he is gay, he will lose his mother's and his friends' support and become one of the people in the school kids segregate because of sexual orientation. These concerns center on his sense of self, his social network, and his sense of personal safety at school as well as family support at home. Does he need supportive counseling to make sense of how he is feeling and build confidence in who he is?

Another Possible Intervention

You know that the school has problems with homophobia, prejudice, and discrimination. You overhear students using gay slurs in the hallways, see a lack of gay affirmative materials in the library, know that the sexual education taught is about abstinence and pregnancy prevention, and know there are no "out" faculty or staff members at the school. You know that it is not a safe place for youth to come out. How could this be addressed? How could a counselor support the development of a Gay–Straight Alliance in the school?

Bob Parlin started the first public school **Gay–Straight Alliance** in Massachusetts in 1991 (Mayo, 2015). He was a teacher who came out to his colleagues after four years in the school and did so at the risk of losing his job because of the attitude that all the students, according to the school administration, were heterosexual. The issue was fundamentally about school safety. He became involved at the state level to implement the recommendations of the "Safe Schools Program for Gay and Lesbian Students" in 1993 and traveled across the state delivering workshops and training for teachers to deal with homophobia in the schools (Toomey & Russell, 2013).

GSAs are youth-led organizations that offer broad-based support for youth who are heterosexual, questioning, gay, lesbian, bisexual, and queer. They provide a safe place for youth who are or are themselves questioning, in an LGBTQ family, or have LGBTQ friends. The efforts include a range of formal and informal activities offered during days, evenings, and weekends in school or in the community. Each GSA has a different size and structure, sponsorships, and levels of formality. They work with their members, share information about relevant issues with those who are not members, and participate in other social change efforts to promote inclusion and safety in their schools and communities (Davis, Stafford, & Pullig, 2014). There are thousands of GSAs across North America.

LGBTQ Psychology

Lesbian, gay, bisexual, trans, and queer psychology developed in response to the pathologization of gender and sexuality by the psychiatric community (Roughley & Morrison, 2013). Psychology was heavily **heteronormative** with deviations from a male and female heterosexual relationship characterized as illness. The focus was explicitly on inclusion and normalization of sexual identities and relationships (Domínguez, Bobele, Coppock, & Peña, 2015).

Origins

LGBTQ psychology started as a response to the pathological view of homo-sexuality and embraced some concepts from within mainstream psychology as well as desensitizing existing practices and informing new developments. Existing practices and standards in mental health led to beliefs that homosex-uality was a developmental maladjustment (Stewart & Roy, 2014). During the political change of the 1960s, the **gay rights movement** began to develop. It was not until the 1970s that the movement gained momentum and gay-affirmative psychology marked the beginning of recognition of healthy normal development (Bullough, 2014). In the 1980s, it became "Lesbian and Gay Psychology," and later LGB, LGBT, and LGBTQ.

LGBTQ psychology is a psychology concerned with the experiences of LGBTQ people (Peel & Riggs, 2014). Although there was early progressive European research on sexuality and gender, Freud's influence on psychology remained pronounced (Alldred & Fox, 2015). The emergence of sex research in the United States opened the possibility of separating identity from behav-ior. Kinsey's seven-point scale of sexual preference was very influential and contributed a scientific perspective to the normalization of bisexuality (Suresha, 2016). Despite emerging research, a great deal of effort was required to educate practicing professionals who held outdated views. While the **Diagnostic and Statistical Manual of Mental Disorders** removed homosexuality as a disorder in 1987 and the World Health Organization removed it from the **International Classification of Diseases** in 1993, heterosexist attitudes remained prevalent within mental health (Drescher, 2015). Conversion thera-pies continued to be practiced, and more change was necessary to challenge heteronormativity. This is reflected in the American Psychological Association's "Appropriate Therapeutic Responses to Sexual Orientation," released in 1997 (Byne, 2014).

A more contemporary view of LGBTQ psychology recognizes impor-tant differences within the LGBTQ population while also acknowledging the population is united by life outside of dominant sexuality and sex/gender norms (Glassgold & Drescher, 2014). Theory development continues against the challenge of heteronormativity because of the need for inclusion and sensitivity of diversity in related research and practice in development, health, and counseling areas (Montgomery & Stewart, 2012). Activism remains as essential as it has ever been to address contemporary human rights abuses within the international community, as well as local issues of discrimination and violence (Swank & Fahs, 2012).

Concepts

Main topics of LGBTQ psychology center on prejudice and discrimination, family and parenting issues, coming out, and identity development (Pereira & Costa, 2013). There has been considerable debate about whether community members should seek therapy for mental health problems because of their history of being treated poorly by counseling professionals; instead, they foster communities of support from within. A more contemporary emphasis is on **gay affirmative** therapy by counselors who have personal experience (Cochran & Robohm, 2015). Depression and relationship problems are frequent issues. Social stress is a major contributor to mental health challenges.

Counselor awareness is essential. Counselors need to be clear about their own beliefs and feelings (Martell, 2014). Recognition of the oppression that all LGBTQ people have experienced is key, and efforts to deprogram internalized stereotypes of people who are LGBTQ, encourage a support network, and promote consciousness-raising are essential (Johnson, 2012). From the literature, additional concepts include the development of the client's own value system, with an awareness of risks of identifying with mainstream societal values, reducing shame and guilt, and affirming sense of self, identity, thoughts, and feelings (O'Shaughnessy & Spokane, 2013). Counselors should be aware of and sensitive to internalized homophobia (Barnes & Meyer, 2012). Activism remains crucial (Thoreson, 2014). Consider the contributions of Richard Isay, an American psychiatrist who practiced psychodynamic therapy. His efforts made significant contributions to counseling that shifted from mental health difficulties as the product of homosexual orientation to mental health difficulties as the product of an oppressive sociopolitical context.

Key Figure: Richard Isay (1934–2012)

Richard Isay grew up in Pittsburgh and attended the University of Rochester Medical School followed by a residency at Yale and the Western New England Psychoanalytic Institute (Roehr, 2012). For ten years, starting in the 1970s, he underwent his own conversion therapy. By the time he completed therapy, he was married with two children (Gelé et al., 2012). In 1980 he came out to his wife and they chose to stay together for another nine years while their children grew up (Kertzner, 2013).

Isay's contributions to psychology and social justice were evident throughout his psychiatric practice. While he himself was closeted, he worked with gay patients to accept themselves and began his writing about homosexuality as normal in the context of a profession where it was considered pathological. The professional pressures he faced were significant. At that time, anyone who was gay was not permitted to train as an analyst accredited by the American Psychoanalytic Association (Yarbrough, 2012).

Isay practiced a subversive form of counseling by teaching acceptance instead of changing patients who were gay. He also started presenting his ideas (Stein & Cohen, 2013). While the American Psychiatric Association stopped classifying homosexuality as a disease in 1973, there was little change among practicing professionals' attitudes (Gelé et al., 2012). Colleagues to whom he confided suggested he needed more therapy himself and stopped sending patients to him. In 1983, Isay organized a panel on "**new perspectives on homosexuality**" based on homosexuality as a normal variant of sexuality and instructed analysts to stop efforts to change the sexual orientations of their patients (Kertzner, 2013). He was the first openly gay member of the American Psychiatric Association. In 1992 he threatened a lawsuit against the APA for discrimination and, in response, the association issued statements that it would not discriminate in training, hiring, or promoting analysts (Kertzner, 2013).

Black Psychology

Black psychology is based on an Afrocentric philosophy, with definitions and concepts, as well as models, procedures, and practices that stem from it (Stevens, 2015). Major contributions have been made by Africans in Africa and abroad (Lindsey & Wilson, 1994). Black psychology is a recognition, description, operationalization, and practice of principles of "African reality structure relative to psychological phenomena" (Azibo, 2015). African American psychology, in contrast, utilizes theories and concepts from mainstream psychology and applies them with African American clients. Black psychology is a cultural psychology and African American psychology is a cross-cultural psychology.

Origins
The origins of black psychology exist in the worldviews of African communities and are embedded within views of health and illness from the earliest times to the present. It is the recognition of the primacy of African people and an African worldview before European contact and influence (Cooper, 2014). In nineteenth-century North America, reactions to **scientific**

racism evident in physical anthropology, evolutionary theory, applied in the scientific method, and within the eugenics movement propelled a strong movement to reclaim African knowledge and organize to resist the messages (Baldwin, 1981). The formal development of black psychology drew from the worldviews and histories of African peoples, and occurred in response to a Western psychology and racist assumptions (Paludi & Haley, 2014). Black psychology is about self-realization, not domination (Neville, Viard, & Turner, 2015).

Concepts

The **Maafa** is a 400-year history of domination, exploitation, genocide, and slavery. It is the recognition of multiple, large- and small-scale, multidirectional efforts to denigrate African peoples (Carroll & Jamison, 2011). These efforts have been described in multiple sources from the past and present. They combine to affect entire nations, communities, and families across generations that together combine to contribute to mental health problems faced (Beasley, Miller, & Cokley, 2015). There is an explicit recognition of and attention to values that have withstood tests over time, including emphasis on community, interdependence, sharing, respect for others, and spirituality (Mbiti, 2015). Functioning is recognized holistically by improving and sustaining interconnections within one's community (Nobles & Cooper, 2013). A rediscovery of traditional African medicine through channels of pharmacology, spiritual healing, and community wellness is proposed (Nobles, 2013).

Six additional characteristics of Afrocentric psychology, in addition to explicit recognition of the Maafa, have been presented (Mukuka, 2012). One characteristic is recognition of the **Ma'at** which refers to the seven cardinal virtues of truth, justice, compassion, harmony, balance, reciprocity, and order (Chapman-Hilliard & Adams-Bass, 2015). There is value in all living beings as well as connections to those who have died. Spirituality is real and its existence is a divine mark of humanity (Dei, 2012). Authenticity and sincerity are essential, as is the recognition of reality as not only what is sensed as tasted, touched, smelled, viewed, and heard, but also as intuited (Parham, Ajamu, & White, 2015). The notion of **Sankofa** is also valued, and means that to go forward one must look back (Grills, 2013).

Contemporary topics include mental health and well-being, personality, racial identity, culture, and health psychology (Cokley, Awosogba, & Taylor, 2014). Blending of Western psychology with traditional therapies has been proposed. For example, **Ntu psychotherapy** is a reconnection of mental life to one's physical, emotional, and spiritual selves (Jackson, 2015). The counselor/healer who has both formal counseling training and traditional medicine training facilitates this transformative process with clients through spiritual, social, and psychological methods (Grothaus, McAuliffe, & Craigen, 2012).

Kenneth B. Clark was a highly influential psychologist who blended African and African American psychologies in his work on racial identity. Dr. Clark made major professional and community service contributions to advance the needs of children and youth. His research led to advocacy efforts resulting in changes in policy and service delivery.

Key Figure: Kenneth B. Clark (1914–2005)
Kenneth B. Clark grew up in Harlem, New York. His mother worked in a sweatshop and was a shop steward as well as an organizer who was instrumental in bringing the union and its protection workers to her workplace (Vasquez, 2012). He attended high school in Manhattan and graduated from Howard University. As a graduate student he worked with Cecil Summer, who was the first African American in the United States to receive his PhD in psychology (Clark, 1988). He attended Columbia University for his own doctoral education and was the first African American at the institution to receive a PhD in psychology.

Clark's contributions to psychology and counseling emerged from his research on children's self-perceptions as related to **racial identity** (Clark & Clark, 1940). He made major contributions to the study of segregation, advocating for de-segregation based on the harmful effects of the practice on child development (Clark & Clark, 1939). He was vocal in calling the problems facing African American children living in poverty an **internal colonialism**, which brought attention to the issues during the time of President Johnson's War on Poverty (Currie, Goddard, & Myers, 2014).

In a landmark 1954 case ***Brown v. Board of Education***, he was an expert witness on the effects of segregated schools (Clark, Chein, & Cook, 2004). The case ended with the decision to declare racially segregated schools unconstitutional. He was a founder of Harlem **Youth Opportunities Unlimited** in 1962, which worked to promote education and employment services (Clark & Hopkins, 1969). Along with his wife, Mamie, also a psychologist, he created the Northside Center for Child Development in 1946 (Chess, Clark, & Thomas, 1953) to provide much needed mental health services for the community (Markowitz & Rosner, 2013).

Indigenous Psychology

Indigenous psychology is psychology based on the worldviews, experiences, and traditions of Indigenous peoples (Allwood, 2011). The psychologies that have developed represent cultural psychologies based on Indigenous teachings and ways (Enriquez, 2013). While Indigenous cultural psychologies differ on perspective and context of development and application, they are united in their reaction to assumptions embedded within mainstream approaches that are rooted in a colonial past and present (Hartnack, 2015). There are multiple colonial examples, among which are included the Ainu in Japan; Kerala in India; Saisiyat, Atayal, and Tsou in Taiwan; Tay, Tai, and Hmong in Vietnam and Laos; Moskito in Mexico and Central America, as well as Native Americans in the United States and Indigenous peoples in Canada. Local development and application of cultural and blended approaches are based in the community's traditions and ways, as well as current realities and priorities (Battiste, 2011).

Origins

Colonial effects have had a powerful influence and positioned the need for an emergence of Indigenous psychology. Colonial effects for Indigenous peoples of **Turtle Island** are rooted in **historical trauma** (Weaver, 2014). The concept of historical trauma emerged from research with Holocaust survivors and their children. Brave Heart was the first to identify **intergenerational trauma** among Indigenous peoples using the same definition, which included the qualities that the actions were community wide, experienced by each person, and undertaken by others with malicious intent (Brave Heart, Chase, Elkins, & Altschul, 2011). The colonists' intentions were **cultural genocide** (Woolford, 2009). In one account of the colonial effects on healing for a Lakota community, colonial forces banned traditional practices and grief processing was not permitted (Dennis, 2014). Following a battle during which many community members died and were buried in mass graves, community members were not permitted to bury in such a way as to release their spirits or grieve properly. Each member of the community lost a family member in the battle and healthy coping with unresolved feelings was disrupted.

Concepts

There are several concepts associated with Indigenous psychology. The colonial effects of multiple losses of people to disease, children to residential schools and the 60s Scoop, cultural practices, and a connection to the land that was severed by the reserve system have affected entire generations and accumulated over time (Adelson, 2005; Kirmayer, Brass, & Tait, 2000; Kubik, Bourassa, & Hampton, 2009). Strengths oriented approaches are used to promote healing, wholeness, and wellness (Gone, 2013b). However, because of the overrepresentation of Indigenous peoples in multiple categories of disadvantage, many counseling efforts use an integrative approach that blends Indigenous and mainstream concepts and practices (Lavallee & Poole, 2010). One approach is to take

Western theories, determine to what extent they fit (Morrissette, McKenzie, & Morrissette, 1993), and apply them within any particular community (e.g., Bennett & Babbage, 2014). Traditional values that guide the work counter the universality beliefs that underlie mainstream psychology (Poonwassie & Charter, 2001).

Traditional healers work in different ways based on how spirituality is incorporated into their treatments (Reeves & Stewart, 2015). There are practitioners who have both psychological and traditional training who incorporate both (Hart, 2002). Many practitioners see the **Grandfather Teachings** and **Medicine Wheel** as important to their counseling work (Mawhiney & Nabigon, 2011). Grandfather Teachings include wisdom, love, respect, bravery, honesty, humility, and truth (Verbos & Humphries, 2014). A Medicine Wheel represents wholeness, inter-relationship, inter-connectedness, and balance/respect (Gray & Rose, 2012).

In the profile that follows, the work of Dr. Joe Couture highlights the interconnections between traditional and Western knowledge and healing (Couture, 2000). In addition, Dr. Couture made significant contributions through his political activism, human service development, and counseling practice.

Key Figure: Joe Couture (1930–2007)

Joe Couture was born to a French-Canadian father and a Cree mother, and attended a private boys' school run by Missionary Oblates of Mary Immaculate where he learned French (Friesen, 2014). As a young adult he went to the seminary and became an ordained priest at age 27. He later became a school teacher and principal. In 1968 he left the church and resumed his university studies (Friesen, 2014). He became the first Aboriginal person in Canada to complete a PhD, in the field of educational psychology (Friesen, 2014).

His contributions to psychology and social justice were evident in his practice as a psychologist in federal corrections where he blended his training in traditional healing and psychology for the benefit of men in the justice system (Couture, 1983). His contributions are also evident in the ways he advocated on behalf of the Aboriginal community for change in the relationship with the federal government (Friedel, Archibald, Head, Martin, & Muñoz, 2012). Couture was a member of the 1970 Citizens Plus (also known as the "**Red Paper**") written by the Indian Chiefs of Alberta in response to the federal government's proposed "White Paper," which would have abolished the Indian Act, all treaty rights and land claims, and relegated Indigenous peoples to the status of any other minority group (Adema, 2014). In 1974 he helped lay the foundations for the Neechi Institute for Alcohol and Drug Education, which opened that year and, in 1975, he became the first chair of Native Studies at

Trent University (Friesen, 2014). In 2007, he won an Aboriginal Achievement Award for his work in health care (Friesen, 2014).

Latina/o Psychology

Latina/o psychology is a cultural psychology focusing on the experiences of people with Latin American heritage who live in North America (Bernal & Domenech Rodríguez, 2012). It is recognized that there is great diversity within this group based on origin, timing of relocation, and pre-migration experiences (Casas, Cabrera, & Vasquez, 2015). However, authors in this area offer prominent elements of a shared culture, including Spanish language, importance of family, connections with the Catholic Church, and sex roles (Liang, Salcedo, Rivera, & Lopez, 2009). In Latina/o psychology, the study of **bicultural identity** has received a great deal of attention (Mazzula, 2009).

Origins
There has been a great deal of recognition of and attention to the educational experiences of Latina/o children and youth in the United States (Cabrera & Bradley, 2012). Significant differences in achievement and early school leaving were notable (Slavin, Calder, & Calderon, 2012). It was educational psychologists who first made connections and academic challenges into experiences of prejudice and discrimination. The first systematic review of literature from a Latina/o perspective was in the 1973 title *Latino Mental Health: A Review of Literature* (Padilla & Ruiz, 1973). In this review, the effects of adapting and meshing with mainstream American values were contrasted against protecting one's own tradition in the areas of childrearing, educational attainment, gender difference, and coping with stress (Umaña-Taylor & Updegraff, 2013).

Concepts
Key issues in contemporary Latina/o psychology include immigration, health, spirituality, mental wellness, identity, and multigenerational families (Gonzalez, Fabrett, & Knight, 2009). There is a major emphasis on the influence of culture, language, group status, and adjustment from acculturation to biculturalism (Kuperminc, Wilkins, Jurkovic, & Perilla, 2013). Counseling practices include both traditional and mainstream elements. The degree to which traditional and mainstream approaches are used depends on the practitioner's qualifications and experience as well as the preferences of the client. There is a need for sensitivity to and understanding of the political and cultural experiences of different groups, which range a great deal in relation to political, social, and economic **pre-migration** and post-migration experiences (Casas, Cabrera, & Vasquez, 2015). The elements

of traditional or culturally based approaches have been articulated. These practices and concepts include **cuento** therapy (e.g., use of cultural folktales), **dichos** (e.g., use of proverbs and sayings), **formalismo** (e.g., formalism), **respeto** (e.g., respect), and **personalismo** (e.g., being personable) (Paniagua, 2013).

Major contributions to Latina/o psychology have been made by Dr. Martha Bernal, a professor who worked to change attitudes and increase the enrollment of women of color in universities. Dr. Bernal also led the development of multicultural competence in psychology by organizing its first professional conferences on multiculturalism.

Key Figure: Martha Bernal (1931–2001)

Martha Bernal was born to first-generation Mexican parents in Texas. She was not allowed to speak Spanish in her school where English was the language of instruction (Denmark & Paludi, 2012). Bernal was in a racially segregated school and encouraged not to take advanced classes in academic subjects (Martinez, Jr., & Mendoza, 2013). Despite these challenges she was able to pursue advanced studies and eventually graduated with a PhD. Bernal was the first Latina in the United States to graduate with a PhD in psychology (Martinez, Jr., & Mendoza, 2013).

She made many contributions to educational psychology, counseling, and social justice through her efforts to organize and support women academics and their students who faced a great deal of criticism and pressure (American Psychological Association, 2015a). Particularly notable was her study of underrepresentation of women of color on university campuses, especially in clinical programs during the 1980s, and the need for explicit attention to increase representation by promoting enrollment (Nettles & Balter, 2011). Her efforts to increase the training opportunities and success of minority psychologists continue to be recognized today. Her contributions to multicultural counseling were also evident through the national conferences she initiated, beginning with the **First National Multicultural Conference and Summit** in 1999 (Johnson & Friedman, 2014). The conference, now in its sixteenth year, "has served to remind us that psychologists must always be mindful of the impact of discriminatory environments and that we ourselves are not exempt from discriminatory views" (American Psychological Association, 2015).

A Culturally and Sociopolitically Informed Perspective

In an effort to make the theoretical and conceptual discussions in this and the preceding chapter more practical, a framework that captures the ideas presented is proposed. This framework for case conceptualization includes an explicit focus on cultural and community dimensions with attention to person and environment orientation as well as mainstream and traditional orientations. It addresses the concepts of cultural identity, cultural account of the issue, the physical and social environment, the cross-cultural counseling relationship, and culturally appropriate interventions. It also includes a reference to each of the examples within categories.

Cultural Identity
- language, reason for seeking service, ethnicity, age, education, health, religion
- immigration (who immigrated, what were the circumstances, when did it take place, where from and to, what made it important to pursue, how connected/similar/different to Canadian or American culture do you feel?)
- mobility history (who is in your family and who has moved, what prompted the relocation, when did this happen, from where to where, how connected/similar or different did/do you feel compared to the new cultures experienced during transition?)

Cultural Account of the Issue
- meaning of symptoms (what are the symptoms, what do you think they mean?)
- causes (what do you think caused them?)
- effects (what are the effects of the symptoms?)
- severity (how bad are they, do they get better?)
- treatments tried (religious, spiritual, medical?)
- treatment desired (openness to talk therapy, desire for culturally based approach?)

Physical and Social Environment
- stressors, supports (partner, family, community)
- religion and spirituality (what activities do you engage in, what are the benefits of engaging in those activities, are there any drawbacks, who are religious leaders that are important, how have your views changed over time?)
- functioning (how do you think you are doing, how do others think you are doing?)

Cross-Cultural Counseling Relationship
- experiences with previous counselors, prior contact and outcome with mental health system, expectations of counseling in present, preference for counselor (e.g., language, sex, or age preferences)

Culturally Appropriate Intervention

- Personal: definition of the "client," roles of professionals, lay helpers and traditional healers, appropriate approaches and methods, anticipated outcomes
- Environmental: sources of oppression (where do you feel pressure to do or be something other than yourself?), actors/agents of oppressive forces (where do those messages or commands come from?), appropriate approaches and methods (how can those be changed and what could be done to change them?), counselor role (is advocacy needed?), client roles (what would change require of the client?), anticipated outcomes (what is hoped for, likely, and achievable?)

Conclusion

Within psychology the concept of oppression has found expression through the development and maintenance of culturally based views that operate in parallel to or in combination with mainstream views. The existence of feminist, LGBTQ, black, Indigenous, and Latina/o psychologies are themselves expressions of collective power acted upon to organize and control professional practice with their members. Despite the independent development and trajectory of each psychology, all identify liberation as a necessary outcome of their efforts. Such efforts are understood to be both collective and individual, which is also the feature that distinguishes cultural psychologies.

Discussion Questions

1. Locate yourself in the culture you identify with. To what extent do you experience advantage and disadvantage relative to others? How do you perceive the forces of sexism, heteronormativity, racism, colonialism, and Eurocentrism in your life? The lives of your clients? How do you address this with clients? Should we, as counselors, address such forces with clients who do not view them as salient contributors to their challenges?

2. Psychology and counseling are primarily focused on the needs of individuals. Do counselors have a responsibility to consider the environment within which clients function as a contributor to their challenges and successes? Are there circumstances under which a counselor could interpret a client's distress as an adaptive solution to an unjust environment?

3. Traditional values and ways are becoming increasingly recognized in cultural psychology. To what extent should counselors develop their knowledge in this area? Should traditional healing be a regulated practice? Who should control its use?

4. Within cultural psychology there is increasing attention to the need for community level intervention, for families and individuals as well as at levels of governance and political arena. How can counselors incorporate social action into their practice, both directly with clients and on behalf of clients, or on their own behalf as citizens in their own communities?

Web Links

- Psychology's Feminist Voices
  http://www.feministvoices.com
- GSA Network: What Is a GSA?
  https://www.gsanetwork.org/resources/building-your-gsa/what-gsa
- The Association of Black Psychologists
  http://www.abpsi.org
- Australian Psychological Association: Bridging Cultures: Psychologists Working with Aboriginal Clients
  https://www.psychology.org.au/publications/inpsych/cultures/
- Aboriginal Multi-Media Society: Indigenizing Psychology Symposium Stakes a Native Worldview
  http://www.ammsa.com/publications/windspeaker/
  indigenizing-psychology-symposium-takes-native-worldview
- National Latina/o Psychological Association
  http://www.nlpa.ws
- Canadian Civil Liberties Association
  https://ccla.org
- Civil Rights Movement
  http://www.history.com/topics/black-history/civil-rights-movement

Key Terms

stereotypes	socialist feminism
pathologized	personal is political
liberal feminism	socially prescribed
cultural feminism	gender socialization
radical feminism	sexism

egalitarian
sex role stereotypes
feminine
masculine
undifferentiated
androgynous
Gay–Straight Alliance
heteronormative
gay rights movement
Diagnostic and Statistical Manual of
    Mental Disorders
International Classification of Diseases
gay affirmative
new perspectives on homosexuality
scientific racism
Maafa
Ma'at
Sankofa
Ntu psychotherapy
racial identity

internal colonialism
Brown v. Board of Education
Youth Opportunities Unlimited
Turtle Island
historical trauma
intergenerational trauma
cultural genocide
Grandfather Teachings
Medicine Wheel
Red Paper
bicultural identity
pre-migration
cuento
dichos
formalismo
respeto
personalismo
First National Multicultural
    Conference and Summit

PART TWO

Changing the Context

In Chapters 5 through 10, it is argued that social change is possible through community action. To connect the personal–political relationship through cultural diversity and at both individual and community levels, a conceptual model is proposed. A key feature of this model is that both individual and collective responsibility are necessary ingredients for personal and community change. Awareness of one's ability to influence also occurs at individual and community levels. This power can be used for action to confront oppression. Counselors, by action and inaction, implicitly and explicitly support either the status quo or social change. Such critical consciousness can be acted upon in a range of ways, from being more deliberate with their support of political and social issues and groups, to becoming directly involved in supporting or leading community change. The type of engagement may be adversarial or collaborative, depending on the issue and target. Each of these carries its own potential risks and rewards for a counselor and for their professional practice. In addition, ethical issues may arise through such involvement. Oftentimes, because of the training and preparation counselors have, our efforts may center on appropriate and responsive human services and supports through community-based organization or program development. Finally, evaluation is a powerful tool to document and support changes and is also useful to others who want to be part of similar efforts in their own communities.

CHAPTER 5

INDIVIDUALS AND CONTEXTS

Chapter Outline

Sociopolitical forces contribute to psychological problems. Both external sources of this oppression and internalized oppression can be altered. However, there has not been a framework to unify these ideas by connecting the individual to the society in a way that recognizes their mutual influence. In the proposed model, liberation at both levels is complementary. The notion of power as opportunity and influence provides the energy and momentum for individual and community change. It is also necessary for liberation.

In this chapter, a conceptual model for counseling is presented. The model is based on notions of oppression and liberation, described in the earlier chapters, and on how together they blend and extend to include all. Culturally based psychologies are united in their explicit recognition of forces of oppression and of people's needs for liberation through internal change and empowerment as well as relationships characterized by equity with others and finally, to the social environment itself to address systemic disadvantage through collective action. The topic of intersectionality is offered to conceptualize personal and collective sites of disadvantage and privilege as well as sources of empowerment and social influence. A description of both the benefits and drawbacks is presented for different uses of this model in counseling and community practice.

Case Example

A sensational case of racially motivated violence took place in the United States as this book was written. Nine members of a black church congregation in South Carolina were shot and killed by a 20-year-old white man. Media reports indicated that the man had been planning the event for several months and selected the church because of its significance in African American history. He entered and sat with the Bible study group that regularly met on Wednesday evenings, and according to one survivor, spent an hour with them during which time he nearly decided not to go through with it "because everyone was so nice to him." On his Facebook page he was pictured with the flags of Southern Rhodesia and South Africa, as well as the Confederate flag of the United States. In his manifesto, published on the Internet, he described the beliefs that supported his racism. He told the arresting officers that his actions were intended to start a race war. There was a great deal of media coverage. Reactions reflected a range of perceived contributing factors.

US President Barack Obama cited racism as the problem in a statement made following the attack: "Racism, we are not cured of it. And it's not just a matter of it not being polite to say n****r in public. That's not the measure of whether racism still exists or not. It's not just a matter of overt discrimination. Societies don't, overnight, completely erase everything that happened 200 to 300 years prior" (Pickler, 2015). A report in the *Washington Post* attributed the attack to accessibility of guns and heightened awareness of the gun control debates, as well as the role of the man's family, as contributing problems: "Because of his criminal record, he would not have been able to buy a gun from a store. Federally licensed gun dealers are required to run background checks on gun purchasers, and Roof's pending charges should have turned up as a red flag. But he didn't need to go to a dealership. According to his uncle, he received a .45-caliber pistol from his father in April for his birthday" (Guo, 2015).

There was also an argument from a psychiatrist that the perpetrator was mentally unstable and had failed to get help for what appeared to be addiction-related problems; the report also noted the failings of his friends to get him treatment: "... if just one of the people in his life had called 911 to report that a family member of theirs (or a friend of theirs) who owned a gun and used drugs was speaking about starting a race war and killing himself, that Roof would have been picked up by police.... And, then, all this might not have happened" (Ablow, 2015).

Counselors are trained to recognize personalities and motives as internal processes that manifest in behavior. However, access to a gun and racist intentions also implicate sociopolitical forces. Racism was named in the president's comment and gun access was identified in the *Washington Post* report. The absence of friends to notice and respond to addiction was reflected in the psychiatrist's comment. What factors do you consider relevant contributors to this behavior? Do you see personality, addiction, peers, and family contributions, as well as community and societal messages, to be relevant forces in behavior? How much responsibility lies with the individual and how much with the context?

The importance of considering the sociopolitical context as influential on psychological functioning, as has been argued in previous chapters, is highlighted by this example. While it is necessary to consider how maturity, emotional processes, beliefs, and expectations lead to such an act of aggression, it is the context that allows for one culture to be valued more highly than another and provides a sanctioned means to enforce it in such an extreme and violent way. The argument here is not to diminish personal responsibility, but rather to elevate collective responsibility to construct a societal context where cultural diversity is not hierarchically arranged.

Conceptual Model

The conceptual model presented here is an effort to construct an approach to counseling practice that explicitly recognizes the sociopolitical context as a legitimate target of change. To do this, it integrates internal processes (i.e., processes that occur within the mind of an individual) and external processes (i.e., processes that occur within the community of that individual). In this model, oppression is experienced both individually (i.e., acceptance of limits imposed by self) and collectively (i.e., acceptance of limits imposed by others). To achieve liberation (i.e., freedom), equality (i.e., opportunity) is necessary. Power is the ability to influence. Exercising power leads to liberation. Power is also culturally based (i.e., resides within one's cultural group affiliations) and intersectional (i.e., one's cultural group affiliations may be multiple and interactive).

This model is needed to connect personal with collective empowerment. It also offers the potential for engaging in community change that improves the lives of clients. It includes what counselors already do while expanding to include efforts that are complementary to individual counseling.

Consider another example. A family is referred to you. The parents are foster parents and the youth, aged 16, is their foster child. The parents are a white middle-class couple, while the youth, David, is from a small community near the city and the son of Mexican immigrants who work in the agriculture industry. He is angry that his foster parents are pressuring him to stay in school. David does not like school and when he is there fights regularly with other students. He is coming to the end of his second suspension this year for aggression and is at risk for expulsion.

In the model as proposed, balance is sought. **Balance** occurs both within and between areas at personal and social levels (e.g., Wallace & Shapiro, 2006). There are individual and community rings in this model that represent the interactions between personal and social experiences (e.g., Hogg & Terry, 2014). In the personal domain, family and peers are also included (e.g., Walrond-Skinner, 2014), while at the community level the larger groupings within which one interacts include society and nation (e.g., Hyde, 2012). The relationship between these rings is bi-directional. They co-exist and interact. They are permeable and flexible. The line can be difficult to draw because they can blend into one another, particularly in relation to family and nation (i.e., what is "family" and what is "community" can vary) (Voydanoff, 2014). For David, the personal experience of feeling bullied by peers because of his modest clothing and language difficulties is contrasted with the experiences of his middle-class, English-speaking foster parents and his working-class, Spanish birth parents. His community, when he is living with his birth family, comprises other families and youth with Spanish as their first language and comparable lifestyles because of the same employer. Living with the foster family, David feels very different than other youth, has no supportive peers, and experiences his school as an unsafe place.

There are **spiritual**, **physical**, and **mental** domains in the proposed model. In the spiritual domain (e.g., Richards & Bergin, 2005), an individual's unique experience of the metaphysical, the unobservable and the intuitive are positioned. At a community level, the sense of interpersonal connections and unity are reflected (Kloos, Hill, Thomas, Wandersman, & Elias, 2011). In the mental domain the cognitive and affective experiences and processes, which occur intra-personally at the individual level and interpersonally at the collective level, exist (e.g., social capital) (Poortinga, 2012). The physical includes behavioral and "natural" qualities or characteristics as well as the built environment experienced at individual and collective levels. These domains also interact. They vary in breadth relative to one another at each level. They also blend into one another. They co-exist and interact. In David's case, his religious beliefs are not the protestant Christian ones his foster parents hold or the agnostic view of his Catholic parents, but rather an atheism that he wishes was untrue. He feels disconnected from his birth and foster family communities because of their lack of spiritual skepticism and feels physically and mentally more aligned with his birth family and its rural, agricultural lifestyle.

Power

Power is influence (Haslam, Reicher, & Platow, 2013). It has internal and external dimensions. Power exists in relation to self (e.g., choice, freedom) and in relation to others (e.g., influence, coercion). It is value neutral. Its types and uses are varied. Self and others determine what is positive and negative. Social power is interrelated with personal power (Smith, Mackie, & Claypool, 2014). They contribute to each other. Strengthening one strengthens the other. Neither exists as a prerequisite, however. The source of this influence comes from **intersectionality**, discussed later in this chapter, which refers to the intersection of sources of social power that is experienced internally as empowerment. David is beginning to recognize his ability to make choices for himself. He does not want to be controlled by adults and considers their advice to be self-serving. His conflict and disengagement from school leaves him with few outlets for relationships with friends or other youth his age. His ability to influence his foster family, living situation, and his birth family and its community are limited.

Sociopolitical Context of Counseling

The focus of counseling is often on the individual and to a lesser extent the family. The attention is drawn to internal experiences of mental processes and to a lesser extent the spiritual and physical factors. The environment and person may be seen to influence each other but the counselor's efforts are to improve the client's personal and social functioning with others in the immediate environment, and neither to question the environment nor promote change to it. One approach to counseling with David may be to have him talk about what he has been through and where he sees himself in the present and future. David may present himself as capable, denied of his want to be "something different" than his families expect, but not yet sure what that is. David's experience with people who are different than him is that they are "better" and while he does not want to be the same color or nationality, he wants the income and lifestyle that this affords. David's experience with people like him, from his community, is that they work very hard but have very little. He does not want that lifestyle. A counselor may encourage David to consider himself as being a combination of the qualities he sees in his family and the qualities he sees in the broader society. Instead of "either-or," David could have "both-and."

The counselor can move beyond focus on individuals and the family, however. The environment is questioned and assessed as well as recognized as a legitimate target for change. Within mental, spiritual, and physical contexts both assets and deficits can be located. The counselor's efforts focus on a determination with the client about whether change within self, between self and environment, or to the environment itself is most important to make. Power as evidenced by social location and personal identity is also attended to. Traditional healing, situated within the spiritual domain, is also recognized and operates at the personal and collective levels. David's ability to connect with other youth in his foster family's community is a significant challenge. But there could be other communities with which he could interact that are not set at school. David's creative abilities could find expression in art or music. His potential in these areas may be recognized through a connection to the local art gallery as a volunteer. The counselor's own connections to the gallery may make it possible for the leadership to consider suggesting to the three or four youth volunteers meeting to explore common ground. Planning for an art or music show, possibly with the help of a local artist, could be a way to organize based on strengths and present an image of self to others that is both authentic and what he is proud of.

Differentiating Features

To further clarify the proposed model, some comparisons between what is proposed herein and what is typically attended to in counseling follows. Typically, emphasis is on the mental processes as described in the conceptual model presented in this chapter. The unit of analysis is the individual and, to a lesser extent, the family. Problems develop within the individual because of a lack of **adaptation** to the environment. The environment influences

behavior most strongly. How clients and counselors interpret that environment greatly influences how they experience and respond to it. There is a
very strong empirical tradition and reliance on measurable phenomena. The
professional role is time limited and symptom oriented. The role is technical
and specialized as well as compartmentalized as a professional activity. From
this view, David's problem may be defined as low self-esteem possibly associated with neglect or trauma. His capability to recognize his abilities and work
to his fullest potential may offer him the best opportunity for an education
and employment that allows him to earn a good living.

From a sociopolitical view, emphasis is on mental, physical, and spiritual
processes. The units of analysis are the individual, the fit between the individual and the environment, and the environment. Problems can develop within
the individual. Problems can also develop within the environment. The lack
of fit is usually due to power imbalance between individual and environment.
The person is influenced by the environment but also influences the environment. There is openness to both empirical and experiential approaches. Focus
is on balance within and between person and environment. The professional
role is lifelong and person oriented, more generic and broadly construed. From
this view, David's problem may be defined as identity formation and expression in a critical environment. His sense of self as the son of a Mexican farmer
with limited English and an accent, who lives in foster care and is failing in
school, is held in low esteem by himself and others. David's ability to find a
community that supports who he is and encourages him to develop himself
according to what he wants offers the best opportunity to develop a healthy
sense of self through support and expression.

Part of the Solution or Problem?

As stated in Chapter 3, the concepts of oppression and liberation are central
to a sociopolitical approach to counseling. In Chapter 5, cultural psychologies are developed in response to recognition of social inequities, historical
influences as well as inadequacies and potential pitfalls associated with a mainstream approach in diverse communities. Within each of Feminist, LGBTQ,
black, Indigenous and Latina/o, efforts have been made to deconstruct and
redevelop, modify or extend mainstream psychology. From each of the psychologies there are issues that center on the nature of oppression and liberation,
with both an internalized and externalized presence.

Considering David, his internalized oppression is evidenced by his perceptions of self as someone who will always be a poor farmer, just like his
father. David is also beginning to identify that his oppression is racialized.

External oppressors are the educational system where his Spanish language is not recognized and his English skills are not enhanced. Another external source is his community system, where the families work for a large producer who controls their income, housing, and most daily activities through employment. Finally, in his foster family, caregivers want his compliance in return for their support of him.

Each of the following cultural psychologies considers the external forces of oppression that advantage some groups over others and the processes of internalization that perpetuate self-oppression. It is important to identify the forces of liberation that, if enhanced in the context, reinforce internal changes.

Feminist Psychology

From a feminist perspective, alternative approaches to development (e.g., independence versus interdependence oriented) are offered, modified (e.g., interrelationship between personal and political), and extended (e.g., gender recognized as a multidimensional concept and construct). Oppression runs through each of these perspectives as male privilege is recognized, identified as **patriarchy**, and expressed as inequality between men and women as well as more broadly through the pursuit of equality for all. The oppression experienced can be internal (e.g., acceptance of rigid gender roles, acceptance of subordinate position relative to others) or external (e.g., discriminatory employment practices, policies that privilege fatherhood over motherhood) (Ali & Lees, 2013). Liberation too has internal and external mechanisms, necessitating recognition of limiting beliefs and values that are apparent to self and encouraged or promoted by others as well as change to social, economic or political structures to remove external barriers to **equality** or **equity** (Moane, 2014).

LGBTQ Psychology

There has been development of affirmative psychological practice that recognizes both the history of **heteronormativity** and the damaging role that psychology plays in the treatment of what had been labeled as psychopathology. Major contributions of this approach are evident in the increasing recognition of problems with hegemonic portrayals of gender and sexuality, openness to diversity in relationships and family issues, as well as a shift of perspective from the treatment of non-heterosexuality to the need to address personal and social contributors to **homophobia**, **transphobia**, and **biphobia** (Whitman & Boyd, 2013). Oppression can be experienced internally (e.g., acceptance of beliefs of inferiority, problematized relationships, and family experiences) as well as externally (e.g., adoption, marriage, military service limitations) (Poteat, 2015). Liberation also has internal and external dimensions, such as personal safety, self-acceptance, family and community acceptance and healthy identity development, as well as equality of eligibility and access to personal health and family entitlements (Glassgold & Drescher, 2014).

Black Psychology

There has been development of both African American psychology and black psychology. The basis of black psychology is an Afrocentric worldview, values, beliefs, and traditions, while African American psychology is oriented toward the modification, extension, and application of mainstream psychology knowledge (Robinson, 2012). Oppression against individuals of African descent in North America was evident through scientific racism and **civil rights** struggles. Both the psychology and politics of the time converged to denigrate, devalue, subordinate, and to justify oppression through "science" (Obasi, Speight, Rowe, & Turner-Essel, 2012). In response, the political struggles and efforts led to the development of both approaches to value African knowledge and experiences in psychology. Internal representations of oppression included perceptions of self-worth according to race, beliefs in hierarchy, and pressure to conform to markers of social status. External barriers created by oppression included scientific racism (e.g., Rushton's research at Western University in Canada), colonial efforts in Africa (e.g., apartheid in South Africa and Southern Rhodesia), and segregation and racism in North America (e.g., symbolic representation by the Confederate flag, Confederate civil "war heroes" honored in some US states) (Bailey, Chung, Williams, Singh, & Terrell, 2011). Liberation also has internal and external routes, such as healthy identity development and full political, economic, and social equality (Case & Hunter, 2012).

Indigenous Psychology

In Indigenous psychology, there are histories of colonial efforts and **genocide** that link Indigenous groups across the globe (Cruz & Sonn, 2011). In a North American context, the issues of **colonization** and attempted cultural genocide by European forces have left a history of losses of life, freedom, and suppression of culture as well as abuses of trust, children, and families and a legacy of strained political relationships between Indigenous and colonial governments. The psychology that developed has occurred both as a return to traditional teachings and as a way to take what works from mainstream psychology and modify, extend, and blend it with cultural knowledge as appropriate to the community that it is intended to benefit (Carriere & Richardson, 2012). Oppression is experienced both internally and externally through **historical**

well! And ain't I a woman? I have borne thirteen children, and seen most
of 'em sold into slavery, and when I cried out with my mother's grief,
none but Jesus heard me—and ain't I a woman? (p. 77)

The initial conceptualization of intersectionality was in race, class, and
gender. Crenshaw notes in her work that intragroup differences are often
overlooked in identity politics to the detriment of women of color and that
these affect the ways that violence is interpreted.

Case Example
Serena, aged 35, moved from Lebanon to Canada, resettled in a medium-
sized city on the Prairies, and is experiencing violence at home from her
husband. The couple has been married for ten years. She has three children,
aged three, five, and six years. Her first language is Arabic and her religion
is Islam (Shi'a). She and her husband arrived three months ago, have a small
apartment, and are in the process of enrolling their oldest child in the local
school. The settlement worker at the school suggested that she see a professional counselor about the challenges she is facing at home, and the settlement
agency provided her with a language interpreter to accompany her to this
appointment.

From a counseling approach, the notion of intersectionalities could be
understood as occurring within the areas of gender, race, ethnicity, and religion within as well as outside at a family level and at a broader mainstream
society level. Serena's social, economic, and political capital is modest. From
the outside, she has the pressures of being a woman of color, with language
and religious differences from the mainstream, and internally to family, she
has the pressures of the traditional woman's role to manage household and
children with deference to her husband. A counselor may question the legitimacy of the husband's treatment of her, but that could conflict with her
personal understanding of her role. From an asset perspective, she has internal strength to care for her children and support them through a relocation
and adjustment to a new home, community, and school. She also has, through
her culture, ways of making sense of the experiences she is encountering as a wife and as a member of her family. Her status as a newcomer also
carries with it the potential to access local social services for newcomers,
including those with an understanding of the range of gendered roles within
her culture, as well as schools and legal and health services that could be
helpful.

From a community approach, however, the intersections of gender, race,
ethnicity, and religion can be viewed as a product of the pressures and structures

of prejudices and discrimination aligned with sexist and racist attitudes as well as the xenophobia and **Islamophobia** that she faces. A collective response to this is the development of newcomer-focused agencies and service providers with links, as necessary, to community-based and government agencies that are for all residents in a community, newcomers and non-newcomers. This transitional approach has been reflected in the development of local community hubs in some cities.

More specifically, in some cities community hubs are social service agencies physically located in public libraries. The hubs provide public space for local organizations to partner with the city to provide services to particular groups, as needed by that community. In some areas, the concentrations of newcomers are such that the hub has a particular focus on services to the population. Some newcomer services are funded at the federal level, while some others are funded at the provincial level, and others receive funding from the local government or charitable agencies.

Intersectionality offers a lens through which unity can be understood for political, economic, and social purposes as well as for agency and program developments that have the critical mass necessary to justify funding. Simultaneously, intersectionality offers a means to view each individual and family receiving services as experiencing several interacting challenges and barriers as well as possessing strengths and assets. While the term *newcomer* references a diverse range of individuals and families as well as races and ethnic communities, financial means, and pre-migration experiences, all experience migration and post-migration trajectories. Agency development can offer newcomers a range of services that recognize differences (e.g., political, language, gender, racial) and are based on meaningful groupings (e.g., job search, English language, income support, health care).

Diversity and the Potential of Intersectionality

Intersectionality is based on social categories relative to a reference group in a community or nation. These factors overlap and blend. In addition, interactions vary across the lifespan and in response to the problems of living. There are **hierarchies** within reference groups for each of these differences, and the extent to which one identifies with (or is seen to identify with) those on the lowest rung of social power determines their location in the hierarchy (Anthias, 2013). As a lens, intersectionality offers a means to view interrelationships between social positions that interact and co-act to produce a representation of privilege and oppression for an individual and a community.

Relationships between social locations (e.g., race) and power dynamics (e.g., racism) are linked but are changeable over time and geography. Privilege and oppression can therefore be felt simultaneously, contributing to social exclusion (e.g., diminished status) as well as social inclusion (e.g., privileged status). Resistance and resilience are key principles (Hankivsky, 2012) underlying coalition building, social justice and transformation. Within the matrix of oppression in Table 5.1 more categories could be added. The more boxes in the table, the smaller the numbers within them and the more competition between them for social change.

Three types of intersectionality have been proposed including **inclusion/voice**, **relational/process**, and **systemic/anticategorical** (Choo & Ferree, 2010). The inclusion/voice model is concerned with a particular disadvantaged group (e.g., black women with low socioeconomic status and disabilities) where a single category at a particular point of intersection, social setting, or ideology is the focus. The relational/process model focuses on how statuses interact (e.g., how race is gendered). In this view, disadvantage and privilege are related. Finally, there is a systemic/anticategorical perspective with a focus on the whole of racialized gender that cannot be separated. From this perspective, intersectionality and its distinctions or categories are irrelevant.

In counseling, a typical focus is on intersectionality as an individualized experience, and from a community perspective, the collective and political experience is most important. The more uniqueness is highlighted in the individual, the greater the potential for isolation of that individual (Cheshire, 2012). For clients who see themselves within the matrix, the potential to recognize areas of oppression and privilege exists (Roughley & Morrison, 2013). The purpose of the **self-location** is to find clarity of identity and insight into how location affects **self-perception**.

Shared interests offer a great deal of collective potential and influence to change circumstances. Locating similarities in interests can assist clients to locate social support. It can also assist with the development of efforts that address sociopolitical forces that affect their lives. From this perspective, while the divisions remain, they have potential use for group identity. The group can decide about the retention of the categorical label while using it as a force to embrace and celebrate, alter, or transcend (Hunting, Grace, & Hankivsky, 2015).

Organizations, social movements, and public policies reference a category, but not the ways it intersects or how others within it are simultaneously privileged in other ways. In other words, the relatively privileged are the organizers who benefit more from their efforts than those multiply oppressed (Busche, Scambor, & Stuve, 2012). For example, efforts to promote racial equality

TABLE 5.1 Matrix of Oppression

PROCESS	GENDER	RACE	ETHNICITY	CLASS	ABILITY	SEXUALITY	FAMILY	RELIGION
Type of oppression	sexism	racism	ethnocentrism	classism	ableism	heterosexism	familialism	exclusivism
Privileged status	Men Masculine	Person from one race	Person of ethnicity X	Upper class Middle class	Person with ability X	Heterosexuality	Person in family type X	Person in religion X
Diminished status	Women Feminine	Person from different race	Person not of ethnicity X	Middle class Working class	Person without ability X	LGBTQ	Person not in family type X	Person not in religion X
Contributed to by …	unjust treatment, fear, sadness, anger, loss, superiority and "right," vilification and condemnation, colonization, imperialism, genocide and eugenics							
Rationalized by …	"less than," "deficient," "incomplete," "weak," "unnatural," "immoral," "savage"							
Evidenced by …	exclude, exploit, dismiss, own, rape, murder							

through employment equity advantage those integrated into the workforce but have no effect on individuals who are unemployed or face other barriers to employment. It is a different way of thinking to organize socially along lines of similarity. One way this becomes possible is by organizing for a particular purpose and goal across difference.

Consider the example that follows, describing an activist organization that focuses on advocacy for people living in poverty. While there are multiple intersections between classism and other types of oppression, the emphasis is on uniting against the sociopolitical forces that create and sustain poverty that dehumanize and disrespect individuals living in those circumstances.

Case Example

The **Ontario Coalition Against Poverty** began in the 1980s in response to welfare reform proposed by the Liberal government of the time. The government proposed a modest increase to welfare rates. Work with labor unions representing both employed and unemployed workers argued for a more substantial increase. Union activity in three cities merged to organize a **March Against Poverty** to the provincial legislature in 1989. The organization was formally founded in 1990 with a focus on the poor and homeless taking direct action (Coulter, 2012). A New Democrat government formed and the organization decided, due to the increasing right wing movement of the left-leaning government, that an alliance was needed with the **Street People's Organization** to put up a tent city near the provincial legislature to stall proposed welfare cuts (Johnson, 2012). A new Progressive Conservative government in 1995 represented a shift in politics to a right-leaning regime. Efforts since that time have focused on creating safe, adequate housing; protecting and reinstating special diet allowances for individuals on welfare with health conditions; funding for emergency shelter beds; and preventing neighborhoods from becoming **gentrified.**

The tactics are controversial, and several members as well as leaders have been arrested for **civil disobedience** (discussed in Chapter 9). The coalition has received funding from organized labor as well as private donations to continue its efforts. The most obvious connection to the oppression matrix is class, but the diversity within that of men and women, those with or without children, individuals with health conditions and activity limitations, as well as ethnic differences and geographical differences are evident within their work. The work includes demonstrations for housing support at national, provincial, and civic levels as well as a variety of local neighborhood-based efforts such as the reclamation of houses that are vacant but could be used as homes for residents without a place to live.

Conclusion

Sociopolitical forces permeate societies and collectives as well as the views and behaviors of the individuals within them. The most intensive and diffuse experience of oppression occurs for members of groups farthest from the top of the social hierarchy in a particular context. A conceptual model is proposed, based on a psychological view that includes spiritual, physical, and mental domains of functioning as well as group identification and membership. In this model, both individual and collective responsibility are necessary. Personal and social change for those experiencing oppression are undertaken to exercise power and by doing so, promote liberation for both self and others.

Discussion Questions

1. How do you define psychology and your counseling work? When you consider the primary influences to your role as a counselor, where do you draw from? Which theories of personality are important? Which, if any, are not as important? Where do you fit in relation to the choice of a cross-cultural or cultural approach to counseling when working with a client from a different culture?

2. How much of an individual's behavior, thought, and emotion, as well as spirit, can be understood through looking at her or his environment? What forces in the environment do you consider to be important? What among those forces can be altered? How could they be changed? When should a counselor limit her or himself to the internal processing for a client and when should a counselor consider emphasis on the context and change to it?

3. What is your theory of oppression and liberation? What is oppression? Where does it come from? How is it sustained? In what ways can it be changed? Liberation has different meanings for different people. What is your definition? What can counselors do to promote liberation in their work? Think broadly about not only what you do directly with clients but also your practice, agency, its location, access, opportunity, and outcomes.

4. Viewing the table on oppression and "isms" where do you locate yourself? What statuses do you occupy? Does this table have any value for your work with clients in identifying their own sources of issues and challenges? Is it more challenging to identify similarities or differences between yourself and clients? Is it challenging to address problematic forms experienced by clients that you experience as privileges?

Web Links

- Women's Empowerment Principles: United Nations
  www.weprinciples.org
- Community Empowerment
  http://cec.vcn.bc.ca/cmp/modules/emp-ce.htm
- Social Change
  https://www.ted.com/topics/social+change
- Social Action
  http://ctb.ku.edu/en/table-of-contents/assessment/promotion-
  strategies/systems-advocacy-and-community-organizing/
  main
- Institute for Intersectionality Research and Policy
  http://www.sfu.ca/iirp/aboutus.html
- An Intersectional Approach to Discrimination
  http://www.ohrc.on.ca/sites/default/files/attachments/
  An_intersectional_approach_to_discrimination%3A_Addressing_
  multiple_grounds_in_human_rights_claims.pdf
- Black Feminism and Intersectionality
  http://isreview.org/issue/91/black-feminism-and-intersectionality
- Amnesty International
  http://www.amnesty.ca

Key Terms

balance	genocide
spiritual	colonization
physical	historical trauma
mental	residential schools
intersectionality	Indian Act
adaptation	ethnic pride
patriarchy	community psychology
equality	Sojourner Truth
equity	Islamophobia
heteronormativity	hierarchies
homophobia	inclusion/voice
transphobia	relational/process
biphobia	systemic/anticategorical
civil rights	self-location

self-perception
Ontario Coalition Against Poverty
March Against Poverty

Street People's Organization
gentrified
civil disobedience

CHAPTER 6

COMMUNITIES

Chapter Outline

Social Participation
    Case Example
Forces Affecting Communities
    Neoliberalism
    Globalization
    Mobility
    Industrialization
    Social Capital
    Case Example
What Is a Community?
    Types of Communities
    Functions of Communities
    Studying Communities
Forces That Strengthen Communities
Forces That Challenge Communities
Myths about Community Change
    It Is Easy
    Anyone Can Do It
    Services Are Well Funded
    Communities Are Democratic
    Communities Speak with One Voice
    Change Is Easy to Measure
    Solutions Are Easy to Find and Implement
    Change Processes Are the Same in All Communities

Sociopolitical forces that oppress members of some groups while privileging members of others reflect an imbalance of power. Counselors can make a positive difference in the lives of those who experience oppression by considering the pressures faced and challenging unhelpful messages that have been internalized. In this chapter, a framework for the externalization of oppressive messages, recognition in the context, and potential for collective action to confront them is offered. In addition to the internal processes of confronting oppression, counselors may also recognize and attend to empowerment and liberation at the community level. The purpose of this chapter is to define and identify qualities of communities related to change processes.

Communities can be considered and approached as legitimate targets for change by counselors. This perspective is particularly useful when working with members of disadvantaged cultural groups living within oppressive circumstances. Liberation at the community level occurs via collective empowerment. Factors affecting contemporary community life include neoliberalism, globalization, mobility, industrialization, and social capital. Communities are collectives of individuals based on geography, interest, or both. They have protective and nurturing functions as well as controlling and constraining functions. For purposes of change, they can also be defined as those who have a particular need for change, those who are the target of change, and those who are the means to that end. These may be similar or different. There is a range of forces that act to either strengthen or challenge communities. An essential concept in community life and change is power and the extent it is mobilized to promote strength and stability or change. Each of these topics is discussed.

Social Participation

In 2000 Robert Putnam, a political science professor at Harvard University, published a well-known commentary titled **Bowling Alone**, in which he described widespread disengagement in community life. Although there has been debate about the extent to which this disengagement is generalizable, the metaphor was an interesting one and has been used since to describe changes that accompany this trend (Turcotte, 2015). It does appear that social isolation is on the rise. Some is chosen and some is a consequence of modern-ization (Rauch, Deker, & Woodside, 2015). Evidence shows that **loneliness** has a strong relationship to mortality (Holt-Lunstad, Smith, Baker, Harris, & Stephenson, 2015). While people can change these beliefs and behaviors to feel worthy of **inclusion** and enjoy social **interaction**, they also need oppor-tunities to participate in a context of **belongingness** and **solidarity** (Aanes, Mittelmark, & Hetland, 2015).

Case Example

Loneliness appears to be increasing among older as well as younger popu-lations (Kearns, Whitley, Tannahill, & Ellaway, 2015). Those who are socially isolated are at elevated risk for mental health concerns (Matthews et al., 2016). Mental health concerns, in turn, make it a challenge to develop and maintain the relationships that would promote connections and inclusion (Leach, 2014). Social support and social action are different forms of empowerment that can be promoted through group counseling. There is the possibility that a group itself, having been initially facilitated by a professional, can become indepen-dent of that professional and develop its own identity and purpose (Leach, 2014). Such is the case of the model of the **Friendship Group** (Hanna & Moore, 2014). Counselors Madeline Novell and Jennifer Newman developed this approach. The purpose was to provide support to women living in high poverty neighborhoods who felt isolated and help them develop connections with others for mutual support and more practical matters such as parent-ing. Types of support offered include **emotional** (e.g., caring and empathy), **informational** (e.g., providing links to resources, such as emergency child care) and **appraisal** (e.g., considering different perspectives on the issue) (Geven, Kalmijn, & van Tubergen, 2016).

They found that it was helpful to develop the comfort and skill of clients to interact more freely with one another (Newman & Lovell, 1993). The group had the purpose of **building community** starting with the building blocks of **friendships** (Mentinis, 2014). The group was focused and directive, with skills development as its primary purpose, including topics such as giving and receiv-ing compliments, taking turns in conversations with listening and speaking, as well as the opportunity to disclose personal or meaningful experiences to others while feeling safe and confident (MacDonald, 2015). Essentially, the outcome was the development of skills in being a community member by interacting with others in a spirit of **mutuality**. Once the skills were developing, the groups were encouraged to develop their own purpose and structure, while counselor involvement gradually decreased and was eventually discontinued (Newman & Lovell, 1993). The groups, given common interests and familiarity, were well placed to take on a broader social purpose (Newman & Lovell, 1993).

Forces Affecting Communities

While there are internal processes that create communities of mutual support, as in the Friendship Group, sociopolitical forces also operate at that level. Such forces affect how communities emerge and maintain themselves as well as stabilize and change over time. These broad level forces exert an influence on the community efforts that a counselor may make. They are important to understand and draw upon or react against as communities develop and strengthen. In this section factors are considered to include effects of neoliberalism, globalization, mobility, and industrialization (Ife, 2013) as well as the presence of social capital (Valencia-Garcia, Simoni, Alegría, & Takeuchi, 2012).

Examples in this section follow from applications of community change efforts that may be engaged in within an inner city context. In North America the term "inner city" describes both locations and populations in central neighborhoods characterized by high rates of poverty, crime, and violence. The existence of these urban communities is influenced by large-scale political, economic, and social forces that are beyond the immediate control of community members. However, community change, like individual change, occurs in a sociopolitical context, and these forces are central to the creation and maintenance of inner cities. Despite these effects, inner city residents can and do create change to buffer the impact of these forces and equalize cultural hierarchies through collective empowerment and social action.

Neoliberalism

Neoliberalism has undergone a range of applications and meanings since the term's inception. Current usage refers to the **free market** economic forces that affect individuals and communities (Duménil & Lévy, 2011). From this perspective, family is the best social service provider, and **charity** picks up where family leaves off because the economy will take care of citizens. A healthy economy is a free economy. The **invisible hand** of competition will organize and regulate the economy. The economy is self-correcting. The approach is associated with **laissez-faire** economics and social policies that favor **private enterprise**, private ownership, **government deregulation**, **free trade**, and a decrease of government intervention in the economy and reduced government expenditures in general. Government **austerity** measures are also favored (Hermann, 2014).

For counselors involved in community work in the inner city, knowledge of neoliberal forces clarifies possibilities for economic growth at a local level. Government austerity has led to reduced funding for social programs while at the same time making it easier to start businesses. The decisions about whether to support the creation and use of a parallel economy or participate more in the formal economy influence the types of efforts to be made.

Globalization

Globalization, or the **interconnectedness of nations**, has existed for a long time (Hirst, Thompson, & Bromley, 2015). For example, between 114 BCE and 1450 CE, the **Silk Road** was a series of trade routes connecting Europe and China, used primarily to transport goods such as silk, but philosophies, technologies, and diseases were also spread via these roads (Mathews, Ribeiro, & Vega, 2012). In North America, frequent contact between Europe and what would become Canada from the 16th century reflected colonial interests in formal trade arrangements across the continents (Pomfret, 2013).

There are several contemporary spin-offs of globalization (Dey, 2013). There is an expanding **market** for and opportunities to increase **imports** and **exports**, and the mobility of both specialized and general workers has increased (Holosko & Barner, 2014). However, a **policy vacuum** exists, without protections in place for workers and nations in the **international marketplace**. The net effect of trade has been increased international privilege in some nations, with increasing disadvantage in others, as wealth has become more centralized (McMichael, 2013).

For counselors involved in community work in the inner city, an understanding of globalization offers the possibility of conceptualizing the current realities of individual survival into a more community-serving approach. The increased global demand and consumption of goods and services have created massive international sites of wealth and poverty. The process of taking cheap materials and labor from poor locations to brand and sell at a profit to wealthier locations is a process similar to the use of local revenue and skills from the inner city for a profit outside. Social assistance, if spent inside the inner city, stays in the community.

Mobility

Movement of people is high. In the United States, about 12 per cent of the population relocates every year and in Canada the proportion is 11 per cent (Corak, 2013). Net migration rates for Canada and the United States in 2014 indicated that both have more people entering than leaving. The rate for the United States is 2.45/1,000, which refers to the total number arriving minus the total number leaving in that year. In Canada, the rate for the same year is 5.66/1,000 (Hollifield, Martin, & Orrenius, 2014). People tend to congregate according to a commonality (e.g., affordable housing, city, employment, organizations, and institutions), which can be a basis for community. Residents are moving into cities and away from rural areas (Thomas, 2016). Nearly 80 per cent of Canadians and Americans live in urban communities with populations over 1,000. The largest cities in both countries are growing (Cullingworth, 2015; Groffman et al., 2014). Each of the top 25 Canadian and American cities grew during the past 20 years.

For counselors involved in community work in the inner city, recognition of mobility is essential. The movement of citizens to cities as well as within cities to areas with affordable housing, and within those areas to capitalize on the best deals available, influences longevity and commitment to community change. Finding ways to make ownership possible is one important way to increase community stability.

Industrialization

Industrialization refers to the movement from the **family farm** to manufacturing jobs. The emergence and prominence of service industry jobs are more recent but widespread (Gohmann, Hobbs, & McCrickard, 2008). Paid work is increasingly owned by a few for the many. In a Forbes article "The **147 companies that control everything**" (Ubpin, 2011), Swiss researchers used a global database of companies and investors to identify the interrelationships and points of convergence. It was found that "global corporate control has a distinct bow-tie shape, with a dominant core of 147 firms radiating out from the middle. Each of these 147 own interlocking stakes of one another and together they control 40% of the wealth in the network. A total of 737 control 80% of it all." Jobs are moving toward contract and part time, many of which are low skilled and in the service industry where pay is lowest (Tilly, 2014).

For counselors involved in community work in the inner city, an awareness is necessary of how the shift to service work, part time, and low pay contract jobs affects possibilities for employment by residents. The types of services that may be in short supply, such as education, job counseling, training, and work placements, are the types that are necessary to make the skills (and jobs) available. Awareness of such issues also contributes to the need for advocacy for a livable wage (Smith, 2015).

Social Capital

The concept of social capital is an important one (Portes & Vickstrom, 2015). With the emphasis on economics and politics, social capital offers a perspective from which to view the social building blocks of community as well as the interconnections and interactions associated with both economic and political development at a local **grassroots** level (DeFilippis & Saegert, 2013). Social capital is a community's networks which, as they diversify and strengthen, produce democratic processes as well as economic benefits. Communities high in social capital have trust, broad participation in decisions, resource sharing, and collective action (Poortinga, 2012). Through high participation in decisions and actions the power of the community to influence both within and outside are heightened (Murayama, Fujiwara & Kawachi, 2012). These factors increase its collective political power in local and civic politics as well as interconnections with other like-minded communities and groups, and state, provincial, and national politics (Mignone & O'Neil, 2005).

For counselors involved in community work in the inner city, the idea of social capital is an important lens through which to view relationships between people, places, and institutions. The networks of associations offer ways to connect resources for mutual benefit and collective strength. Consider the following descriptions of cooperatives as ways to bring individuals and groups together to solidify and represent community interests.

Case Example

Economic cooperatives have a long history in Canada (McMurtry & Brouard, 2015). While there has been a more concerted effort to organize cooperation, the earliest efforts were both informal and spontaneous responses to need. The agricultural practice of cooperation has and does occur during planting and harvesting times in many communities (Nilsson, Svendsen, & Svendsen, 2012). Also, the collective purchase of goods when opportunities arose reflected more spontaneous efforts to come together for a particular purpose (Selsky & Smith, 1994). Before there were any rules or principles guiding the practice, cooperatives emerged in areas of banking and insurance, cheese factories, and grain distribution, as well as housing, workers' rights, and in the fishing industry and health care (Cheney, Santa Cruz, Peredo, & Nazareno, 2014).

The **consumer movement** of the 1920s was an import by European working class immigrants (Larsen & Lawson, 2013). Stores sprang up to buy wholesale and sell at cheaper prices to members. Financial cooperatives and **credit unions** developed and broadened under provincial legislation modeled after similar developments in the United States (Goddard, McKillop, & Wilson, 2014). Efforts have combined savings and expansion of services in more recent years to be competitive (MacPherson, 2010).

During the 1950s the practice became much more formalized in agricultural efforts (Chaddad & Iliopoulos, 2013). For example, in the sale of milk, butter, and cheese, families joined together to have their own factories for production and sale (Gentzoglanis, 1997). With the railways, better transportation made it possible to move the product to market, which was exported to Britain as well (Ortmann & King, 2007). A market developed for grain both domestically as well as internationally. Today, there are over 1,000 **agricultural co-ops** serving rural needs across Canada (Fulton, 1995).

Cooperative housing emerged in urban or company towns during the 1930s, where the housing provided was of poor quality (Penfold, Rethoret, & MacDonald 2016). The notion was for families to build their own shared housing. This effort took a more modern form after World War II with government incentives. In the 1980s critics started to take notice of these developments and concluded that the users of this housing were unfairly benefiting from government support, so support immediately declined and later ended (Dreier & Hulchanski, 1993).

Worker co-ops were very localized and responsive, but the forestry industry was particularly successful in organizing to sell harvesting services to farmers to clear land and harvest wood (Staber, 1989). Fishing co-ops, which are discussed in more detail in Chapter 8 with the **Antigonish Movement**, were highly successful (Dodaro & Pluta, 2012). They created cooperatives to pool efforts in fishing harvest and sell directly from the co-op itself. The middlemen, known as the cod lords, were removed from the sale and the workers benefited directly.

An important contemporary example is the **Northern Star Worker Cooperative** (Northern Star, 2016). Started in Winnipeg, Manitoba, in 1998, it began as a Friendship Group. Women met for emotional (i.e., affect, esteem, concern), informational (i.e., suggestion, advice, informational), appraisal (i.e., feedback, affirmation) and **instrumental** support (i.e., location, equipment, business advice) in a local inner city community resource center. They started a sewing group. Initially, the projects were independent projects, but over time the group began to consider the potential for larger projects they could work on together (Loxley, 2003). They formed a collective and then a cooperative, which was incorporated in 2000. The business is in operation today and their products sell worldwide.

What Is a Community?

The term *community* is used many ways. In a review of over 90 definitions of community, shared interaction, connections, and location were common elements (Warren & Lyon, 1988). Commonalities in interests, beliefs, and behaviors are also often mentioned. Galbraith (1990) suggested that community may be defined as "the combination and interrelationships of geographic, locational and non-locational units, systems, and characteristics that provide relevance and growth to individuals, groups, and organizations" (p. 5). Using this definition, the inner city would qualify as a community. Other definitions emphasize the interaction of members. For example, community is "a human system of more than two people in which the members interact personally over time, in which behavior and activity are guided by collectively-evolved norms or collective decisions, and from which members may freely secede" (Boothroyd, 1996). There were several examples of communities based on this definition within the section on cooperatives, such as the cooperatives in agriculture or housing. Community can also be formed in the spirit of change, as found in the following definition: "a collection of people who have become aware of some problem or some broad goal, who have gone through a process of learning about themselves and about their environment, and have formulated a group objective" (Roberts, 1979, p. 10). Examples of community change were evident in the efforts of individuals involved in the Antigonish Movement as well as the Northern Star Worker Cooperative.

Types of Communities

Communities can also be understood in relation to their attributes and purposes. Pre-industrial to industrialized nations will be described below as well as functional attributes of communities and finally subcategories of community for the purpose of community change efforts.

Ferdinand Tönnies (1855–1936) described two fundamental types of community, including **Gemeinschaft** (pre-industrial) and **Gesellschaft** (modern) (translation in 1957). According to Tönnies, Gemeinschaft were pre-industrial communities with interacting, reciprocal relationships involving face-to-face dealings with the whole person, rather than segmented, bureaucratized, and role-determined components. They were rooted in reciprocity. Gesellschaft communities are based on contract, legal/rational notions, and the achievement of individual rather than collective goals. They are rooted in competition.

A more recent distinction between aspects of community life in modern Gesellschaft communities is based in **geographic**, **function**, or **attribute** as well as interest (Lee, 1986). A geographic community refers to a group of people that reside in the same physical area (e.g., inner city neighborhood). A function or attribute community refers to a group that shares commonality, such as gender, religion, or workplace (e.g., immigrants living in an inner city neighborhood). An interest community refers to a group of people who have a particular interest with a focal issue or concern in mind (e.g., immigrants who have English as a second language living in an inner city neighborhood).

A very helpful definition of community for the purposes of social change is based on the interest type of community. Within an interest community there are those who identify a need for change (i.e., **need community**), those who are the target for change (i.e., **target community**), and those who are the promoters of change (i.e., **action community**) (Israel, 1985). These groups can overlap, but may also be distinct depending on the issue. For example, distinct groups may be defined when the need for change is local banking services

for residents whose first language is not English. In this case, the credit institutions are the target of change; the residents and supporters recognize the
need for change, but it is a small group of banking institution members who
can persuade the financial institution to become capable of communicating
in other languages that are relevant to the community. In another example, a
local group of individual residents seeking employment determines that they
have the potential to develop their own service to market locally. They take
action to learn about small business practices that allow them to develop the
structure necessary to advertise and provide the service. In this case, the same
group is the need, target, and action community.

Functions of Communities

Communities can be defined by the different functions taken up within
them. They have **production**, **distribution**, and **consumption** functions,
as well as socialization, social control, participation, and mutual support functions (Cohen, Gottlieb, & Underwood, 2000). Production, distribution, and
consumption refer to the goods and services produced by that community and
how they are shared among members as well as used by them. **Socialization**
refers to the norms of behavior, expected conduct of members including
observance of proper protocols. **Social control** is the system of rewards and
punishments for appropriate and inappropriate behavior. **Social participation** refers to the involvement of members in everyday life as well as decision
making. Finally, **mutual support** is the cohesion or solidarity that exists as a
function of interdependence of members.

In addition to social capital, or the networks of relationships within a
community, there are several other forms that together represent a range of
sources of influence. These include environmental, physical, economic, human,
political, and information (Lin, 1999). There is a high degree of overlap and
influence between these functions, and strengths in some make up for lack
thereof in others. **Environmental capital** refers to the natural environment,
while physical capital refers to the human-created environment (Roseland,
2000). The **economic capital** of a community refers to the financial resources
within or within easy access of the community for the community's benefit
(DeFilippis, 2001). **Human capital** is the collective gifts of individuals within
that community, including knowledge, skills, and contributions (Putnam,
1993). **Political capital** refers to the influence on decision making within
the community, evidenced by participation and engagement as well as influence on decisions about the community or concerning the community from
those outside of the community (Emery & Flora, 2006). **Information capital** is the local knowledge that exists or is created and reproduced, used locally
or outside of the community (Neuman & Celano, 2012).

Of key importance are the mental health functions of community. Communities decrease isolation, offer mutual support, recognize interdependence, mobilize all resources, influence policy decisions, provide services locally, and scale up needed services from the outside, as well as ensuring that those from the outside are culturally appropriate and community driven (Barter, 2001). Communities offer opportunities to interact, help out, and mobilize to meet the needs of members more broadly and formally for basic needs such as food, clothing, and shelter, as well as for higher level needs of affiliation and belonging (Arcidiacono, Procentese, & Di Napoli, 2007). When services are initiated from outside, the community can influence the nature and extent of those services (Bowles & Gintis, 2002). Communities can also organize to influence decision making internally as well as with other communities and governments.

Studying Communities

There are many ways to study communities. A visual representation of major forces and their interconnections can be done with social network maps and community asset maps. Considering the example of banking services for inner city residents with English as a second language, the relevant networks and assets could be referenced in respective maps.

A **social network map** is a visual representation of relationships between families and institutions (Tracy & Whittaker, 1990). Such maps are typically used to identify significant relationships for individuals within and between communities (Bott & Spillius, 2014). They have been used to identify interactions between employees in a workplace, teams in competitive sports, and high-level security applications on cellular telephone use (Klasnja & Pratt, 2012). The sophistication ranges from simple paper and pencil exercises, the type most familiar and useful to counselors, to complex representations of many data points represented by computer-generated analyses and outputs (Scott, 2012). The main components of such a map, whether small or large, are the points and lines (Cotterell, 2013). The points can represent people, and the lines, their relationships. The purpose of a social network map is to identify **patterns** in the actors and their **interrelationships** (Tracy & Abell, 1994). In the inner city for example, the map could be drawn using dwellings, workplaces, and banking institutions near residents' homes. In some inner cities, the major banks do not have locations and residents may be left to use money lenders, pawn brokers, and check cashing businesses. The relationships with such businesses could be compared to the actual and potential relationships with formal banking institutions and the map could also represent barriers to accessing those institutions such as distance and transit routes.

A **community asset map** is a visual representation of relevant components of a community. A key component is the asset focus (Phillips & Pittman,

2014).This is a decidedly optimistic view of what exists in the community. These maps, in contrast to the other types presented, include people, places, and things.The people are typically represented as groups who share a particular gift, strength, or ability that is recognized by the authors and other community members (Green & Haines, 2015). Examples of these people are artisans, youth, and elderly, while places may include a park or main street.Things often include institutions, such as a school or a community center, as well as associations such as art clubs, businesses such as a grocery store, and services such as a health center.The relationships between these assets are represented by the distances between them on the map (Lightfoot, McCleary, & Lum, 2014).The purpose of an asset map is not to avoid or minimize problems or needs, but rather to recognize what positive **building blocks** of a community exist that can be mobilized or enhanced to tackle concerns. In the inner city example, the potential for local businesses that operate within the community to connect with residents who have goods and services to sell using a profit-sharing arrangement could lay the foundation for the development of local banking services based on a profit-sharing model.

Forces That Strengthen Communities

What makes it possible, in the presence of multiple challenges, to enhance community cohesion, identity, and power? Forces that strengthen communities include active voluntary organizations, community centers, a common need or enemy, good transportation, and balanced land use.

Active voluntary organizations offer residents opportunities to participate in community efforts that give purpose and meaning as well as ways to make a difference in the lives of other people within and outside the community (Orozco & Rouse, 2013). Examples of such initiatives include traditional service clubs as well as local theater companies, food cooperatives, and youth councils.

Community centers offer residents a place to meet to develop and engage in voluntary activities (Ledwith, 2015). Many voluntary organizations lack resources for meeting space, which is essential to a sense of identity and purpose as well as meeting an obvious need to have a physical location for their efforts.These can be dual purpose or multipurpose buildings, which in some communities are the local school by day; during evenings and weekends, community members can book space. In some neighborhoods, public libraries can be booked for community meetings.

Common needs or enemies provide focus to efforts that solidify support in the community (Phillimore & McCabe, 2015). Groups within a community that build support for a problem have undertaken some of the most success-ful neighborhood organizing. For example, poor housing has origins either outside the community, such as zoning bylaws, or within the community, such as lack of training for home building.

Good transportation is essential for strong communities (Webber, 2015). Far too often, underserved neighborhoods are forgotten in planning or particu-larly harmed by cuts to public transportation services. In some communities, private vehicle travel is essential but not affordable. The physical structure may not offer safe pathways for walking or bike riding. The climate and spread of the community also play a role in the viability of different types of transpor-tation for residents.

Balanced land use requires green space, public space, and residential spaces that are safe for children, youth, and families (Kaiser, Godschalk & Chapin, 1995). Inexpensive housing is high density, and affordable land makes some communities attractive to developers for business or factory locations (Ferguson & Dickens, 2011). It is essential that members of the community be involved in decisions about zoning and changes to the composition of land with differ-ent uses.

Forces That Challenge Communities

Forces that challenge communities include lack of collective history, stigma, high mobility, fragmentation, lack of services, lack of decision-making author-ity, and lack of boundaries.

Lack of collective history is associated with divisions and rivalries within a community that can hamper efforts to voice concerns or promote changes that benefit all residents (Fodor, 1999). There can be great value in explor-ing the history of the place and finding a way to be inclusive in the telling of such a story to build potential for cooperation between different groups.

Stigma is a negative label applied by outsiders to insiders, and one that if not carefully scrutinized and actively resisted may become internalized and self-fulfilling (Bradshaw, 2007). The terms used to describe some communities and groups have powerful effects. Members of the community need to self-define and identify in ways that make sense and help the community represent itself appropriately for the intended purpose.

High mobility is a challenge to communities because of frequent changes in interests and goals of those coming and going (Scanlon & Devine, 2001). A core group of members can provide stability throughout periods of change, but care is needed to ensure that inclusion is pursued and barriers assessed. Ways to promote longer-term residency may be considered as a goal.

Fragmentation is the result of divergent skills, interests, and goals between families and groups within a community (Laska & Spain, 2013). While diversity can be a strength, the absence of some sense of shared experience is potentially divisive. Communities with a history of internal conflict need to put effort into combining resources for a common purpose.

Lack of services locally available and accessible to members is problematic for communities (Steiner & Markantoni, 2014). The need to constantly leave the community for services whether they are health, educational, social, financial, or employment-related leaves little control within the community. Such a problem locates major resources outside of the community and leaves less opportunity to congregate, organize, and make decisions locally.

Lack of decision-making authority is a major challenge to communities (Connelly, Markey, & Roseland, 2013). Despite an existence within a layer of authority, such as in the case of an urban neighborhood within a civic political riding, local decision making can be facilitated, promoted, and enacted. The more influence local residents have over the conditions that affect their lives, the more opportunity there is for empowerment and motivation to make positive change (Aiyer, Zimmerman, Morrel-Samuels, & Reischl, 2015).

Lack of boundaries creates potential for divisions within communities making collective decision making and action difficult to achieve (Purcell, 2014). Communities that have a clear sense of where, who, or what they are, or claim an identity that, if shared, can form the basis for efforts to support themselves internally and interact in an organized way with external forces that affect them.

Myths about Community Change

Community change is fraught with challenges. There are several assumptions that can be made about the nature and effects of this type of professional work. Some common beliefs are that it is easy, anyone can do it, services are well funded, communities are democratic, communities speak with one voice, change is easy to measure, solutions are easy to find and implement, and finally, that change processes are the same in all communities.

It Is Easy

Despite the seeming simplicity of building cohesion, support, and action for an idea, there are many potential derailments throughout this process (Gough & Accordino, 2013). The preparation that counseling professionals have sets us up well to recognize that community change, like individual or family change, is possible, but not necessarily easy for the professional or the client.

Anyone Can Do It

Like counseling practice, community work requires more than just having a good attitude and interest (Warburton, 2013). While those are important qualities of practitioners, training and experience are also necessary. Each of us has known individuals who have great education but struggle with their professional work as well as those who have little formal education but a real knack for the work.

Services Are Well Funded

The nature of community work is that the recognition of demands on practitioners is not well understood by private and public funders (Feit & Bonds, 2014). The effort necessary to pursue this work is not compensated as counseling practice is, and services in the helping field are subjected to tighter controls, with less funding, greater accountability, and continual pressure for outcome evidence.

Communities Are Democratic

Cooperation, collaboration, and coalitions, which will be described in further detail in Chapter 8, all require the identification of commonality (DeFilippis & Saegert, 2013). Commonality is not necessarily shared by all members of a community. While democratic processes are important means to promote access and contribution to decision making, many members do not participate (Mattern & Love, 2013).

Communities Speak with One Voice

Even with the best democratic procedures and local governance structure, disagreements are inevitable. While consensus is ideal, it is rarely achieved (Munn-Giddings & Winter, 2013). The recognition of multiple interests and priorities within those interests can be a more practical way to represent the realities in many communities (Phillips & Pittman, 2014).

Change Is Easy to Measure

Community change is very difficult to determine. While there are a range of techniques to establish which change efforts made a difference, how they made a difference, and even how much of a difference, results are often achieved incrementally and over the long term (Goldstein, 2012). There are many forces interacting and co-acting within communities making it difficult to isolate causes and effects, which are often held in high esteem by funders as evidence.

Solutions Are Easy to Find and Implement

Causes and effects are difficult to identify in relation to complex social problems (Minkler, 2012). There are multiple lenses through which to identify and locate the "problem" and as many or more for potential "solutions." Even after a confident decision about the nature of an appropriate solution, the means to achieve it can be elusive.

Change Processes Are the Same in All Communities

While the description of change presented in Chapters 8 and 9 offers a model to identify stages and steps, the actual process is far more fluid and circular in nature. Each community process follows its own trajectory and stages occur simultaneously or in a different sequence (Omoto, 2014).

Power: Energy for Community Change

Power is the essential ingredient for community change (Stoecker, 2012). It exists in all communities and is expressed in all efforts to promote consistency and change. It is important to define power in community change, describe why it is needed, locate its presence and expression, and promote it within others.

Power is the capacity to move people in a desired direction to accomplish some end (Homan, 2015). It is something a person or organization possesses and is willing to use that involves some sense of purpose or intention and is used to meet some need or achieve some benefit. It is necessary to turn good ideas into brilliant plans and thinking into doing. Power is situational in that it does not solely reside within a particular person, but depends on social context, including other people, at a particular time, a particular place, and for a particular purpose. Expressions of power can be positive (e.g., collaboration, noble, cooperation) and negative (e.g., dominance, manipulation, coercion).

Because power is value neutral and its use can be positive and negative, it is incumbent on the practitioner to use ethical judgment about when and how to use it (Zeldin, Christens, & Powers, 2013). It is important to recognize that change is difficult and will be met with reluctance or resistance, which are not necessarily reliable indicators of in/appropriate use. Responsible use begins with awareness of others as well as their rights and legitimate interests, and all use must be with respect for rights and legitimate interests of others.

In a community there are several potential sources of power. A series of types have been proposed for power in groups (Northouse, 2015), which includes: **reward power** (i.e., something positive given in exchange for compliance), **coercive power** (i.e., something negative given in response to noncompliance), **legitimate power** (i.e., sanctioned by an office or recognized authority), **referent power** (i.e., charisma, convincingness, and credibility), **expert power** (i.e., specialized knowledge or experience), and finally **informational power** (i.e., sources, types, and access to knowledge).

From the example earlier in this chapter concerning banking needs of inner city residents, a community network that linked residents with similar interests through the development of a local neighborhood association could be a very useful vehicle to represent itself in discussions with banking institutions to bring services to the community. Such an organization would represent legitimate power because of its formal status as a representing body for the community. Ideally, it would have leadership with a charismatic presence to be motivational. While its presence could be subject to the coercive power of city hall, reward power could exist via elected representatives. To build its membership, it would be important to assemble informational power about community needs and directions.

There are also several bases of power in a community that are consistent with some of the sources of power in groups presented (Homan, 2015). **Information** includes access to relevant data that are public or private, as well as locally existing or obtained cultural or sacred knowledge. **Money** is another source of power, which could include sources such as residents or members with economic power, as well as businesses or groups within the community that have financial holdings or easy access through loans. **Laws** as a source of power within a community are legal requirements to conform behavior in specific ways that have legal consequences. **Constituencies** are small groups within a community who have particular levels of engagement, solidarity, and activism, and who exercise the strength in proactive or reactive ways. Energy and **natural resources** refer to existing physical characteristics that have economic, cultural, social, or political value to a community. **Goods and services** refer to sources of power that are harvested, created, or developed that can be bought and sold. **Network participation** as a source of power includes the involvement of members of relevant social networks and interconnections between individuals and groups within a community that do not always, but can, act cohesively when necessary. **Families** have power in a community not only through their relationships with primary and extended members but over time in that the history of collaborations and achievements carry influence into the present day. **Status occupations** including professionals, cultural, or religious leaders have positions of power that confer a standard of training or expertise. **Illegal actions**, those that run counter to the laws in place, are also a source of power within a community. Finally, **personality**, or the kind of interpersonal qualities that are possessed by an individual can add to her or his potential to be a formal or informal leader in a community.

Power and Programs in Community Change

Owing to the importance of power in relation to community change, a well-known model of development has been proposed that distinguishes between two types. In **power-based development**, change is rooted in the view that society comprises the "haves" and the "have-nots" (Stoecker, 2001). Community change requires the "have-nots" to take power from the "haves." Often, confrontational tactics are used. In **program-based development**, change is rooted in the view that distribution of power is the problem and that cooperation and collaboration between those with relatively more and less power can serve the interests of the society and create fair conditions for those who have been disadvantaged. In both models, change depends on economic, social, and political power. Their views of society and the nature of differences lead to different choices about tactics to achieve goals.

Conclusion

A community is a collective that has influence on forces both outside of it and within it. Communities may be large or small, defined by a particular characteristic or set of qualities, and have power to act. They are complex, including both healthy and unhealthy aspects, as well as regressive, stabilizing, and progressive factions. In some cases, the power may need to be awakened or stimulated. But counselors who are aware of either the potential or presence of collective representation to combat oppression can facilitate this process indirectly and directly.

Discussion Questions

1. Do you agree with the metaphor that Canadians and Americans are "bowling alone"? Are each of us becoming more isolated from one another? Do you see pockets of greater and lesser interconnectedness? Under what circumstances do you see people coming together for a common purpose? What makes that happen? How does it start, sustain itself, and possibly discontinue?
2. What communities are you a member of? Think about communities that you identify with based on where you live, the people you associate with, the places you spend time, the hobbies or activities you enjoy, the place you worship and work. Draw circles on a piece of paper for each and use the size to indicate how many people are members of each community, and position them to show how much the communities overlap. What conclusions about your community life do you draw?
3. When you shop, do you think about where the products were made, who made them, what the producers were paid, and who else is making

a profit? If not, consider the possibilities for the clothes you are wearing right now, the food you ate in the last meal you had, and where you live. What do you know about the people who played roles in having these needs met? Who are they? Do you see forces of neoliberalism, globalization, industrialization, or mobility playing a part?

4. From your thoughts about the questions above, consider writing your own list of forces that strengthen and challenge communities. First consider what you would define as a healthy community. Use your senses to start with and from there create an image. What would you include as positive aspects of community life? What do you see as detractors from a healthy community? How can these challenges be addressed?

Web Links

- Ontario Healthy Communities Coalition
  http://www.ohcc-ccso.ca/en/what-makes-a-healthy-community
- Supporting Local Business Development to Build Wealth
  http://community-wealth.org/policy-brief/
  Supporting-Local-Business-Development-to-Build-Wealth
- A Primer on Neoliberalism
  http://www.globalissues.org/article/39/a-primer-on-neoliberalism
- IndexMundi
  http://www.indexmundi.com
- Mental Health: A State of Wellbeing (World Health Organization)
  http://www.who.int/features/factfiles/mental_health/en/
- Mapping Community Assets
  http://www.abcdinstitute.org/docs/Diane%20Dorfman-Mapping-
  Community-Assets-WorkBook(1)-1.pdf
- Understanding Community Power Structures
  http://www.nrcs.usda.gov/Internet/FSE_DOCUMENTS/
  stelprdb1045565.pdf
- Power or Programs? Two Paths to Community Development
  http://comm-org.wisc.edu/drafts/twopathsb2.htm

Key Terms

Bowling Alone	interaction
loneliness	belongingness
inclusion	solidarity

Friendship Group
emotional
informational
appraisal
building community
friendships
mutuality
free market
charity
invisible hand
laissez-faire
private enterprise
government deregulation
free trade
austerity
interconnectedness of nations
Silk Road
market
imports
exports
policy vacuum
international marketplace
family farm
147 companies that control everything
grassroots
consumer movement
credit unions
agricultural co-ops
cooperative housing
worker co-ops
Antigonish Movement
Northern Star Worker Cooperative
instrumental
Gemeinschaft
Gesellschaft
geographic
function
attribute
need community

target community
action community
production
distribution
consumption
socialization
social control
social participation
mutual support
environmental capital
economic capital
human capital
political capital
information capital
social network map
patterns
interrelationships
community asset map
building blocks
stigma
reward power
coercive power
legitimate power
referent power
expert power
informational power
information
money
laws
constituencies
natural resources
goods and services
network participation
families
status occupations
illegal actions
personality
power-based development
program-based development

CHAPTER 7

COMMUNITY CHANGE

Chapter Outline

Counselors can challenge oppression and promote empowerment through participation in group efforts at the community level. The same sociopolitical influences that operate within the individual operate within and between groups as well as in communities. In addition, while there is diversity within communities, there are also commonalities that offer possibilities for groups to form and merge as well as create opportunities for members. There are many examples of social change agents who have made major contributions at the community level to promote liberation for members of oppressed groups. The ways that change can be viewed and engaged in provide direction for counselors to interpret, become involved, and possibly even lead such initiatives in their own or their clients' communities.

The purpose of this chapter is to provide a perspective on ways that counselors can partner with others in the interests of community-level change and ways that change could be undertaken. Profiles of major contributors to community change processes and practices provide some examples of types of community change, principles used, and outcomes achieved. Based on existing literature regarding the efforts of professionals leading community change, three major approaches are defined, including locality development, social planning, and social action. Some areas of practice where these approaches have been used are offered, including employment development, neighborhood development, community-based housing, and social enterprise. Finally, specific tactics of community change including confrontation, negotiation, collaboration, and cooptation are presented.

Partnerships

Different partnerships exist in the professional lives of counselors and clients. These include **professional to professional**, **professional to client**, **client to client**, and **professional to organized group** (Corey, Corey, Corey, & Callanan, 2014). In relation to the sociopolitical context of counseling, the efforts that counselors engage in with clients typically occur as professional to client. These can be, as has been noted, oppressive or liberating, both internally and externally. However, counselors can and do interact with colleagues, both within and outside of the counseling profession and can use those connections to influence change that benefits clients. They can also, in ways that respect the privacy and informed consent of clients, make it possible for clients to interact in ways that offer mutual support and assistance. Finally, there is the possibility of counselors interacting with organized groups that make a difference in the lives of individuals and clients negatively affected by forces of oppression.

An important consideration in the development of a liberating relationship in direct work with clients, as well as indirect work that affects clients, is the recognition of a bottom–up and **democratic process** (Bannister, 2015). One of the most valuable assets counselors have is their own experiences of oppression and, most importantly, for the purposes of the approach proposed in this book, their relationships with clients who have experienced oppression. This empathetic awareness is essential to the momentum of efforts that address oppressive forces. The key message here is that the experience of community change, given the need for members themselves to determine its nature and expression, ought to be driven by the members' experiences and efforts in a democratic way. The reason for this suggestion is that the forces of oppression are put upon people from the outside and often experienced as though they are dictated and beyond one's control. The need for agency, voice, and influence on social conditions is therapeutically and interpersonally helpful, as well as economically and politically empowering (Hoener, Stiles, Luka, & Gordon, 2012).

Key Figures

Social change can be undertaken to alter the power structure itself or align with it in a way that benefits oppressed groups in a community or entire communities. It can be **reactive** (e.g., response to zoning bylaws) or **proactive** (e.g., political leadership), **formal** (e.g., a social service) or **informal** (e.g., a neighborhood barbeque). Development efforts that are program-based are rooted in a functionalist philosophy, primarily collaborative in nature with a focus on building organizations and programs that operate in **partnership** with the prominent power structures to attend to social and technical aspects of community needs (Cels, De Jong, & Nauta, 2012). In contrast, development efforts that are power-based are rooted in a conflict philosophy, are primarily **confrontational** and focus on taking power from the major power structures in the community to develop power in those who have less, often by holding public officials and private leaders accountable (Ganesh & Zoller, 2012).

In the following profiles, well-known leaders of community change are presented. As you read these descriptions, consider the reactive or proactive orientations taken, and the formal and informal partnerships used, as well as the extent to which each aligned with the power structure or challenged it. Jane Addams, Myles Horton, Saul Alinsky, Paulo Friere, Moses Coady, and Georges Erasmus made major contributions to the theory and practice of community change in Canada and the United States.

Jane Addams and the Settlement House Movement

Jane Addams (1860–1935) grew up in Cedarville, Illinois. On vacation to Europe, she witnessed severe poverty and learned of Toynbee Hall in London where university students lived and worked with people in the community (Watts, 2015). She found the practice to be inspirational. In 1889 Addams opened the first settlement house in North America based on the approach taken at Toynbee Hall. It was located in Chicago.

Addams and a colleague rented an abandoned mansion in an industrial neighborhood. They invited residents in for community book and art events, and eventually expanded to include a kindergarten, gathering space for mothers, teen clubs, and a cultural space (Beauboeuf-Lafontant, 2014). **Hull House** grew to 13 buildings and over 70 residents. Its purpose was to help local immigrants adjust to life in their new community. They provided support and services as well as political activism to improve conditions in the community for residents. Addams was also heavily invested in policy level efforts and made contributions to issues of child labor, factory safety, and youth justice, and specifically, practices to regulate working hours and recognize labor unions (Shields, 2011). She founded the American Civil Liberties Union and the National Association for the Advancement of Colored People. Addams won the Nobel Peace Prize in 1931. A quote from one of her many books, reflects her desire to make a difference:

> We all know that each generation has its own test, the contemporaneous and current standard by which alone it can adequately judge of its own moral achievements, and that it may not legitimately use a previous and less vigorous test. The advanced test must indeed include that which has already been attained; but if it includes no more, we shall fail to go forward, thinking complacently that we have "arrived" when in reality we have not yet started. (Addams, 1902, p. 38)

Myles Horton and the Highlander Folk School

Myles Horton (1905–1990) grew up in a rural community where his family experienced severe poverty. As an adult he went to seminary school, traveled to Denmark, and learned of folk schools in Copenhagen. Upon his return to the United States and Tennessee, he brought neighboring farmers, miners, woodcutters, and mill hands together. His focus was on workers' rights to organize using discussion groups to share experiences, problems, and solutions (Keefe, 2015). The process was peer education. He believed that people should do their own research and become their own experts. They need to test out ideas in practice, learn from them, and reapply what worked (Loder-Jackson, 2013). Horton and the school became active in the Civil Rights Movement, focusing on desegregation, voter education, and citizenship schools. The **Highlander Center** replaced the original School in the 1960s with a broader mandate and federal funding (Chang, 2013). The Center was also nominated for a Nobel Peace Prize. His belief about the importance of a grassroots-led process is apparent in a quote from his autobiography (Kohl & Horton, 1988): "Instead of thinking that you put pieces together that will add up to a whole, I think you have to start with the premise that they're already together and you try to keep from destroying life by segmenting it, over organizing it and dehumanizing it. You try to keep things together. The educative process must be organic, and not an assortment of unrelated methods and ideas" (p. 21).

Saul Alinsky and the Industrial Areas Foundation

Saul Alinsky (1909–1972) was the son of Jewish Russian immigrants who grew up in Chicago's west side, living in the back of the family's tailor shop. Alinsky went to the University of Chicago to study archeology and sociology. After graduation, he was hired to do research on crime and observed the efforts and benefits of trade union organizers. Alinsky fought against the recreation, camping, and "character building" programs proposed at the time that did little to address the real issues of power and powerlessness as causes of crime (Horwitt, 1989).

Alinsky was a professional activist. He founded the **Industrial Areas Foundation** and trained organizers to work in poor communities (Alinsky, 1941). The approach was confrontational. A favorite tactic employed by Alinsky's organizers was to bring groups of people together to demand better jobs or pay and put it on display for the media where the reactions of those responsible were caught on film (Finks, 1984). He found allies who could fund his activities in movie stars and the Christian church. His well-known tactics for community change follow from the book *Rules for Radicals* (1971):

Power is not only what you have, but what the enemy thinks you have.
Never go outside the expertise of your people.
Whenever possible, go outside the expertise of the enemy.
Make the enemy live up to its own book of rules.
Ridicule is man's most potent weapon.
A good tactic is one your people enjoy.
A tactic that drags on too long becomes a drag.
Keep the pressure on.
The threat is usually more terrifying than the thing itself.
The major premise for tactics is the development of operations that will maintain a constant pressure upon the opposition.
If you push a negative hard and deep enough, it will break through into its counterside.

The price of a successful attack is a constructive alternative.
Pick the target, freeze it, personalize it, and polarize it. (pp. 34–38)

Paulo Friere and Conscientization

Paulo Friere (1921–1997) grew up in Brazil in extreme poverty. He observed the oppressed as accepting of their situations. Friere saw the internalizing of oppression via a personal devaluing of experience and potential, belief in inability, low confidence, and the power of the oppressor, which together contributed to a culture of silence. He saw that the focus of the poor was survival and not the opportunity to develop **critical consciousness,** as evidenced in the famous quote, "The oppressed, having internalized the image of the oppressor and adopted his guidelines, are fearful of freedom" (Freire, 1970). He characterized the relationships between oppressors and the oppressed as dehumanizing, and outlined the characteristics of this approach to education in his book *Pedagogy of the Oppressed* (1970, pp. 54–55):

the teacher teaches and the students are taught;
the teacher knows everything and the students know nothing;
the teacher thinks and the students are thought about;
the teacher talks and the students listen—meekly;
the teacher disciplines and the students are disciplined;
the teacher chooses and enforces his choice, and the students comply;
the teacher acts and the students have the illusion of acting through the action of the teacher;
the teacher chooses the program content, and the students (who were not consulted) adapt to it;
the teacher confuses the authority of knowledge with his or her own professional authority, which she and he sets in opposition to the freedom of the students;
the teacher is the Subject of the learning process, while the pupils are mere objects.

His efforts centered on **literacy education** for adults, through recognition of social, political, and economic contradictions that surrounded them (Freire & Macedo, 2013). He encouraged action in solidarity and against oppressors. Education, from this perspective, had to be liberating. Its purpose was not to fit people into roles, but to open them up to their fullest potential. To Friere, learning was the integration of knowledge. It was authentic and relevant and took the form of genuine dialogue between teachers and students. Educators needed to establish a climate for learning where learners did not become docile listeners, but co-constructors of knowledge (Freire, 2014).

Moses Coady and Economic Cooperatives

Moses Coady (1882–1959) had a rural Cape Breton upbringing. He attended St. Francis Xavier University and graduated in 1905. His cousin convinced him to enter the priesthood. He traveled to Rome to study theology and philosophy and returned as a Roman Catholic priest serving in Antigonish, Nova Scotia (Stabler, 1986). Main industries in the area were farming and fishing. People were leaving the area because they could no longer earn a decent living. Farms were too small to support families and the "cod lords," middlemen who bought and sold fish, controlled the local economies.

Social change required education. Coady would call mass meetings in the fishing communities. Then, from there, **study clubs** were formed to look at the ways they could take control of the benefits of their labor (Lovett, Clarke & Kilmurray, 1983). There was a partnership with the university which began to offer a **Peoples School** in 1921, which was a six-week course focusing on principles of cooperation and self-help (Coady, 1939). The practices expanded and grew to reach other communities. At the time of World War II, 2,265 study clubs in the Maritimes led to the formation of 451 credit unions and 210 cooperative retail stores (McManus, 2013). The Coady Institute today focuses on asset-based community development, including topics in microfinance, advocacy and networking, youth programs, peace building, and conflict resolution (Mathie & Cunningham, 2005). Coady describes the approach to education in the following passage from *The Antigonish Way* (pp. 63–64): "The technique was discovered by facing the actual situation and planning a way by which the people of eastern Canada could be mobilized to think, to study, and to get enlightenment. We found the discussion circle. This did not involve any teachers. It was in line with our whole co-operative idea. We would make people come together by themselves and discuss their problems."

Georges Erasmus and Indigenous Self Government

Georges Erasmus (b. 1948) was born in Fort Rae and raised in Yellowknife, Northwest Territories. The Dene people had lived in the Mackenzie Valley and Barren Grounds in the Northwest Territories for centuries. The arrival of Europeans brought the fur trade in the eighteenth century and mineral deposits brought increasing numbers to the area in the nineteenth and twentieth centuries (Erasmus, 1977). Treaties were signed between the Dene and the Europeans. To the Dene, these were friendship and peace agreements. The Europeans believed that they were taking title to the land. A lack of respect for the treaties led to the emergence of an organization called the Indian Brotherhood of the Northwest Territories in the 1970s (Richardson, 1989).

Erasmus made major efforts to protect Dene ways and the land. He became president of the Dene Nation at the age of 28 and brought together

25 communities to work out the details of a land claim. He became vice-chief of the **National Assembly of First Nations**, and was elected chief in 1985 where he remained until 1991 (Joseph, 2015). Of major note were his contributions to discussions about the Constitution, for which he became known as the "11th Premier." Erasmus became a member of the Order of Canada in 1987. He was also the co-chair of the **Royal Commission on Aboriginal Peoples** (Russell, 2014). In the report (Dussault & Erasmus, 1996), the following was stated:

> To bring about this fundamental change, Canadians need to understand that Aboriginal peoples are nations. That is, they are political and cultural groups with values and lifeways distinct from those of other Canadians. They lived as nations—highly centralized, loosely federated, or small and clan-based—for thousands of years before the arrival of Europeans. As nations, they forged trade and military alliances among themselves and with the new arrivals. To this day, Aboriginal people's sense of confidence and well-being as individuals remain tied to the strength of their nations. Only as members of restored nations can they reach their potential in the twenty-first century (pp. x-xi).

Erasmus was chair of the **Aboriginal Healing Foundation** (AHF) from 1998 to 2010, with the "mission to encourage and support Aboriginal people in building and reinforcing sustainable healing processes that address the legacy of Physical Abuse and Sexual Abuse in the Residential School system, including intergenerational impacts" (Castellano & Archibald, 2006).

Approaches to Community Change

The 1960s and 1970s were the heydays of community intervention. However, there was no analysis of the scientific literature until the 1990s. Jack Rothman (1996) has written extensively about community change and has proposed three main approaches: locality development, social planning, and social action. The distinguishing features of each are presented in Table 7.1.

Locality Development
In locality development, the focus is on cooperation (Rothman, 1996). Locality development often occurs in the context of limited resources where expansion of those resources is undertaken for mutual benefit. Local leadership development is important. Often education is a piece of this approach. There is an assumption that residents can and want to work together, and when people work together, benefits can take place for each (Schriner & Fawcett, 1988).

TABLE 7.1 Approaches to Community Change

LOCALITY DEVELOPMENT	SOCIAL PLANNING	SOCIAL ACTION
• emphasis on self help	• emphasis on rational, technical problem solving	• emphasis on redistribution of power and resources
• focus is on broad-based social and economic progress	• focus is on social problems	• focus is on social justice issues
• partnership with power structure	• sponsorship by the power structure	• variable orientation to power structure

From this approach, all people are viewed as worthy, capable, and having growth potential. Results are long-lasting. It has a broad focus and maintains that by bringing people in, moving slowly, and making small changes to build momentum toward larger changes, a consensus-based ideal can be achieved (Bailey & Chatterjee, 2015).

Process. Leadership development is crucial to success in this approach. Local leaders carry the most local credibility but outsiders can be useful to minimize divisions within the community or effort (Maton, 2008). The purpose of leadership is to engage members. There are several benefits including instrumental, immediate (e.g., a new playground), and anticipated (e.g., hope for a new school), as well as expressive (e.g., friendships, social activities) and symbolic (e.g., awards or mentions in a newspaper) (Stockdale, 2014).

Benefits. A main benefit of locality development is a reduction in isolation and loneliness. By promoting a sense of community through citizen involvement, and fostering **mutuality** and achievement the community can grow its sense of identity and purpose (Pilisuk, McAllister, & Rothman, 1996). Additional benefits are the cultivation of **local leadership** and **internal power structures** as well as the development of communication with external power structures (Basch, 2014).

Drawbacks. In locality development, the efforts and change are local, not regional or national in scope. The approach generally does not directly alter distribution of wealth or tackle complex financial problems such as unemployment. It does little to directly change structural oppression, such as sexism or classism. Local leadership can have a dark side, too. In some cases it allows the most vocal in a community to take control and silence the voices of those who were and continue to be oppressed. While such a narrow view of the community and its challenges and strengths helps bring focus, it can also be alienating to those outside of those priorities.

Social Planning

Social planning is a technical process of problem documentation (Rein, 1969). This approach is research-oriented and assumes outside expertise is needed. An assumption is made that there is a complex and multifaceted environment for which a highly controlled and careful process of study and documentation is required (Weil, Reisch, & Ohmer, 2012). The outcome of a social planning effort is typically a description of the problem and its causes, as well as a plan to move forward, often including policy change (O'Hara, 2006). The product is typically a document. For example, such efforts may explore the need for coordination or delivery of services, ways to incorporate community views into a city, efforts to solve a particular concern, or social impacts of an existing policy.

Process. There are six basic stages to a comprehensive social planning process (Weil, 2014): (1) preparation, (2) needs assessment, (3) policy development, (4) program development, (5) implementation, and (6) monitoring and evaluation. These are very similar to the problem-solving model with which most counselors are familiar. The idea is to begin by setting the terms of reference or how the process will be carried out including who will do what and when. The needs are assessed using research methodologies that produce results for intended uses (Neuman, 2005). Typically, there are policy- and program-development implications for the findings. Unfortunately, the report is often where this process stalls. But, ideally, the process includes change at a policy- or, more likely, a program-level, which is then monitored and evaluated.

Benefits. One of the benefits of this approach is the **expert credibility** that accompanies the right person from the outside to act as a **consultant** for this process. Another possibility is that the issues be framed so they are evident across silos—for example, the presence of unemployment among youth in the community and effects in health, social service, justice, and adult education services for the community. The sophistication of this analysis can carry some weight with the external power structure by providing "hard evidence" of the issue, problem, need, or service (Brueggemann, 2013). These efforts can translate research into funding/development/services.

Drawbacks. One challenge is that the process and outcome becomes so technical that it has little validity or utility for the community. It can be so consultant-heavy that it is disconnected from the needs of the community. The politics of "evidence" can make it known what the findings "ought" to say before the work is done (Kaplan, 1973). For example, the process could be a consultation exercise geared to a particular outcome, and one that may not be in the community stakeholder's best interests. There is a risk for a process that does not have a predetermined outcome, insofar as the results may not be politically or locally palatable. Deliberate attempts to document issues that funders want buried will be problematic.

Social Action

Social action is, as the name states, about action (Omoto, 2014). The assumption made is that change is necessary and good (Ife, 2012). Efforts from this approach are direct and often confrontational. Leadership can come from both outside and inside the community. Power, located in those from the outside, is to be relocated to the community (Rowbotham, 2013). Often these efforts disrupt the activities of those who have the power to provoke a public reaction. Efforts are made to personalize the attacks and create specific, meaningful, realizable goals with clear short-term outcomes. While the intention is quick action leading to quick reaction and change, the actual change can also take a long time to achieve (Rivlin, 2015). The approach is practical and realistic but the action is radical.

Process. A five-step process has been proposed: (1) defining, (2) researching, (3) formulating an action goal, (4) developing a method, and (5) evaluating the action (Cameron & Kerans, 1985). Framing the problem is important (e.g., who has been hurt by the policy?). It is helpful to research the problem through the solutions as stated by leaders of action groups, experts on the problem, and those who have an opinion about what to change. The action goal is to decide who will do what in order to bring about a change that benefits those who are being harmed. What methods are being pursued? Several possibilities exist, such as awareness building, **lobbying**, **demonstrations**, **boycotts**, **petitions**, and **lawsuits**. Evaluation depends on the intended beneficiaries' perceptions of the change and what it has done for their quality of life.

Benefits. Social action can be exciting. It is often high-profile and even fun. The collective effort to thwart a common enemy can be socially cohesive, provide an emotional high, and involve focused attention with intense effort (Reisch & Andrews, 2014). The social action taken is typically very gritty but with a heightened moral purpose. The direct consequences of the actions are immediately apparent. The confidence of those involved can increase.

Drawbacks. A major drawback to this type of effort is that one can upset groups who might, under different circumstances, be supportive. It can be very difficult to find sources of funding for these efforts because of their often controversial nature. In addition, a charismatic leader is essential. Without someone who has the potential to bring people together and lead the charge, these efforts fade away quickly. The downside to a charismatic leader is that she or he takes the attention from the effort (Sutherland, Land, & Böhm, 2013). Sometimes those involved do so for the opportunity to take the action and not because of commitment to the issue and desire for change. It is problematic to the effort when the action is more important than the change.

Types of Community Change

At a major community gathering in Winnipeg, Manitoba, a series of working documents were presented and discussed (Loewen, Cates, & Chorney, 2003). This conference represented local thinking about the ways that community change was being pursued. While the categories are not exhaustive, they provide a very useful framework for thinking about types of community change efforts, as well as the efforts that counselors may consider becoming involved with to benefit their clients. They include employment development, neighborhood development, community-based housing, and social enterprise.

Employment Development

In employment development the work is with both prospective employees and employers. There is a range of services provided from preparation (e.g., to ensure housing and health for prospective employees), to pre-employment training (e.g., training in ESL or high school education, as needed). In addition, efforts geared toward specific **employment training** (Michaelides & Benus, 2012) and self-employment skills are offered. Finally, **job placement** (Frank-Miller, Lambert, & Henly, 2015) and retention services are needed.

Neighborhood Development

Neighborhood development is locally based and focused on a social community within a geographic area. The goal is to strengthen connections between individuals and promote local governance. **Local governance** can range from encouragement of residents to vote in elections, speak to their elected representatives, or discuss issues with their neighbors (Chaskin & Greenberg, 2013). It can also develop into a residents' association that could speak for the neighborhood and be proactive by developing its own plan with priorities. Such efforts need connections with those on the outside of the community as well as the development of connections within it.

Community-Based Housing

Community-based housing is often locally based and clearly focused on the physical and social aspects of housing. These efforts center on planning, developing, or managing housing. The work can be directed toward the occupants of the houses to recruit occupants and maintain the building. Another area of work is to facilitate transition to housing and link prospective buyers or renters to homes. Another important focus of the work is in providing informational as well as emotional support to the occupants. An overriding purpose of these efforts is to promote stable housing for individuals and families as well as **local**

ownership and **long-term residency** for stability in neighborhoods and control over the housing (Aminzadeh et al., 2013).

Social Enterprise

Social enterprise is a relatively new development. The expertise to oversee these efforts exists within traditional business operation and social action (Phillips, 2015). The goal is to develop a viable and successful business that meets a social need. It is about using business approaches and techniques to reach social goals. These efforts can bring in revenue for social service organizations, provide **local employment**, keep income from the community within the community, and be environmentally conscious about how these efforts are pursued.

Tactics of Community Change

There are four major ways of taking action for community change, including confrontation, negotiation, collaboration, and cooptation (Homan, 2015). The choice depends on the purpose, outcomes, and risks one is willing to take. One way to think about this is by considering the issues, the target, the group, and other resources needed. For example, the issues include basic facts, causes and effects thereof, what has worked in other places, and what rights and responsibilities do those involved have. In relation to the target or the location where the change needs to take place, one needs to consider who the key players are, how much they would support or resist your group's solution, and what their strengths and challenges, as well as particular vulnerabilities, are. It is also essential to honestly evaluate your group's commitment and number as well as what the positive and negative effects of the intended action are, all in the context of what is culturally appropriate. It is necessary to determine what resources, other than the group itself, are needed and how to get them.

Confrontation

Confrontation is used to irritate an opponent and force concessions that become an agreement. It is used when there is a clear enemy or target that a group wants to force to change. It is a competition with a clear winner and loser. Such a tactic may be necessary when there is no possibility of reaching a compromise, or the target does not expect a confrontation from you or wants to keep a low profile (Gutierrez & Lewis, 2012). This can be used to promote your group's agenda publicly, by drawing attention to the conflict. It can solidify the issue as well as show anger and willingness to battle. Benefits include internal strengthening, showing the group's collective power to others, and upsetting opponents. Downsides include the need for a very cohesive and committed group that does not detach when things get difficult, as well as the potential to make a long-term enemy and other consequences of defeat (Somerville, 2011). Uses of this tactic are exemplified by personalizing the issue, freezing the target, having an "accountability" meeting, being disruptive, lawsuits, cutting off support, and **civil disobedience** (Alinsky, 1971).

Negotiation

Negotiation is used when your group is skeptical about the intentions of the other. There is potential for trust to develop here and awareness that the other side has something to gain from the agreement. It is potentially useful when your group wants to work with the other side, when you see that you cannot clearly "win" a confrontation, when your group needs to make some progress, or when you see legitimacy to both positions (Slavin & Morrison, 2013). Benefits are that you can get something, though not everything, and that the groups can work together, which opens the door to a relationship that could be beneficial in the future. A downside is the risk of giving away too much in negotiation, taking away from the main issue by focusing on small "wins," and looking weak if your group does not come away with a significant result. Uses of negotiation are **positional** (i.e., interests are hidden and positions are in conflict) and **principled** (i.e., interests are out and positions can advance both sides' interests). Uses of these tactics are evident in having a clear purpose and outcome, being willing to concede or package some things, involving a third party, if helpful, and breaking from the negotiation when needed (Minkler & Wallerstein, 2011).

Collaboration

Collaboration is used when trust is beginning to develop between groups that have the potential to grow stronger, and there are clear winners on both sides in favor of working together. This can be useful when groups see commonality and want to establish a more formal relationship through this effort (Soska & Butterfield, 2013). The benefits are that each side gets resources—shared and new—as well as the possibility to work together in the future. In addition, an **interdependence** or dependence can be facilitated. Potential downsides are that the relationship is focused on only a single issue while significant differences remain, or that your group loses some freedom of independent action. Finally, as counselors know very well, relationships take time and effort. This tactic can be used to make agreements, clarify ownership, acknowledge a partner's involvement, offer rewards to a partner, take on a fair share of the work, and get to know each other personally.

Cooptation

Cooptation is a formal alliance that usually begins by bringing a target for change into the fold. It is used when your group wants to share information and resources and develop a relationship for the purpose of influencing that target group (Fields, 2015). This is tricky depending on the intentions. If intentions are only strategic, the other side may feel duped or take advantage of your group. If there are genuine intentions on both sides, this can work well. It is most appropriate when your group cannot confront the other side and does not have anything the other side wants through negotiation or cooperation (Ostrander, 2013). Potential benefits are silencing a critic from the outside by bringing her or him inside, learning about the other side's operations with little investment of time and effort. Drawbacks are the time it takes for this to develop and potentially giving away information or connections. Uses of this tactic may be to place particular people on committees together, share a message that teamwork is being shown on the other side, and invite advice from the other group.

Conclusion

There are several approaches to community change. Well-known mobilizers in communities struggling against oppression have developed approaches that can be used in other settings. Major ways of mobilizing and using power within the community are based in three general approaches including development, planning, and action. These approaches have been expressed in the development of employment opportunities, neighborhood governance, housing, and small business.

Discussion Questions

1. Considering the descriptions of the Key Figures presented in this chapter, which of those individuals' approaches and contributions resonate most clearly with your own experiences? Were there any who you found yourself reacting to negatively? Where we locate ourselves in relation to the interests we hold and the type of change we believe in can be very useful guides for the community work we support and engage in.

2. The Key Figures in this chapter each favored an educational approach within their work in a community. How do you define and apply education in your counseling work? Do you direct it? To what extent do clients direct it? Does the influence of this education extend both ways (i.e., to you and the client)? Consciousness raising requires effort by the educator to introduce the idea that oppression is happening and the ways it is happening in the lives of clients. Do you use this in your counseling? Why or why not?

3. From the three approaches to community change presented, including locality development, social planning, and social action, which do you favor?

In which style of work do you see your particular strengths emerging? The next time you read a local newspaper or community newsletter, or watch the news on television, consider the social issues that reappear, or the underlying problems that are faced. How is community change being pursued in your community on these issues? How could it be?

4. The tactics of community change include negotiation, collaboration, confrontation, and cooptation. While cooptation, if done by withholding information, is not permitted under professional ethics, the other tactics are, when used appropriately and intentionally for a client's benefit. Which of these tactics do you find yourself emphasizing in your counseling practice? Would they be the same or different in your professional and interpersonal interactions outside of the office? How familiar and comfortable are you with these tactics of community change?

Web Links

- Settlement House Movement
  http://ocp.hul.harvard.edu/immigration/settlement.html
- Jane Addams Biography
  http://www.biography.com/people/jane-addams-9176298
- Simcoe Hall
  http://www.simcoehall.com
- Highlander Research and Educate Center
  http://highlandercenter.org
- Industrial Areas Foundation
  http://www.industrialareasfoundation.org
- Paulo Friere: Dialogue, Praxis and Education
  http://infed.org/mobi/paulo-freire-dialogue-praxis-and-education/
- Coady International Institute
  http://coady.stfx.ca/coady/
- Assembly of First Nations
  http://www.afn.ca/index.php/en
- Aboriginal Healing Foundation
  http://www.ahf.ca

Key Terms

professional to professional
professional to client

client to client
professional to organized group

democratic process
reactive
proactive
formal
informal
partnership
confrontational
Hull House
Highlander Center
Industrial Areas Foundation
critical consciousness
literacy education
study clubs
Peoples School
National Assembly of First Nations
Royal Commission on Aboriginal
    Peoples
Aboriginal Healing Foundation
mutuality

local leadership
internal power structures
expert credibility
consultant
lobbying
demonstrations
boycotts
petitions
lawsuits
employment training
job placement
local governance
local ownership
long-term residency
local employment
civil disobedience
positional
principled
interdependence

CHAPTER 8

GETTING STARTED

Chapter Outline

Based on the preceding chapter with its focus on major concepts, strategies, and tactics for community change, there are several ways that counselors may engage. Few can, or desire to, take on community change efforts to the extent that the contributors described in Chapter 8 have. However, a sociopolitical view and recognition of challenges associated with oppression at a community level does not necessitate radical changes to one's practice. Indeed, counselors already engage in activities with clients in ways that challenge internalized oppression. However, there are possibilities for extending one's efforts into communities. There are different levels, as well as benefits and drawbacks for each. In this chapter, a process of community change is offered that counselors may use to guide their efforts. While there are many ways that involvement can be pursued and support provided, in this chapter the focus is on general ways that counselors may consider and approach community change.

Involvement in Community Change

Counselors already understand the context within which their clients live and the sociopolitical influences on their daily lives. Counselors can be involved in a more direct way through participation in community events and change efforts. Counselors can increase involvement by putting their personal and professional names and credentials to their contributions of time and addressing oppressive forces as they appear in their daily lives. Taking on leadership requires more time and energy, but can also be personally rewarding and helpful to larger groups. Each layer of involvement is presented in this section, followed by potential advantages and disadvantages. A case example also provides more detail on these ideas.

Awareness
At this level, counselors are sensitive to the ways that oppression operates in clients' lives (Reeve, 2000). This awareness is achieved and sensitivity maintained by following the news and reading about social justice issues, including what has been and is happening, as well as what has worked and is working

for positive change. Counselors also listen to clients about oppression in their lives. They are open to viewing oppression as a contributor to their challenges and liberation to be of benefit. Counselors also watch in their personal lives for oppression as well as notice its contributors and effects.

The main benefit of this understanding is an increased ability to empathize with clients. Counselors can develop faster connections with clients. They can also deepen and extend an understanding of both the challenges faced and the strengths evident. Finally, these efforts potentially assist in the effectiveness of the work (Shepard, O'Neill, & Guenette, 2006).

The main drawbacks of this awareness can be that the additional information and skill dilute from the focus with clients. Some may argue that the use of contextual information and forces on the lives of clients takes away from the science underlying intrapersonal factors that are a hallmark of counseling and therapeutic practice. This additional information can take more time with clients and perhaps take away from the purpose clients themselves have for being in counseling.

"Behind the Scenes"

At this level, counselors contribute quietly to community initiatives in a variety of ways. Such efforts can include anonymous donations to collective efforts expressed through groups and organizations, and reflected in programs and campaigns. In addition, counselors vote in elections for candidates that reflect important values and priorities (Sullivan, McNamara, Ybarra, & Bulatao, 1995).

A main benefit to this involvement is that counselors take actions as part of professional practice or personal duty to improve causes or address issues that they believe in. They avoid the potential risks associated with extensive time commitments and public involvement. They are also involved in civic affairs and see the "big picture" potential of political or policy change.

Some drawbacks of this involvement are that the "bigger issues" remain at a personal and professional distance. In addition, this type of participation is separate from direct action that may be needed. It may also fail to recognize ways the profession contributes to or could better address oppression.

Sideline Contributions

At this level, counselors contribute openly to community initiatives. They do this in multiple ways. They may address micro-aggressions in daily life (e.g., challenge "jokes," stereotypes, and social hierarchies). They may choose to provide formal and public support for political parties and candidates. They may also make named contributions of time and money to collective efforts (e.g., mail-outs, donations) for international, national, or local causes (Olson-Buchanan, Bryan, & Thompson, 2013).

recent editorial in the newspaper about the challenges of older workers entering the workforce for the first time, and know that her options are very limited.

Thinking about her personal experiences, the expectations of her role, and the forces that contribute to those, you as her counselor reflect on the trauma, depression, and anxiety, childrearing, education, and employment, as well as housing situation, and recognize that within these experiences are the issues of sexism, ageism, and classism.

Awareness. You are aware of the demands she puts on herself to be "everything" to her grandchildren and children. They are taking an emotional, physical, and financial toll on her. You are also aware of the need to "not trust anyone" in a residential place where getting involved in the happenings can be dangerous. Finally, you are aware of the potential for women, if they are interested, to enter the workforce at a late age to gain freedom and financial security. You can use this understanding therapeutically to check with Donna about her situation and how she sees it, what she believes has the potential to change, and how she can move in that direction.

Behind the Scenes. You could take some action behind the scenes that does not involve your client but does involve yourself as a citizen or professional. You can be sure to vote in the next civic election after informing yourself about women's issues, children's issues, as well as homelessness efforts and employment-creation initiatives. You could also contribute financially to organizations that make a difference, such as those that support women's transitions

TABLE 8.1 Issues Faced by a Client

PERSONAL	< - >	SOCIOPOLITICAL
Trauma		
Depression		
Anxiety		
Childrearing Responsibilities		
	Education and Employment	
	Residence Type and Location	
		Sexism
		Ageism
		Classism

from violent situations and those that have a clear anti-poverty focus, such as a local **food bank**.

Sideline Contributions. To get involved from the sideline, you could put specific effort into interactions in your daily life that limit opportunities, such as confronting micro-aggressions (e.g., "jokes," stereotypes) made about women, the "poor," or older people at home, in the workplace, or in public. You could also become involved in sideline efforts by helping **campaign** for a political group, or volunteer with the food bank or **meal program** in the community.

Direct Involvement. This could involve being part of the change as a major contributor by identifying causes and organizations that make a positive differ-ence in the lives of all residents, or your clients in particular. These can involve, for the purposes of Donna's situation, attendance at a housing meeting for public housing and questions about the quality and quantity, as well as offering participation in working groups or citizens' advisory groups. Another possi-bility may be to be more formally involved in the food bank, to ensure that your involvement can lead to changes that make it easier for busy caregivers to access the benefits (e.g., organize a delivery service for some residents or a distribution center to public housing locations).

Leadership. Leadership positions usually involve the greatest commitment of time, energy, and money. These efforts are most directly related to the issue and offer the most ability to direct and inform in ways that make a difference. Although much of this book is written about the work of grass-roots groups and leadership within such groups, the principles apply and can be used by anyone who wants to be involved in community change at any level or type of involvement. In the case of leadership, there is the possibility to be involved in the issues affecting Donna in her community by orga-nizing a housing meeting with a local community development agency for interested individuals facing struggles in **public housing**. Another possi-bility is to look at connecting with a temporary services agency in the area to determine the likelihood of specialized job recruitment and **job place-ment** for women entering the workforce later in life. You could also become a member of a board of directors for agencies in the areas of community housing, women's services, or mental health.

Community Change Model

In the proposed model there are four major steps in community change. It is a circular model and the steps do not necessarily occur in the sequence presented, nor do they occur independently of each other. What each adds to the effort is likely addressed at some point along the way. The assumption underlying this process is that a leader or facilitator or staff person with the role to inspire and coordinate as well as oversee the change is in place. However, counselors who recognize the pieces of this process can be very helpful, if not as leaders of change, to those leaders and the community as supporters of change.

The change process includes preparation, organization, building momentum, and, finally, taking and sustaining action. Issues to be addressed during preparation concern the role of the counselor in the community change effort and the determination of information necessary to be obtained about the community or focal community issue as well as potential processes. In organization, the issues to be addressed include the actual engagement in the community and ways of identifying and raising interest in doing something about the challenges faced. In building momentum, the strengths and needs of the community are assessed and goals for the change are identified. Taking and sustaining action is the last step and includes both engagement and motivation in the identified solution at the onset of the effort as well as the important role of maintaining levels of engagement in the effort after the initial undertaking.

Preparation

Although one could start with a determination of the type of community change that is needed, it is often worthwhile to begin with a quick inventory of one's own internal and external resources as well as potential challenges to involvement (Fawcett et al., 1995). In consideration of the role of the counselor in the change effort, it is suggested that counselors identify anticipated facilitators and constraints to your desired type of involvement. It is suggested that counselors also consider personal and professional goals and expectations, as well as the type of role(s) that one could play, and finally, the recognition and management of **dual relationships** anticipated during one's involvement (Borys & Pope, 1989).

Goals and Expectations

For counselors considering involvement in community change efforts, there are some basic considerations in terms of time, results orientation, contexts of the work, and both employer and peer evaluations. Much of this involvement comes either in addition to or in place of income-generating efforts through employment. There are few if any sources of funding that will pay for professional time or expertise in these efforts, with the potential exception of some income from activities related to a proposal that typically requires a considerable effort to construct, and entry into a competition for limited funding dollars. **Research consultation** is the most likely role for which a professional counselor may be financially compensated in community work

(Rubin & Babbie, 2013), but for many counseling professionals, working directly with people is their interest.

A related issue is the personal need to see results from efforts. In counseling there are typically aspects to a client's situation that are remediated as a result of the efforts both parties contribute to the process. Employers, funders, and clients themselves often expect these results to be achieved quickly and explicitly. A marked contrast is evident in community work where the outcomes, depending how they are framed, are far more distant and broad in orientation, requiring a collective effort over a significant period (Minkler & Wallerstein, 2011). Good community work takes time, and short-term results, comparable to a counseling process for many clients, are difficult to come by.

It is also important to recognize the limitations on one's personal energy for responsibilities outside of work. Given the likelihood that involvement can cut into billable hours, direct financial contributions, or add to the workday, which extends into evening and weekend work, the energy for community work can be drawn from other activities or if simply added on, contribute to fatigue and burnout (Philp, Egan, & Kane, 2012).

It is also worthwhile to consider the effects of involvement in the eyes of employers and colleagues. While it can be worthwhile to approach an employer about the possibility of using some **company time** to engage in these efforts, particularly if they are seen to contribute to the agency's mission, there may be no sanction for this effort granted by an employer (Baldwin & Gould, 2012). One issue that can emerge in such a discussion or negotiation is the legitimacy of community work (Hardina, 2013). While there is evidence from the literature concerning the need for social change and the benefits thereof on clients (Fawcett et al., 1995; Flynn & Hodgkinson, 2013; Rivlin, 2015; Stringer, 2013), including individuals, families, and entire communities, this may not be apparent to others who have a focused understanding in counseling about human development and change. There are cases where the **legitimacy** of community work itself will need to be defended.

The nature of community work is also very political (Rivlin, 2015). The assessments and judgments about who deserves what and who is responsible in a society, as has been described in Chapters 4 and 5, factor into the reception such involvement will obtain by an employer and professional colleagues. Depending on the nature of one's practice and the source of funding, it is also worthwhile to consider the perceptions of those contributors (Weinberg & Campbell, 2014). For example, being seen to bite the hand that feeds can severely limit or end a relationship with a funder (e.g., being a contractor for provincial mental health funding with counseling clients, and pushing for change with survivors of the mental health system as a community worker, may make one a target of budget cuts).

Potential Roles

The types of roles counselors in community efforts may take on include organizing, teaching, coaching, facilitating, advocating, negotiating, and functioning as a broker or researcher (Banks, Butcher, Orton, & Robertson, 2013). **Organizers** view the resources and challenges to the change effort, making decisions about who will be involved in what way to achieve the goal, as well as strategies to be pursued as part of that change effort. **Teachers** raise consciousness and critique of the unsatisfactory situation that exists, as well as share information about the tactics, roles, and specific actions of the change effort. **Coaches** function as motivators who reinforce the gains made, efforts needed, and the confidence and capacity to execute the plans that lead to the change. **Facilitators** can function both with the ranks of those involved in the change effort and between those ranks and an external group, agency, or institution. They represent the process within the ranks and assist with the movement forward. Between the ranks and the external world, they can organize potential meetings and chair them.

Advocates represent a particular set of interests, have done their research, and have a good rationale for the changes they seek. They can advocate on behalf of a particular participant, an interest group of participants, or the entire change effort in relation to some identified external group, agency, or institution. **Negotiators** find ways to achieve goals through reason and discussion. They work to find outcomes or agreements that offer maximum benefit for the side they represent while preserving the relationship between parties as much as possible. They can manage conflicts between members of the change effort itself, as well as those between the group pursuing change and an external group, agency, or institution. **Brokers** keep their options open between different tactics and strategies (as presented in Chapter 7) with a rational view of what will work best for which end at what time and with a particular set of individuals and groups involved. They can be very helpful strategists and consultants as the group moves forward with its efforts. **Researchers** collect or locate information, synthesize and interpret it, and prepare reports for their constituents. Often, their involvement occurs as a representative of a particular interest in community change and the identification and representation of information is done for a particular purpose, to a particular group, at a particular time.

Dual Relationships

There is the potential that, as a result of involvement in community work, a counselor may meet up with or be part of groups sharing similar interests. Dual roles for many counselors to some extent are unavoidable (e.g., small communities where a counselor shops, gets her or his car serviced, and goes to restaurants), and we are required by ethical codes and guidelines for practice to avoid or manage these in ways that do not put us in a position of advantage or **power over** a client (Reamer, 2012). The responsibility is always on the counselor to ensure this occurs and never on the client. The best way to manage dual roles is to prevent them from occurring in the first place.

It seems very clear that it is inappropriate to have a personal or another professional relationship with a client outside of sessions. A major concern here is that the counselor will be in a position of **authority** over the client in another capacity (e.g., chair of an organization). This is not appropriate. In such cases, a referral to another counselor or withdrawal from the position of authority is necessary.

Less preventable are instances where the counselor may have unexpected and casual contact outside of the office by being involved in similar initiatives. A major issue here is that the counselor could potentially identify a counseling client. A possible way forward is to discuss such incidents in sessions and make plans for handling them in the future. For example, the author was a volunteer server and dishwasher in a weekly lunch program for single men in an inner-city church. I was surprised when one of my counseling clients was staring back at me over the meal that I helped to serve. I said hello and he did as well, similarly to the others who came through the line. I approached him quietly and privately after the lunch and made sure he recognized me, told him that I was surprised but pleased to see him and that I had not nor would ever identify knowing him outside of the lunch. He was satisfied and at our next scheduled session we laughed about how surprised each of us was to see one another in this small world.

Information

In relation to the community, it is important to begin with information about the issues and their resolution. Communities refer to people and places. It can be helpful to consider both the physical and social aspects of community when considering the nature of the issues and the means for their resolution. Although many residents will already know what the problems and solutions are, it can be invaluable to collect information to promote **responsibility** (e.g., due diligence to ensure different views represented), **credibility** (e.g., that the important sources such as census data and key informants are incorporated), **versatility** (e.g., that the data can be used to profile the community for different purposes), and **accountability** (e.g., to perform the collection and analysis as required by funders or other stakeholders). Both **primary sources** (e.g., community members' perspectives) and **secondary sources** (e.g., census data) should be used. In addition, the power sources and structure of the community are important to recognize. The following is a guide that may be useful in identifying relevant community information:

Physical Community [sources: government documents, census, planning reports (city, county, province/state, federal), observations, consultations with key informants]

1. Boundaries
   a. What are the boundaries of the community?
   b. When did the boundaries first appear?
   c. What was the purpose of the boundaries at the time?
2. Governance
   a. What local formal and informal governance exists in the community?
   b. What layers of formal and informal governance is the community subsumed within?
3. History
   a. Who were the founders of the community?
   b. What was the vision the founders had for the community?
   c. What efforts have been made by whom to change the boundaries and why?
   d. What natural resources existed within the boundaries?
   e. Who owned the resources?
4. Present
   a. What physical landmarks characterize the community today?
   b. What physical resources exist within the community? (both person-made and naturally occurring)
      i. Housing, schools, government offices, local businesses, human services, food sources, financial institutions
      ii. Green space, play space, meeting space, transportation within and between community and outside
   c. What climate-related, natural resource-related, size-related, and location-related issues are pressing for the community?

Social Community [sources: government documents, census, planning reports (city, county, province/state, federal), observations, consultations with key informants]

1. Demographics
   a. Population size, mobility (within and outside of community)
   b. Age of population, family status, children, ethnicities, religions
   c. Income sources and amounts
2. Participation
   a. Community organizations
   b. Communication (newsletters, newspapers, Internet)
   c. Festivals, celebrations

3. History
   a. Founding interests of the community? Is this contested?
   b. Which interests have been prominent over time?
   c. Which interests have been marginalized over time?
   d. Which interests are most prominent in the present?
4. Present
   a. What social functions characterize the community today?
   b. What social resources exist within the community?
      i. Formal and informal cooperatives, gatherings
      ii. Associations, clubs
   c. What age-related, ethnicity-related, and class-related issues are pressing for the community?

Power Structure [sources: government documents, census, planning reports (city, county, province/state, federal), observations, consultations with key informants]

- Conduits for income into the community
- Conduits for income out of the community
- Location of political power internal (informal and formal)
- Location of political power external (informal and formal)
- Ethnic or religious leadership
- Advocacy organizations or groups

Organization

Armed with information about the community, its history, resources, and challenges, as well as thoughts about the nature of involvement, the process of getting to know the community more personally can be undertaken. In this step, the more specific considerations for becoming involved as a change agent in a community are important to address. This will help to build credibility needed to be involved more centrally in the change effort. Oftentimes, critical consciousness (presented in Chapter 6) is needed for motivation to pursue change by community members, and if this is not already present, attention is likely to be needed in this area.

Taking Steps into the Community

It is important to know the social networks that are in operation within a community. The concept of social capital (presented in Chapter 5) is useful to identify assets in the community that reflect the contributions of people and their collectives as well as associations that make a difference (Green & Haines, 2015). There are multiple ways to conceptualize social capital in a community and one way is to develop an **asset map** of the social groups that exist. Major benefits of constructing an asset map are that it is easily drafted, open to change as new information appears, easily understandable, and accessible. An example of an asset map for a rural community in a moderately populated prairie area concerning the need for youth activities is shown in Table 8.2 below. It represents through size and location the relationships between different groups and could be altered to display overlaps between them as well as, in other cases, distance between them (Delgado & Humm-Delgado, 2013).

The status of a person involved in the community change effort can also be represented differently for different purposes, but an important consideration and relevant to credibility as well as ability to influence is related to **insider** and **outsider** status. Much has been written about this distinction and, rather than a dichotomy, it is now best understood as interrelated statuses that vary according to the context and application (Kerstetter, 2012). For example, someone who was involved in community change for youth as presented in the asset map by virtue of his residence might be an outsider (i.e., lives out of the rural area), but by virtue of his participation be an insider (e.g., as president of the softball association). He may not be viewed as an insider by church leadership, but by the members of the softball association he has some local connection and potentially insider status for matters related to the use of the sports equipment, scheduling, and by extension, the ability to schedule games in evenings and weekends for the youth. It is important to note that insiders are not necessarily favored, as they come with baggage (because of their family, relationships, and past behavior) that can challenge the perceptions of competence, objectivity, or trustworthiness by others in the community. Indeed, as noted in Chapter 7, Saul Alinsky, a well-known organizer, was sometimes brought in from outside of communities for this reason.

A related topic is **boundaries**. Boundaries can be physical or social. They can exist around a community as well as function as separations within a community (Cohen, 2013). A community with high fragmentation has high internal differentiation and boundaries, while a community with high solidarity has

TABLE 8.2 Asset Map of a Sample Rural Community

Seniors	Parents	Softball Association
Women	YOUTH	Crime Watch
Church Leadership	School Parent Council	Children

high internal-external differentiation and boundaries. The different interests within a community and where these already merge or have the potential to do so is important information for community change.

Some of the "baggage" that counselors carry by virtue of their profession and possibly their position in a community is their own history in a community. The experiences that community members have with "people like you" can be positive and negative (Shakil, 2015). They can be specific about the kinds of roles that are undertaken. For example, a group of professionals (including the author) traveled to fly-in First Nations communities to assist with community development efforts. When we arrived, our training as social workers, psychologists and psychiatrists greatly influenced how we were perceived. While cautiously welcomed, we were asked often why we were in meetings with community members about local issues and not sitting in a nursing station waiting to meet individually with people for medication or talk therapy.

Raising Consciousness

Critical consciousness is a term from the works of Friere who was profiled in Chapter 4 and Chapter 8, and translated from the word *conscientização* which appears in his writings. The purpose of this approach is to explore economic, political, and social meanings in everyday events, to recognize the forces of oppression that are evident within those events, and to consider ways to interpret and address those events in a liberating way. Education is an essential means to achieve this (Iddings, McCafferty, & Silva, 2011). However, the ways that education is used vary a great deal, in the amount of community involvement in the topics and process as well as the intended outcome.

The field of adult education is a broad and diverse one. There are several approaches that have been described. **Formal adult education** is organized, guided by formal curriculum, and leads to a credential that is recognized by governing authorities (e.g., university or college degree, diploma) (Knowles, Holton, & Swanson, 2014). **Non-formal adult education** is also organized and may or may not be guided by formal curriculum, but there is no certificate at the end that is recognized by a governing authority or institution of learning (Merriam & Brockett, 2011). **Community education** can be organized and guided by a formal curriculum, but the development of that content and process is a collaborative one between the learners involved. In this type of education approach, the teacher is also a learner and the learners are also teachers. The involvement, collaboration, and collective determination of the process and content are the defining features of this approach. **Radical adult education** is organized around the pursuit of social justice (Coben, 2013). It too can be organized and have a formal curriculum, and while it also has a collaborative emphasis, it is more explicitly political in nature. It has a critical consciousness emphasis and recognizes the need to attend to alternative views of issues, the structural contributors to personal problems, and how social change is a means to achieve these ends.

Challenges at this stage are both within the counselor and within the community. The challenges that counselors may bring are associated with the biases carried. Most counseling education includes a heavy emphasis on self-awareness, recognition of biases, and openness to address blind spots, so these are familiar concepts and practices. As described in Chapter 4, perspectives and views of internal and external events occur though a perspective which is culturally based and shaped by such factors as our gender, social class, age, ethnic background, and the level of education we have received. Another challenge that can appear during this stage is the desire of the community. Communities may not speak with one voice or have a clearly defined understanding of their needs. In fact, many communities that need help are fractured and divided. So who should one listen to?

One process that has been used is to have a **community meeting**. The meeting should be as inclusive as necessary to bring together diverse perspectives (Pyles, 2013). In one effort, the author and colleagues were involved with newcomer youth and their parents in a mid-sized city. The youth and parents arrived together, met separately with different facilitators simultaneously, and at the end of those independent meetings each group identified key issues they wanted to share with the other. We had a lunch and conversation sessions before concluding with a presentation by each group and another discussion to share perspectives and identify key points of convergence from which to move forward.

Building Momentum

Once there appears to be some collective will to move forward on a particular issue or issues, to work on the identification of issues and strategies for positive community change, or to trust the organizer or organizing group, a depth of understanding and commitment to the process can be pursued. A more formal assessment of community needs and assets can be developed. A range of considerations should be attended to before the assessment is undertaken to ensure that the results are useful. In addition, goal setting and the means to achieve goals are selected. This decision should align with the assessment.

Assessing Assets and Needs

The assessment of needs and assets can serve a variety of purposes. It is important that the process and product are part of a strategy for change to highlight the most pressing issues, their nature, and extent of impact as well as barriers to their resolution from the perspectives of those who are integral to the effort. In this way, the process can serve a motivational function as well as an information, problem definition, and solution selection outcome (Ferdinand, Fudrow, Calhoun, & Wisniewski, 2013). While it is essential from a motivational and community wellness perspective to view assets in the community, it is likely more important for a process designed to challenge a particular set of circumstances to focus on the problem and its resolution. While assets are key to the resolution (Griffiths, Connor, Robertson, & Phelan, 2013), they may not, depending on the purpose, provide the rationale for community support, or political or financial motives for change.

Community needs are likely to be familiar to all members of a community. In significantly oppressed and disadvantaged communities these needs are multiple and interconnected. The clarity of the problem is important for a focus, but too narrow a focus may leave out key issues or interests of community members (McIntyre, Patterson, Anderson, & Mah, 2016). It can be useful to consider again which positioning of the problem is best for clarifying, giving focus to the effort while encouraging the involvement of most, if not all, members of the community.

For an assessment plan, it can be useful to consider the **purpose**, **means**, and **audience**. It can be helpful to define the purpose of the plan and whether the intended outcome is to document the situation as it is, describe what has already occurred, or outline what is needed (Weil, 2014). The questions will follow a similar pattern of past, present, or future orientation and will have a particular focus on specific forces (e.g., neighborhood infrastructure or land claim status, poverty or homelessness, racism or discrimination) that are essential to address. Regardless of the temporal emphasis in the assessment plan, the desired future as a process (e.g., local governance structure is developed or improves), outcome (e.g., food bank-type distribution system for clothing), or both (e.g., community garden) should be considered at the onset.

Methods for data collection can be **qualitative** or **quantitative** (Creswell, 2013) and can utilize existing or original data. The main advantage of qualitative data is its depth of coverage, while for quantitative data the main advantage is breadth. While qualitative data can be used to explain, it is more often used to describe. Quantitative data can be used to describe as well, but it can be particularly useful to explain. Existing data can be found in census, government records, and reports. Original data can be collected from residents; **key informants**, selected on the basis of an important characteristic (e.g., long term residents, politically active residents); and other experts from outside the community if appropriate (McKenna & Main, 2013). Often, mixed methods work well, offering the advantages of each approach.

Two commonly used approaches to data collection and analysis are **focus groups** (Stewart & Shamdasani, 2014) and **surveys** (Ledwith, 2011). Focus groups are in-depth, qualitative interviews with groups of people having similar or different experiences. The purpose is the gathering of rich information in an efficient manner to identify similarities or represent differences. A moderator guides the process and the responses are usually recorded. The advantages lie in the modest cost, potential depth, quick timeframe, and opportunity for unanticipated responses. The disadvantages are lack of generalizability, comparison, and potential facilitator costs, with the quality of data influenced by the background and skill of the facilitator. Surveys offer an opportunity for gathering specific, usually quantifiable, information that can be collected in person, by telephone, mail, or via the Internet. While interviewer skill may not factor into the data quality as much as it does for a focus group, often many surveys are required. The analysis of the data can be complex and costly.

Setting Goals

The process of setting goals should follow from and be supported by the findings of the assessment. The goals themselves can be **short term**, **long term**, and **visionary** (Swanepoel & De Beer, 2012). The vision can provide a desired state that is aspirational and far into the future. Goals are more specific, observable, and changeable outcomes that can be realized in a particular timeframe. Short-term goals are often within the next 6 to 12 months and long term between 2 and 3 years. It is essential that they are reasonable in number and commensurate with the resources available so that they are viewed as achievable. As presented in Chapter 8, there are several approaches and tactics for achieving social change. Each of these has benefits and drawbacks. It is important to factor in the resources including people, funding, and information as well as experience with the means proposed. More will be presented on the identification of goals and objectives in Chapter 10 on organization and program development.

Taking and Sustaining Action

Requisites for change at the community level include an awareness of a problem, identification of an action that can be taken, competency and resources for taking that action, safety in taking action, and reinforcement for taking action. At every point along the change effort, communication is essential, and the same ways can be used for efforts within the community as well as between the community and others as needed. In addition, there are particular outcomes that may be pursued.

Communication

It is essential for community change that the word gets out about the effort. Benefits of making efforts known include letting people know you and the change effort exist, and it can stir interest. In addition, communication can expose the issue, educate for action, and attract new support. Finally, communication can serve to strengthen the affiliation between existing and potential future members as well as promoting credibility of the issue and proposed change.

It can be helpful to consider who you want to reach with the message. These audiences can include supporters, active or general, and the target or response community, who are those the group wants to change as well as the general public. An effective message has three aspects including the **Market** (recipients of the message, from whom you want a reaction), the **Medium** (technique or device used to get the message to the market), and the **Message** (what the market needs to hear to respond) (Lefebvre & Flora, 1988). A communication effectiveness hierarchy has been developed (Homan, 2015). From the highest and most effective to the lowest and least effective, it includes the following: one-to-one conversation, small group discussion, large group discussion, telephone conversation, handwritten letter, typewritten letter, mass-produced letter, newsletter, brochure, news item, and finally, an advertisement handout.

Outcomes

Major outcomes of efforts over time include mutual support, program planning, and organization building. Mutual support is often a starting point for community change and often a prerequisite for program or organization development (Lucero et al., 2016). In the next chapter, different approaches to community change are presented, followed by a more detailed description of the components of organization and program development. The main difference between these two types of community change activities is that for organization development a great deal of effort and resources over a longer period are needed while in program planning a partnership with an existing and sponsoring organization is necessary.

Conclusion

Counselors may become involved in community change efforts in several different ways. A very fundamental and powerful way of being involved in community change is through sociopolitical consciousness and deliberate action, as well as inaction, in support of a particular agenda. Involvement can scale up in different ways to the point of assuming a leadership role. Regardless of role, knowing personal and professional boundaries is key. In addition, an awareness of processes of community change can be very helpful.

Discussion Questions

1. Reflecting on the experiences you have had as a counselor, what underlying issues have you faced? What do you see as the most pressing concern? What do you see as the concern that has most potential to be altered? What community change efforts are underway to take action that makes a difference? What are the biggest barriers you face to becoming involved in that effort or a new effort to make community change?

2. What community change efforts have you been involved with? What made those efforts gratifying, either personally or professionally? What kind of involvement did you have? How did what you learned influence your counseling practice? What kind of difference do you think it made to the clients you had who experienced that particular challenge?

3. What potential use do you see for asset assessments in community work? Although it is helpful to document the strengths of a community to respect the capacities it holds, are there potential downsides to an asset-based community assessment, such as the resources it has available or the motivation to mobilize in response to a particular issue, if they are presented favorably? For example, would funders see the need to provide money to an already "wealthy" community?

4. Given the breadth and quantity of information that flows around us every day in email, Internet, newspaper, newsletter, television, and radio, what makes a message stand out from the rest? How can community change efforts make the best use of technology to reach the people who are important to the effort?

Web Links

- Community Toolbox
  http://ctb.ku.edu/en
- A Social Justice Approach to Advocacy Counselling
  http://www.ccpa-accp.ca/
  what-is-a-social-justice-approach-to-advocacy-counselling/
- Conducting a Needs Assessment
  https://cyfernetsearch.org/ilm_1_9

- Community Power Structure
  http://srdc.msstate.edu/fop/levelone/trainarc/09fall/session4_kahl_ppt.pdf
- Asset Mapping Handbook
  http://volunteer.ca/content/asset-mapping-handbook
- Insiders and Outsiders
  https://www.brynmawr.edu/ethics-fieldwork/insiders-and-outsiders
- Social Justice Issues in Adult Education
  https://www.youtube.com/watch?v=oPwOqiElWt8
- Key Informant Interviews
  http://www.cgh.uottawa.ca/whocc/projects/nb_toolkit/chp1/t_kii.htm

Key Terms

social contribution	primary sources
leadership	secondary sources
food bank	asset map
campaign	insider
meal program	outsider
public housing	boundaries
job placement	formal adult education
dual relationships	non-formal adult education
research consultation	community education
company time	radical adult education
legitimacy	community meeting
organizers	purpose
teachers	means
coaches	audience
facilitators	qualitative
advocates	quantitative
negotiators	key informants
brokers	focus groups
researchers	surveys
power over	short term
authority	long term
responsibility	visionary
credibility	Market
versatility	Medium
accountability	Message

175

CHAPTER 9

TAKING ACTION

Chapter Outline

Issues and Approaches
   The Occupy Movement
   Detroit Water Crisis
Organization Building and Program Development
   The Family Centre
Community-Based Organizations
   Development
Community-Based Program Development
   Internal and External Assessment
   Processes
   Structure
   Potential Barriers
Conclusion
Discussion Questions
Web Links
Key Terms

The levels of counselor involvement in community change are varied. Choices will depend on personal style, interests, experience, and resources that can be brought to bear. While it is important to have a purpose and align efforts with it, the actual outcomes of community change are sometimes difficult to observe. Counselors may feel a personal responsibility to participate in political activities by supporting candidates, bringing awareness to issues, or voting. Counselors can often, by virtue of their professional training and experience, make a contribution in the areas of community agencies and service gaps as well as in the content of effective programs in education and psychology. Of course, they also have research skills that can be brought to bear at each point in a community effort.

In this chapter, several community change efforts are presented to illustrate different possibilities for counselor involvement. While involvement may take many forms, as described in Chapter 8, it can also occur in response to different issues and general approaches. Well-publicized community change efforts such as the Occupy movement and the Detroit Water Crisis illustrate large-scale political activism and locally responsive social development. Many counselors also choose to be involved in organization and program development that challenge oppression and make a positive difference in communities. The work of the Family Centre in New Zealand is highlighted, followed by a process that counselors may consider for the development of responsive, culturally based, anti-oppressive organizations and practices that have local credibility and impact as well as national and international significance.

Issues and Approaches

Both the Occupy movement and the Detroit Water Crisis reflect a desire for community change in response to oppressive forces in the environment. Many of us may have clients who are affected by similar issues or live in communities where these issues are apparent. In both cases, the issues of classism, sexism, and racism are evident in political and economic structures that lead to social disadvantage and poverty. Poverty is a product of forces that are operating well beyond the control of individuals and families (Sullivan, 2012). These forces exist in the environment. While individuals and families may have adapted to its presence in their lives, they actively resist as well. These examples locate the problem in the environment and view the personal experience of poverty as something that can be altered through collective action. For Occupy, poverty is the product of global market forces that advantage a few and disadvantage the many (Van Stekelenburg, 2012). For Detroit, poverty is the product of local employment that disappeared, and with it, others who had the means to leave (Ewen, 2015). For Occupy, a goal is to show the power of the many, and for Detroit, a goal is to meet a basic survival need for clean water.

In contrast, the Occupy movement and the Detroit Water Crisis reflect different issues, approaches, processes, scale, tactics, and philosophies. For Occupy, the issue is diffuse and global, while for Detroit, it is focused and localized. The development of Occupy was emergent and for Detroit, predefined.

For Occupy, the issue was crystalized through collective action, while for Detroit the issue invited a response. Efforts to scale down the movement were apparent in Occupy to be locally effective, and for Detroit, efforts were made to scale up the movement to be locally effective. Occupy has an anarchic orientation with freedom as a basis. Detroit has a socialist orientation with equality as a basis. The approach to community change taken by Occupy is social action, and for Detroit, it is primarily locality development. While Occupy uses largely confrontational tactics and some internal negotiation, Detroit focuses primarily on collaborative tactics and, to a lesser extent, confrontation.

The Occupy Movement

The Occupy movement is a global effort by local groups in many communities to organize and protest massive economic and political inequality. The influence of corporations that exert large-scale control over the world's resources benefiting a small minority threatens democracy and is neither stable nor sustainable.

The roots of Occupy lie in the **Arab Spring**, which was a wave of protests, demonstrations, and civil wars in the Arab world beginning in 2010 with the Tunisian revolution and continuing with the Arab League through to 2012 (Gitlin, 2012). Rulers in Tunisia, Egypt, Yemen, and Libya were removed from power and protests were held in Algeria, Iraq, Jordan, Kuwait, Morocco, and Sudan. Although the protests were non-violent and included strikes, demonstrations, marches, and rallies as well as social media for consciousness-raising about state censorship, violent responses from authorities led, in some cases, to violent responses from protesters (Gamson & Sifry, 2013).

Anti-austerity efforts in Portugal and Spain as well as student protests in the US were additional influences on the development of Occupy (Fuchs, 2014). In Portugal, citizens organized through a Facebook event protested in ten cities against the economic crisis and violations of labor rights, without the help of unions or political parties. In Spain, social networks also played a major part in organizing demonstrations in 58 cities. In the US, California students protested rising tuition and pay cuts for the university system.

In 2011 Adbusters Media Foundation, a Canadian group, proposed a peaceful occupation of Wall Street to protest corporate influence, economic disparity, and lack of legal consequence from the global financial crisis. On June 9, 2011, OccupyWallStreet.org was registered as an Internet address. On September 17, over 2,000 people organized and moved on Wall Street where police blocked them from entrance, so they gathered in nearby Zuccotti Park, which they renamed Liberty Square. By October 2011 Occupy protests had occurred in over 951 cities across 82 countries, including over 600 communities in the United States and 35 in Canada.

According to their website, Occupy's efforts are organized through three main means, namely resist, restructure, and remix:

> In the spirit and tradition of civil disobedience #occupy takes to the streets to protest corporate greed, abuse of power, and growing economic disparity.
>
> #occupy empowers individuals to lead others into action by gathering in the commons (public spaces, parks and online) as engaged citizens to demonstrate a culture based on community and mutual aid. We will be the change we are seeking in the world.
>
> Work to make fundamental changes in the system. (#occupy, 2015)

The issues that are of interest to Occupy include influence in government through officials acting in corporate interest, corporate personhood in financial contributions to promote government influence, for-profit education that leaves graduates in debt and without good paying jobs, wrongful foreclosures that leave residents homeless or damaged rendering them uninhabitable, banks that are "too big to fail," private health care that leaves people vulnerable, a living wage for workers, and budget cuts that reduce public services, including schools (#OCCUPY, 2015). Occupy maintains a strong presence on the Internet (Dorf, 2012). However, its attention-grabbing efforts are no longer prominent in the media. The outcomes of this effort are now reflected in the work of more localized groups taking action on community priorities.

Detroit Water Crisis
The water shortage in Detroit, Michigan, is a consequence of making the water business attractive to potential buyers by a city that is selling its assets. Residents who cannot afford their utility bills because of the lack of jobs and income due to the economic downturn are having their service turned off, worsening their situations and creating new challenges.

Detroit has experienced many shifts to its once-strong national presence (Sugrue, 2014). The developments have been well documented, and the city, once thriving, has been humbled. Corporations have moved to cheap overseas labor and wealthy residents have moved to suburbs; the **financial emergency** of 2013 was based on the city's inability to maintain debt and expenditure levels based on income (Kasdan, 2014). In the absence of state intervention, the city had lost nearly two-thirds of its population over the past 60 years and was on the path to bankruptcy (Boyle, 2001). Residents who wanted to leave and could afford to leave did so.

Media fueled the fear about bankruptcy, and politicians allowed the dismantling of infrastructure and public services for residents (Borden, 2013). Efforts were made to close schools, cut pensions, and sell parks and art holdings to private corporations. The public water system is worth billions and sits on the Great Lakes. To make it attractive to potential buyers, it needed to be a viable business in which to invest. This has meant large scale shut-offs of water to customers who could not afford to pay. Many have been in arrears for some time and have bills in the hundreds or thousands of dollars. Health and family problems faced by residents living in poverty were exacerbated (Mosley, Bouse, & Stidham Hall, 2015). There have been reports of children being removed from their families because the home did not have running water.

Despite these efforts, local gardens for community members flourished, as did a rich culture of music and art. In addition to the common cause achieving some solidarity among community members, a variety of informal and formal coordinated efforts to change the situation have emerged.

Community organizations brought the issue to the attention of the United Nations with the proposal for a statewide moratorium on water shut-offs. The UN High Commissioner for Human Rights, Catarina de Albuquerque, responded that the city was violating international standards by removing access to water for residents. She stated that "[w]hen there is genuine inability to pay, human rights simply forbid disconnections" (United Nations, 2015).

New community organizations have emerged to coordinate responses of water to neighbors who have been cut off. For example, the **Detroit Water Brigade** accepts donations and supplies from across the US and internationally. In addition, the **Detroit People's Water Board** is a coalition of several organizations focused together on the human right to water with community responsibility and judicious use of this resource for all (Presbey, 2015). Social action measures undertaken by residents include parking vehicles over water valves so they cannot be shut off and neighbors helping one another to physically turn the water valve back on themselves (Wahowiak, 2014). They have blocked trucks sent to shut off water to homes.

Organization Building and Program Development

Efforts that counselors can engage in to create a power structure or partner with a power structure often occur through organization building and program development. These can be in response to a particular issue or organized in a preventive way to represent a community's strengths. In organization building the focus is to develop a formal entity that can represent the needs of a particular community and exist over the long term to ensure that the change is sustained (Edwards & McCarthy, 2004). Program development exists within an organization as a direct means to provide a service to a particular group within a community (Elder, Schmid, Dower, & Hedlund, 1993). The service can have self-help (e.g., women helping women), political or organizational (e.g., building support for appropriate ethnic representation in city council) purposes, as well as educational (e.g., skills and information), therapeutic (e.g., treatment or service) or caregiving (e.g., child minding, day programs) emphases. In the following example, an organization emerged in response to a need for community and counseling support, and from within the organization, a well-known and highly credible counseling approach was developed.

The Family Centre

The Family Centre is a community organization in New Zealand that provides a rare balance of counseling service, policy research, and community education (Tennant, O'Brien, & Sanders, 2008). The organization was developed on the recognition that culturally based services and advocacy were necessary to serve the needs of the community and that partnerships between cultural groups were essential (Tamasese, Peteru, Waldegrave, & Bush, 2005). The organizational structure includes representation of the three cultural groups it serves, including the Māori, Pacific Island, and Pākehā (European) (The Family Centre, 2015).

Social policy research undertaken by the Centre is done with a range of local, national, and international agencies and organizations and focuses on issues of social justice (e.g., Salmond, Crampton, King, & Waldegrave, 2006). The topics upon which these studies are based focus on equity, poverty, social and economic policy interaction, research on aging, cultural appropriateness, social impacts, and evaluation. The many reports and peer-reviewed publications authored by staff are available on their website (The Family Centre, 2015).

Community education efforts are also varied and responsive to local strengths and needs as well as international requests for presentations about the approaches used. Community development efforts center on participation, resource access, equity of cultural groups, and healthy communities. Public education efforts center on partnerships with social and business agencies, community groups, and government departments to deliver programs that meet local need.

The counseling approach developed and used by the Centre's staff is known as **Just Therapy**, which is an approach to family counseling that addresses the intersections of socioeconomic status, gender, and race. It is a values-based approach that emphasizes belonging, sacredness, and liberation, which refer to the "essence of identity, who we are, our cultured and gendered histories, and our ancestry ... the deepest respect for humanity, its qualities and the environment ..." and "freedom, wholeness and justice" (Tamasese & Waldgrave, 2012).

Staff recognized the sexist, classist and racist forces that many of the clients they saw for counseling were experiencing and sought to do something different (Vodde & Gallant, 2002). Spirituality, justice, and simplicity became fundamental bases of the approach. The "web of meaning" through which families view their situations is often felt as personal failure. The alternative proposed in Just Therapy is to recognize the challenges as symptoms of an oppressive environment and offer possibilities for hope and personal change as well as community action (Frankel & Frankel, 2007).

Waldegrave (2009) outlines the approach in relation to the work of counselors with families facing poverty. It is suggested that asking questions about day-to-day survival on low to no income, as well as managing a tenuous housing situation from strengths perspectives are important to do through the use of metaphor. The nature of the conversation turns to the structural issues clients are dealing with and their creative and strong responses to those issues. In addition, counselors are challenged to be "thermometers of pain" (Waldegrave, 2005) who need to share the injustices of economic and social inequality as well as problems with housing and poverty outside of their sessions.

Community-Based Organizations

An organization is a formalized structure with a purpose, procedures, and members. There are several ways of describing organizations that exist for social purposes. According to Katz & Kahn (1978), there are three distinct types, including both **temporary** and **ongoing** as well as **single issue** and **multi-issue** organizations. Rubin & Rubin (2008) define organizations in relation to their purposes including **self-help**, **partnership**, **coproduction**, **pressure**, and **protest**. Organizations that are for self-help focus on local issues for the community in which they are located, with little outside help. Partnership organizations also focus on community-defined problems, but do so in partnership with outside funders who support their work. In coproduction organizations, the community, through the organization, takes on government functions. While they are typically subject to the same rules as government-run organizations, there is more opportunity for the community to influence the nature and delivery of local services in ways that are culturally appropriate and meet community need. Pressure organizations take community-defined issues and conventional approaches, usually in partnership or collaboration or at least consultation with those who determine the policies with which they are concerned and want change. Protest organizations focus on economic and social change in a more radical way, looking at taking direct social action that can be confrontational and forcing a competition. Coalitions are also important connections between organizations of different types to focus on a joint goal or specific initiative. Networks are often more inclusive of different stakeholders and have more modest requirements for membership and a broader focus.

Development

Organizations that are newly developing usually have an immediate and compelling issue in focus. In many cases community organizations develop over long periods and undergo shifts in priorities and activities. Sometimes they begin with that level of clarity about mission and purpose, but often start with a group of citizens who all recognize a particular issue or need and have enough interest to do something concrete about it.

As counselors we hear experiences that are common among our clients, which leads us to the desire to be involved in a collective effort that makes a difference. It is important to check on the agencies and services that exist locally to ensure that what you are considering as a new development has not been already identified within the mandate of a government or community group. Making contact with an existing organization about an issue of concern can lead down a fruitful path for collaboration, or at least help you determine what your idea could add to the community as a supplement to what already exists. Bringing a select group of people together is a good way to start. It can be helpful to invite those with the expertise and other resources needed to identify and address the issue. From that meeting, setting specific next steps can assist in keeping motivation and focus. Taking action early can be very helpful for cohesion and confidence.

A series of stages of organizational development has been proposed. These stages include **introduction**, **initial action**, **emergence of leadership and structure**, **letdown and floundering**, **recommitment and new members**, **sustained action**, and finally, **growth/decline/ending** (Cummings & Worley, 2014). In the introduction, a purpose for meeting is needed. A recent event or growing awareness of a particular problem can be a compelling reason to gather and discuss. It is necessary to consider who it might be important to involve at the beginning, such as those who have political power, funding potential, local credibility, research expertise, and practice experience. The initial action may be a public statement about the problem, an assessment of the need and response, a proposal for funding, or another meeting or event to bring in other stakeholders. The leadership will emerge by this time, and the group will know those who have a strong interest for personal, professional, or political reasons. The beginning of a formal structure can be exemplified by meeting times and locations, minute takers, and meeting chairs and can become more formalized over time. Often, a letdown of interest and loss of members occurs once the initial action and excitement fades, leaving a core of those who are most committed to keep the effort alive. Bringing in new stakeholders with enthusiasm and resources to contribute can revitalize the effort and bring along the potential for another event with concrete action, and ideally, a significant infusion of resources to continue.

Community-Based Program Development

There are several considerations for community-based program development within an existing organization. An initial determination of the nature and operations of the organization is important to consider. The history of the organization is important. For example, it is important to know who the stakeholders were at the beginning, how and from where the organization obtained its funding, and major changes that have occurred since its inception. The **mission statement** can also be very informative. It should reference the overall direction and purpose for the organization, its philosophy, its major functions and services, where those services are provided, and its interconnections with other services and the community.

Additional initial considerations include the **service area**, **population served**, current programs, and **staffing** as well as future plans (O'Neill, Albin, Storey, Horner, & Sprague, 2014). Funding sources and other agencies providing similar services along with informal contacts and formal connections with them are important to identify. The service area is geographic and indicates to which areas of the community, town, city, or outlying areas are potential or actual recipients of service. The population served refers to the qualifications of eligible participants in the organization, based on factors such as age, sex, income, or ability status. Current programs are an overview of the services provided and for what purpose. Staffing refers to the number and qualifications of those providing services. Funding sources include core and contact funding, based on nonprofit or charitable status, from government and nongovernment as well as fundraising and in-kind contributions. Connections to other organizations and programs that provide similar or different services to the same or different populations are important to be aware of. Finally, the direction of the organization in terms of expansion and openness to new program development is a relevant consideration.

Internal and External Assessment
Once a relationship and trust exists between a program developer and an organization, a more formal assessment can be undertaken to specifically inform

its components and potential delivery. An essential piece of information is the organization's administrative structure (Dolgoff & Feldstein, 2012). These exist formally in the form of an **organizational chart** with lines between positions that indicate routes of communication and levels of responsibility. However, an informal structure always exists, and it is good to know who makes and influences which decisions about what.

An analysis of an organization's resources can inform development by reflecting what already exists, can be used, or needs to be added. For example, attributes of relevant resources may include unallocated or allocated funding that is available internally; physical space both within and surrounding the building; whether there are relevant spaces for cooking, child minding, reading, prayer, private and large meetings or presentations; adequate bathroom facilities; or possibly a gymnasium. The staffing and their allocations to different organization functions can inform development of a new program by indicating where there may be administrative, secretarial, or professional support. Transportation is often an issue and the existence and possible use of the organization's own means, if available, can be a major asset, though potentially costly, to the program. Equipment and materials refer to a range of possible resources, for example, office and communications, recreation, or equipment specialized for accessibility purposes (e.g., wheelchairs). The expertise within the organization to inform the development and support the delivery is also important to recognize, as is its general level of motivation, commitment, and support for the idea.

An assessment of the community is also important. Similar to the issues presented in Chapter 9 the physical, demographic, institutional, and social indicators relevant to the community and potential participants are important to recognize and consider in planning. In particular, for program development purposes, it is important to consider both the needs and strengths within each of eight areas (Holzemer, Klainberg, Murphy, Rondello, & Smith, 2014). These areas include the **physical environment** (e.g., location), **education facilities** and services (e.g., schools or higher education institutions), **transportation sources** and adequacy (e.g., public transportation and private access with parking), local and regional **government** (e.g., national, regional, and local government representatives), health and **social services** (e.g., children's services, income support, disability services, health care), businesses and **employment** opportunities (e.g., locations, hiring staff), **communication** networks (e.g., local newspapers, bulletin boards, electronic newsletters, or blogs), and **recreation** facilities (e.g., parks, swimming pools, ice rinks) and their use.

Processes

The internal and external assessments are usually directed to where the organization is in its history and mandate, and on the level of commitment to pursuing its goals further. The priorities of an organization are essential to understand. These interests will be apparent, but can vary considerably depending on the interests represented. It is essential to find commonalities between these interests. Different **stakeholders** include the potential participants themselves, the sponsoring organization's mission, the mandate of the funder, or oftentimes, the funders. Through the assessment process, the preparation, background, and skills of service providers within the organization in relation to the general direction for program development will be evident. Finally, the broader community and its stakeholders, including grassroots activists, neighbors, local politicians, and vocal residents should be consulted.

The ways that decisions are made can also vary a great deal. These decisions are made within the organization, following the relevant consultations as described. Different processes have been suggested, including **rational**, **bureaucratic**, **anarchic**, and **political** (Schwenk, 1988). A rational decision process includes a focus on a question, such as which service is needed by a particular group within a community to help achieve improved quality of life. Alternatives and their likely outcomes are considered and the best choice is made. In a bureaucratic decision-making process, the best choice is made by those at the top of the organization's hierarchy, based on which service fits most clearly with the mandate, structure, and function of the organization. An anarchic decision process is not subject to clear procedures or participation and is determined vaguely, typically by the collective, based on the strongest voices. A political decision is based on who the power holders are in a community, and often those are the funders, with whom the organization has established a good relationship, or with a new funder that the organization wants to impress by its ability to produce outcomes.

Structure

Program development can occur in a variety of different ways. The types of programs developed by community organizations involved in social justice-related efforts may include those with a focus on training (e.g., food management certificate), education (e.g., positive parenting), information (e.g., community news), case management (e.g., coordination of government services), advocacy (e.g., tenant rights, accommodations), counseling (e.g., drop-in, crisis or mediation), meeting basic needs for social support (e.g., collective kitchen), food (e.g., food depot), clothing (e.g., donations and pick up), or shelter assistance (e.g., emergency accommodation). A key component is the provision of a service that helps not only the participants in attendance but that can be used by those participants to help others as well. Implicit or explicit theories of change are evident. A **theory of change** includes the framework linking what program participants directly experience in the program to a particular change (Funnell & Rogers, 2011). For example, a training program that provides a food management certificate upon completion offers information, support, and hands-on practice, which together lead to a competency. This competency, evidenced by a certificate, provides a qualification for employment in a restaurant.

Programs are often organized around three components. These components include **goals**, **objectives**, and **activities** (Klor, 2012). Program goals are the most general statements about what the program will achieve for participants and the community. Program goals may be to increase skills, connect people, share or blend resources, promote ownership, or promote action. Other examples of goals are to foster self-reliance and confidence or to enhance the quality of life. Objectives are the evidence that goals have been met. They are specific and measurable indicators. There may be several for each goal which together, in the judgment of the developer, reflect accomplishment or success in relation to that goal. Activities are the actions taken by the program to lead to objectives. They are the functions of the program that include who will do what with whom using which resources during a particular timeframe.

Potential Barriers

Barriers to services include **availability**, **accessibility**, **affordability**, **acceptability**, **appropriateness**, and **adequacy**. Availability refers to the presence or perceived presence of a service. Accessibility includes the ability of potential participants to use services. Acceptability refers to the degree to which participants feel that they can use the services. Affordability of services includes both tangible and intangible costs to participants for use. Appropriateness of services depends on the right kind of assistance for the participants. Finally, adequacy of service refers to the quality and completeness of service for the level of diversity and need.

Conclusion

While sociopolitical forces are not actionable at their highest levels, their impact at the community level can be diluted or exchanged by well-formed collective efforts to target particular issues. Local organizations can make a positive difference in communities through programs and can be responsive by making needed resources available to families and individuals. Local neighborhood governance processes can add to the credibility and political influence of a community to plan for its own future, or when it is threatened by some unwanted, outside force. While counselors may engage in direct social action, oftentimes a more collaborative and consultative role is desired.

Discussion Questions

1. Reflect on your knowledge of the Occupy movement, its origins, and tactics. How do you feel about confrontational approaches to community change? How can longevity be promoted in social action organizations functioning solely on the basis of confrontational tactics? How well can social action efforts function without leaders? What risks and rewards are involved for counselors participating in such efforts?
2. In Detroit, mass water shut-offs put pressure on local residents to organize and collectively respond to the source of the problem. How do you feel about collaborative tactics to community change? Can collaboration by itself produce results that would help residents facing a significant threat? Is collaboration best undertaken as a preventive or reactive tactic? What are the risks and rewards for counselors participating in such efforts?
3. To what extent are problems that clients present in counseling all symptomatic of living in a racist, classist, and sexist society? What are the arguments for and against this assertion? Do different actions follow from the opposing arguments?
4. What program would you envision making a difference in your community for clients you are working with? Where could such a program be located? Who would it serve? What would be the goal, and how would it be delivered and reach its objectives? What difference would it make? How would you ensure that it remained effective in addressing racism, classism, and sexism?

Web Links

- Arab Uprisings (BBC)
  http://www.bbc.com/news/world-middle-east-12813859
- #OCCUPYTOGETHER
  http://www.occupytogether.org
- Detroit Water Brigade
  http://detroitwaterbrigade.org
- The Family Centre
  http://www.familycentre.org.nz

Key Terms

Arab Spring
anti–austerity
financial emergency
Detroit Water Brigade
Detroit People's Water Board
social policy research
community education
Just Therapy
temporary
ongoing
single issue
multi–issue
self–help
partnership
coproduction
pressure
protest
introduction
initial action
emergence of leadership and structure
letdown and floundering
recommitment and new members
sustained action
growth/decline/ending
mission statement
service area

population served
staffing
organizational chart
physical environment
education facilities
transportation sources
government
social services
employment
communication
recreation
stakeholders
rational
bureaucratic
anarchic
political
theory of change
goals
objectives
activities
availability
accessibility
affordability
acceptability
appropriateness
adequacy

CHAPTER 10

TAKING STOCK

Chapter Outline

The forces of sexism, racism, ethnocentrism, classism, ableism, heterosexism, familialism, exclusivism, and their intersections are evidenced through values and beliefs reflected within dominant institutions and policies. While these forces are beyond any single individual's ability to influence in abstraction or at a global level, they become much more amenable to change through community-based efforts. Community change efforts include social action and local development with organization building and program development. As has been discussed throughout this book, oppressive contexts can be altered and lives liberated through personal empowerment and collective action.

Local community governance and ownership provide the means to support people, as well as competing with or sheltering them from oppressive forces that negatively affect personal, family, and community life.

In this chapter some considerations for counselors involved in community change efforts are offered in the area of evaluation. The chapter begins with an example of a well-studied educational program followed by an overview of purposes, types, and approaches to the evaluation of large scale as well as smaller scale initiatives.

Why Evaluate?

There are personal and collective benefits associated with community change. The expressed value of its measurement, via evaluation, can be an influential means to document the existence, change effort, and outcome. An evaluation can provide information for other communities and other leaders of change. It can benefit the originating community by documenting history to provide motivation for new changes or evidence for funding applications.

While the specific content of the evaluation will vary based on the issue, effort, and use of the results, different approaches to its conduct provide some useful guidelines for counselors involved in community change efforts to consider. In the example that follows, forces involved are classism, sexism, and racism that weigh on families living in poverty, which are disproportionately led by women and overrepresented by members of racialized groups. **Early childhood education** (Roopnarine & Johnson, 2013) can provide a way for children at risk for difficulty in school to be prepared and successful. The logic underlying these programs is that compensatory preschool education can combat poverty through increased potential for success in primary and secondary school, employment, and a better income.

Case Example

The HighScope mission is to lift lives through education (HighScope, 2015). It is an early childhood education program that was developed in Ypsilanti, Michigan. David Weikart (1931–2003), a school psychologist in the local district, worked with a group of interested individuals considering ways to improve the academic problems encountered often by children living in neighborhoods affected by poverty (Weikart, Bond, & McNeil, 1978). The idea was to prepare children at ages three and four for school entry. The program was delivered for the first time in 1962 at the **Perry Elementary School** (Nores, Belfield, Barnett, & Schweinhart, 2005). The educational activities became known as the HighScope curriculum. In 1970 the HighScope Educational Research

Foundation was established and has subsequently published a great deal of research on the curriculum model.

Main concepts of the curriculum include **active learning**, adult–child interactions, daily routine, learning environment, child and program assessment, and **developmental indicators** (Schweinhart & Weikart, 1997). Active learning is hands-on learning with people, objects, ideas, and events. Adult–child interactions refer to the importance of children and adults interacting together both in the classroom and at home in their families and communities. A routine offers structure to the daily activities, creating expectations and promoting security. Learning environment is a setting rich with opportunities, activities, and materials for play and learning. Assessment is important and occurs before, during, and after participation to ensure that the children are progressing and the program activities are in place. Finally, key developmental indicators concern the curriculum contents, which are approaches to learning, social and emotional development, physical development and health, language, literacy and communication, mathematics, creative arts, science and technology, and social studies (Holt, 2010).

HighScope has a large research base. A **randomized controlled trial**, which included children randomly assigned to intervention (i.e., those who received the program) and control (i.e., those who did not receive the program) was performed. These children have been followed into their adult years. In the age-27 follow-up (Schweinhart & Weikart, 1993), HighScope participants had accomplished more school completion, spent less time in receipt of special education services, were more likely to graduate from high school or with a **General Educational Development** (GED), and were less likely to have become pregnant as teens. At age 40 (Belfield, Nores, Barnett, & Schweinhart, 2006), the program participants were less likely to have served jail time, been convicted of a violent crime, or received government assistance. The median monthly income of participants was also higher than for non-participants.

The Head Start mission is "Helping people. Changing lives. Building communities" (Family Resource Alliance, 2015). The program started in 1965 with federal funding in the United States. Initially an eight-week summer program, Head Start became a year-round program in 1966. Head Start is an early education model of bringing children in at ages three and four to help prepare them for school (Zigler & Styfco, 2004). Head Start is delivered in high poverty neighborhoods and for children at risk for difficulty in kindergarten. Many of these programs use the HighScope curriculum (Roopnarine & Johnson, 2013).

Some differences between the two programs have been noted (Barnett, 2011). Head Start is usually offered by community agencies and HighScope is offered by the school district. HighScope teachers have higher qualifications in general, and are paid more, than Head Start teachers. Head Start programs will take children for less than two full years while HighScope has a two-year requirement for participation. Head Start parent involvement varies considerably while HighScope has required and consistent parental involvement.

In a recent follow-up of participants and non-participants in both Head Start and HighScope programs, similar positive effects were found. The magnitude of positive effect was slightly larger for the HighScope participants, and both early intervention participants, at age 22, were more likely to obtain a high school diploma or GED and less likely to have been arrested (Oden, Schweinhart, Weikart, Marcus, & Xie, 2000).

In Edmonton, Alberta, parents and staff have evaluated Head Start programs delivered in the city (Edmonton Head Start Project, 2015). The results are very positive reflecting an average of 4 on a scale from 1 (no impact at all) to 5 (very significant impact) from parents and staff in relation to the desired outcomes. These outcomes include helping parents to assist their children with learning activities at home, preparing children for kindergarten, and making connections for the children with other needed services. In addition, Head Start helps parents with their own parenting, problem solving and planning, making connections and friends for social support, and connecting with other needed community services.

Staff members have noticed an increase in the ethnic diversity of those attending programs (Edmonton Head Start Project, 2015), in particular, large numbers of new Canadians who are settling into a new community and country and need assistance with housing and language services as well as parenting support and children's services. The number of working poor families who have employment but no government support and not enough income to meet basic needs is growing. The family issues of abuse, addictions, and violence are apparent. They have noticed that family configurations are changing, including more blended families. Finally, they recognized physical health needs of children, including diet and activities that promote health.

The next steps for development in the Head Start programs in Edmonton focus on multicultural sensitivity, transition to school, scheduling, and connections (Edmonton Head Start Project, 2015). Efforts to enhance sensitivity to cultural diversity include ways to represent it in the physical and social spaces, making the school and program a community hub for interactions, and building support, including services specifically for parents such as a resume writing class or a community kitchen. The efforts for transition to school include making more information about local schools available to parents, including details such as the expectations and requirements of children and their parents. Scheduling is based on the recognition that families have busy lives and that some programs and services may need to be offered in the evenings or on particular days of the week to make it possible for parents to attend. For connections, there is potential to link program alumni with current participants, providing a mentorship program, buddy system, or information hotline for support.

The Public Health Agency of Canada (2015) funds Head Start programs for Aboriginal children in urban and northern communities. The program is similarly targeted for children aged three and four as well as their families, including relatives, parents, and communities. The programs as funded have a large family participation component. Languages and culture are woven throughout the content and delivery. Staff members are hired from within the community and the local oversight for the program rests with the local sponsor and its community interconnections.

Stakeholders from communities, parents, children, and staff are pleased with the program. School readiness effects are noteworthy and positive. Language, motor, social, and academic skill improvements are noted. Cultural literacy and exposure to languages are viewed as important. In addition, health behaviors for children and families improved, including physical activity and access to health services (Public Health Agency of Canada, 2015). An unintended positive effect was noted in the creation of a "hub" experience and facilitating a sense of community. There was recognition of the need for additional training of staff and staff retention efforts as the initiative and the programs move forward. In addition, there was also mention of the need for expansion to extend reach to more children and families.

What Is an Evaluation?

Evaluation means "measuring value" (Royse, Thyer, & Padgett, 2015) and, while measurement has a common use in counseling research, value is a more contested and relative term. There are multiple ways and means available to perform an evaluation. Evaluations are a form of research and have theoretical and operational meaning (Donaldson, 2012). Theoretical meaning refers to the need for information to be collected, interpreted, and used in a clear and consistent way. Operational meaning refers to the need for information to be useful to those who have it collected and interpreted for a particular purpose.

Several overall considerations can be identified for an evaluation. These include **utility**, **feasibility**, **propriety**, and **accuracy** (Grinnell, Gabor, & Unrau, 2012). Utility refers to the recognition of whom the evaluation is for and the purpose it is intended to serve for that person or group. Feasibility refers to the practicality of the evaluation given the money, time, and expertise available. Propriety is about the process of evaluation, the ethics of the procedures as well as its use and fairness. Accuracy concerns the appropriateness of the approaches taken in the evaluation, given its purpose.

Stages

There are three stages for an evaluation, including planning, implementing, and using (Brinkerhoff, Brethower, Nowakowski, & Hluchyj, 2012). In planning the evaluation, it is essential to define the project, determine the goals for the project, and get the support of stakeholders. In addition, having **funders** on board is important, as well as determination that the initiative itself and the individuals involved are ready to be evaluated. The individuals involved in the actual design and conduct of the evaluation should be selected, and some appreciation of the types of challenges that may be encountered and strategies to respond to them should be considered.

During the planning stage the evaluation team should look to the evidence that has been published about the type of initiative as well as the processes of evaluation that have been used by previous researchers. The **theory of change** underlying the initiative should be articulated so that major points can be identified and targeted within the evaluation (Funnell & Rogers, 2011). The questions for which the data will lead to an answer should be determined. The data are information collected in a specified way (e.g., focus group, questionnaire) and from a specified source (e.g., key informants, funders, clients, community members). In addition, the ways that this information will be analyzed need to be determined. Finally, it can be very helpful to **pilot test** the instruments and procedures to identify any unanticipated problems with the evaluation.

During the implementation stage a more in-depth review of the literature is often conducted (Fink, 2013). This review references the types of initiatives that are comparable to the focus of the evaluation as well as the approaches taken to evaluation and results thereof. Simultaneously, the collection of data and their analyses are started. Once the results of the analyses are summarized an evaluation of the evaluation is performed. The evaluation of the evaluation is often an informal discussion about the ways the plan was implemented, any difficulties experienced along the way, changes made on the fly once in process, and the impact these had on results.

An essential component of the implementation follows completion of data collection and preliminary analyses. A discussion with the evaluation stakeholders about the evaluation process and findings is necessary at this point. Because evaluation reports always have a particular purpose, it is essential that those involved in the use of the results be included in discussions about what was done and what it means. The determination of main points and conclusions, based on the data, are made in consultation and with the endorsement of stakeholders. In addition, directions for future work, efforts, funding as well as facilities and staffing, for example, are discussed so that they can be incorporated into the final report (Bryson, Patton, & Bowman, 2011).

Based on the success of the discussion with stakeholders, the proposed directions that the results inform are clear. The evaluation report provides a review of the literature, a summary of the research methodology with description of the data, the analyses thereof, findings, and next steps (Schalock & Thornton, 2013). The next steps are for the stakeholders to take forward, implement, and subsequently evaluate.

Policy Evaluation

Social policy concerns human well-being: the social relations necessary for it as well as the systems of its promotion (Blakemore & Warwick-Booth, 2013). Oftentimes, areas within which social policies are studied include health, education, and justice, as well as social services such as income security, housing, and child welfare. The Perry Preschool Project was an educational program that, based on its success, informed the development of a school district policy to provide educational services to children living in communities affected by poverty. The Head Start initiative in the United States is a federal social policy to provide compensatory preschool education for children at risk by a community group that meets specific funding criteria. In Canada, Head Start is a federal health policy initiative for Aboriginal children living in urban and northern communities. Federal funding is also provided through the Community Action Plan for Children to provide early intervention (0–6 years) services to families facing "challenging life circumstances," which includes community Head Start programs (Public Health Agency of Canada, 2015). Local Head Start initiatives, including several in Edmonton, receive funding from the charitable sector and offer service in collaboration with local schools. The social issue of child poverty, as evidenced with this example, has policies associated with funding in education, health, and social services in the United States and Canada.

The evaluation of social policy is complex and varies between constituencies, mandates, and scopes of service. If agreement can be reached and codified in government that child poverty is a social problem for which the government has the responsibility and capacity to address, the ways in which it is implemented can be incredibly diverse. For example, in Canada, the recently announced Enhanced Universal Child Care Benefit is a policy to provide a taxable income supplement to all parents with children under the age of 18 years. Provincial social service benefits for adults with children are higher than for those without children. In addition, many cities provide activities for children during the summer months. These activities all follow from policies that have a poverty reduction orientation.

Policy evaluation judges the effects of a policy on large groups of people. The determination can be based on whether the policy does what it is intended to do, whether it disadvantages certain groups, duplicates other initiatives, or does harm (Spiro & Yuchtman-Yaar, 2013). The advantages and disadvantages of the policy are viewed from a particular perspective or stakeholder group, and aspects that should be retained or eliminated are considered. Suggested actions may include replacing, strengthening, or improving the policy.

Major challenges associated with performing policy evaluation stem from the diversity of interests in the process. If the interests are too diverse, there will be difficulty in reaching enough of a consensus to move forward with a focused evaluation. If the interests are too narrow, the concerns raised will have little generalizability and impact. In a policy evaluation, decision power is distributed among multiple stakeholders, often with different understandings of the problems and solutions.

Program Evaluation

In contrast, a program evaluation has the benefits of more narrowly defined levels of analysis, control, comparison, and scale. The evaluation of a program offers greater control and clearer boundaries than the evaluation of a policy. **Comparison groups**, required for some forms of evaluation, are easier to obtain at a program level than an entire community, city, province, or state. The sheer numbers of stakeholders and participants are smaller in a program evaluation, allowing for the possibility of more expensive data collection methods that would be prohibitive at the policy evaluation level.

There are two main types of program evaluation. Formative evaluations center on the early development of the program, including groundwork before it begins operation as well as feedback on the processes and effects of the program. Summative evaluations focus on the effects of the program and include program, participant, and costing studies (Spaulding, 2014). In the case example, formative evaluations were performed by the Edmonton group on local Head Start programs to determine the effects of the programs on parents and the degree to which parent experiences and needs were reflected in the programs as offered. Summative evaluations were apparent in the HighScope and Head Start longitudinal data on outcomes at follow-up.

Formative Evaluation

There are three types of formative evaluations. These types include **needs assessment**, **implementation evaluation**, and **process evaluation** (Schalock & Thornton, 2013). In a needs assessment, as described in Chapter 9, the issues, problems, strengths, and solutions are identified outlining what type of program, how much (e.g. duration, intensity), and for whom it is intended. An implementation evaluation concerns the degree to which the planned implementation of the program matches the structure and function of the program as implemented. In a process evaluation, the functions of the program are studied to determine their actual performance and the extent to which they function as intended.

Summative Evaluation

There are five types of summative evaluations. In a **goal evaluation** the emphasis is on the degree to which the goals of the program were reached. In an **outcome evaluation** the emphasis is on the effects of the program on those who participated in the program. An **impact evaluation** includes the changes to the organization and community as well as the system of the program's operations. Costing studies include **cost benefit**, which is how much cost per unit of benefit the program provides, and **cost effectiveness**, which is which interventions provide more benefit for the same cost (Royse, Thyer, & Padgett, 2015). There are HighScope data that indicate cost benefits for the program at $12.90 in return based on taxpayer costs in justice and social services for every $1 of cost for delivery (Belfield, Nores, Barnett, & Schweinhart, 2006).

Approaches to Evaluation

There are five major approaches to evaluation research. These include scientific, management, anthropological, participatory, and mixed. In a scientific approach, traditional **quantitative** research methods and designs are employed (Punch, 2013). Examples include posttest and pretest-posttest, as well as randomized designs with increasing specificity to isolate the changes associated with program participation and sampling across large and diverse groups of participants to determine how robust the changes are, with immediate, short-term, and longitudinal measures to measure changes over time. A **management** approach to evaluation refers to the attainment of objectives based on a particular information need for a particular audience and purpose. The actual methods themselves are selected based on the types of information required. In an anthropological approach, traditional qualitative research methods and analysis procedures are employed (Creswell, 2013). Examples include **narrative** with its focus on stories, **phenomenological** with its emphasis on the essence of experiences, **grounded theory** with its emphasis on theorizing from experience, ethnographic with its emphasis on the culture of participants and program, and **case study** with its emphasis on experience within a particular narrowly defined context. In a **participatory** approach, the stakeholders determine collectively whether the purpose, design, data, and analyses are most appropriate given their experiences and intentions for the evaluation process and outcome. Mixed approaches to evaluation use elements from two or more of the other four approaches listed here. These approaches can be blended or separate to provide information that neither could adequately capture on its own.

Self-Evaluation

Counselor self-evaluation is also very important. Throughout this book there has been attention to cultural, political, and social assumptions counselors bring to their roles. These views also filter through three major areas for self-evaluation. These areas are normative, formative, and restorative (O'Donovan, Halford, & Walters, 2011). **Normative self-evaluation** concerns the knowledge and skills of the profession, including ethics, practice guidelines, standards to follow, and laws that are reflected in our practice with individuals and communities.

Formative self-evaluation reflects personal and interpersonal qualities, theories, and skills applied in everyday professional practice. An important area for reflection is the distinction between academic theory, espoused theory, and theory-in-practice. There are six important components of a theory (Patterson, 1986 cited in Austin, 2013), including precision and clarity (i.e., consistent language and assumptions), simplicity (i.e., fewest words to express an idea), comprehensiveness (i.e., based on relevant evidence), operationality (i.e., the ideas can be evaluated), practicality (i.e., useful to counselors in practice), and falsifiability (i.e., the theory itself can be proven incorrect). The notion of espoused theory refers to the theory or theories that counselors adhere to with colleagues and clients, while theory-in-use is what counselors actually do in practice (Savaya & Gardner, 2012). It can be helpful for counselors, particularly after working through this book, to consider the theories they find useful for practice, how they envision their use of theories, and then remain aware of the way they apply these beliefs in practice.

Restorative self-evaluation refers to the support and challenges, as well as the doubts and insecurities that counselors experience. Usually these insights are prompted through reflections on our interactions with others, such as clients, colleagues, supervisors, and family members. The intent of this self-evaluation is self-improvement. An essential area for restorative self-evaluation concerns vigilance for the potential of emancipatory experience (Miller & Sendrowitz, 2011). This is a process of liberation from oppressive internal and external forces that counselors, like their clients and the communities and societies we live in, all carry. While the particular experience of oppression varies considerably in nature and extent, the underlying process of identifying the oppression and liberating self and others from it is the same.

Case Example

Take a moment to reflect on the case example presented in Chapter 2. The case, as you may recall, is a new referral to you as an intern at a university counseling center. The client is 28 years old and identifies as a First Nations person. She is in her first year of general arts studies and her parents live in a northern fly-in community. Mary lives with her aunt and uncle in the city, worries constantly, and is having trouble sleeping. Her studies have suffered, her grades are falling, and she is questioning her decision to attend university.

There is undoubtedly a major cultural difference between where she was living and where she is living now, including what is around her, how people interact, and the expectations placed upon her by others at home and at school, as well as her own expectations of self. She is immersed in a culture with which she may have limited experience or a dislike for, disconnection with or desire to fit in. How do these expectations function as challenges to her sense of self and abilities?

The questions that can arise when considering these potential challenges are the extent to which these cultural differences, evidenced by the oppressive forces of "isms" through the institution as well as those who work for and attend it, can be liberated. More specifically, how can Mary and her counselor address these issues? What role are you, as her counseling intern, comfortable taking? What supporting, processing, and challenging do you believe can make a difference for Mary in counseling? What kind of environment would make it possible for Mary to feel more connected and supported? How could that be located, created, or mandated?

Conclusion

Evaluation consumes resources. However, evidence can be helpful for documenting the nature of the efforts made and outcomes in communities. Such evidence may be useful to convince new supporters, make the case against a proposed change, show responsible use of resources, and encourage other communities to organize effectively for change.

Discussion Questions

1. What is your experience with evaluation? In what roles have you been involved? What effects have you felt as a result of your participation?

2. Though evaluations are usually done to improve a policy area, community initiative, social program, or counseling service, they often have a negative connotation for participants or stakeholders because the results can be negative or actions stemming from them can impose change. How could you mitigate this potential in your work?

3. Evaluators, as applied researchers, are often taught to understand a range of approaches and to select the best approach for the project and purpose. However, in practice, most researchers and counselors have preferences for research and theories that resonate best with them and with which they are most familiar and experienced. Does evaluation, like counseling practice, necessitate that the practitioner, when faced with an issue and apparent need by a client that is not within their expertise, refer the client to someone else?

4. How can counselors engage in a practice of critical self-reflection on their work? Do counselors need to have their own counseling to identify areas to work on? Or can counselors be self-reflective without any "outside" assistance? If so, what methods can they use?

Web Links

- Policy Evaluation (Centers for Disease Control)
  http://www.cdc.gov/injury/pdfs/policy/Brief%201-a.pdf
- HighScope Research Foundation
  http://www.highscope.org
- Head Start Impact Study
  http://www.acf.hhs.gov/programs/opre/resource/
  head-start-impact-study-final-report-executive-summary
- A Framework for Program Evaluation
  http://ctb.ku.edu/en/table-of-contents/evaluate/evaluation/
  framework-for-evaluation/main
- Community Sustainability Engagement Evaluation Toolbox
  http://evaluationtoolbox.net.au
- Reflective Practice, Supervision and Self-Care
  http://www.counsellingconnection.com/wp-content/uploads/2009/10/
  report-4-reflective-practice-supervision-self-care.pdf

- Indigenous Student Centre (University of Manitoba)
  http://umanitoba.ca/student/indigenous/

Key Terms

early childhood education
Perry Elementary School
active learning
developmental indicators
randomized controlled trial
General Educational Development
utility
feasibility
propriety
accuracy
funders
theory of change
pilot test
social policy
comparison groups
needs assessment
implementation evaluation

process evaluation
goal evaluation
outcome evaluation
impact evaluation
cost benefit
cost effectiveness
quantitative
management
narrative
phenomenological
grounded theory
case study
participatory
normative self-evaluation
formative self-evaluation
restorative self-evaluation

REFERENCES

#OCCUPY. 2015. Issues. Retrieved November 30, 2016, from: https://webarchive. org/web/20130502073425/http://www.occupytogether.org/aboutoccupy/ #issues

Aanes, M.M., M.B. Mittelmark, & J. Hetland. 2015. "Interpersonal stress and poor health." *European Psychologist* 22: 321–33.

Ablow, K. 2015. "Charleston: Why didn't anyone help Dylann Roof?" Retrieved September 4, 2016, from: http://www.foxnews.com/opinion/2015/06/22/ charleston-why-didnt-anyone-help-dylann-roof.html

Aboriginal Affairs and Northern Development Canada. 1996. *Royal Commission Report on Aboriginal Peoples.* Ottawa: AANDC.

Addams, J. 1902. *Democracy and social ethics.* New York: Macmillan.

Adelson, N. 2005. "The embodiment of inequity: Health disparities in Aboriginal Canada." *Canadian Journal of Public Health* 96 (Suppl 2): S45–61.

Adema, S. 2014. "Tradition and transitions: Elders working in Canadian prisons, 1967–1992." *Journal of the Canadian Historical Association/Revue de la Société Historique du Canada* 25 (1): 243–75.

Afuape, T. 2015. "A passion for change." In *Liberation practices: Towards emotional wellbeing through dialogue,* edited by T. Afuape & G. Hughes, 225–39. London: Routledge.

Aiyer, S.M., M.A. Zimmerman, S. Morrel-Samuels, & T.M. Reischl. 2015. "From broken windows to busy streets: A community empowerment perspective." *Health Education & Behavior* 42 (2): 137–47.

Alang, S.M., E.M. McCreedy, & D.D. McAlpine. 2015. "Race, ethnicity, and self-rated health among immigrants in the United States." *Journal of Racial and Ethnic Health Disparities* 2 (4): 565–72.

Alegría, M., N. Mulvaney-Day, M. Woo, & E.A. Viruell-Fuentes. 2012. "Psychology of Latino adults: Challenges and an agenda for action." In *Handbook of race and development in mental health,* edited by E.C. Chang & C.A. Downey, 279–306. New York: Springer.

Alessandrini, A.C., ed. 2005. *Frantz Fanon: Critical perspectives.* London: Routledge.

Alexander, J. 2014. "The major ideologies of liberalism, socialism and conservatism." *Political Studies* 32: 112–20.

Ali, A., & K.E. Lees. 2013. "The therapist as advocate: Anti-oppression advocacy in psychological practice." *Journal of Clinical Psychology* 69 (2): 162–71.

Ali, S.R., W.M. Liu, A. Mahmood, & J. Arguello. 2008. "Social justice and applied psychology: Practical ideas for training the next generation of psychologists." *Journal for Social Action in Counseling and Psychology* 1 (2): 1–13.

Alinsky, S. 1971. *Rules for radicals.* New York: Vintage.

Alinsky, S.D. 1941. "Community analysis and organization." *American Journal of Sociology* 46: 797–808.

Alldred, P., & N. Fox. 2015. "From 'lesbian and gay psychology' to a critical psychology of sexualities." In *Handbook of Critical Psychology*, edited by I. Parker, 200–10. New York: Routledge.

Allen, J., R. Balfour, R. Bell, & M. Marmot. 2014. "Social determinants of mental health." *International Review of Psychiatry* 26 (4): 392–407.

Allwood, C.M. 2011. "On the foundation of the indigenous psychologies." *Social Epistemology* 25 (1): 3–14.

Almond, G.A. 2015. *Appeals of Communism.* Princeton, NJ: Princeton University Press.

Álvarez, A.S., M. Pagani, & P. Meucci. 2012. "The clinical application of the biopsychosocial model in mental health: A research critique." *American Journal of Physical Medicine & Rehabilitation* 91 (13): S173–80.

Amer, M.M., & A. Bagasra. 2013. "Psychological research with Muslim Americans in the age of Islamophobia: Trends, challenges, and recommendations." *American Psychologist* 68 (3): 134–44.

American Psychological Association. 2010. *Ethical principles of psychologists and code of conduct.* Washington, DC: American Psychological Association.

American Psychological Association. 2015a. Martha Bernal. Retrieved August 18, 2015, from: http://www.apadivisions.org/division-35/about/heritage/martha-bernal-biography.aspx

American Psychological Association. 2015b. 2015 National Multicultural Conference and Summit. Retrieved August 18, 2015, from: http://www.apadivisions.org/multicultural-summit.aspx

Aminzadeh, K., S. Denny, J. Utter, T.L. Milfont, S. Ameratunga, T. Teevale, & T. Clark. 2013. "Neighbourhood social capital and adolescent self-reported wellbeing in New Zealand: A multilevel analysis." *Social Science & Medicine* 84: 13–21.

Anthias, F. 2013. "Hierarchies of social location, class and intersectionality: Towards a translocational frame." *International Sociology* 28 (1): 121–38.

Arcidiacono, C., F. Procentese, & I. Di Napoli. 2007. "Youth, community belonging, planning and power." *Journal of Community & Applied Social Psychology* 17 (4): 280–95.

Aron, A., & S. Corne. 1994. *Writings for a liberation psychology: Ignacio Martin-Baro.* Cambridge, MA: Harvard University Press.

Arpaci, I., & M. Baloğlu. 2016. "The impact of cultural collectivism on knowledge sharing among information technology majoring undergraduates." *Computers in Human Behavior* 56: 65–71.

Arredondo, P., & P. Perez. 2003. "Expanding multicultural competence through social justice leadership." *Counseling Psychologist* 31 (3): 282–89.

Arthur, N., & S. Collins. 2015. "Multicultural counselling in Canada: Education, supervision and research." In *Canadian counselling and counselling psychology in the twenty-first century*, edited by A. Sinacore and F. Ginsberg, 42–67. Montreal: McGill-Queen's University Press.

Arthur, N., & S. Collins. 2014. Counselors, counselling, and social justice: The professional is political. *Canadian Journal of Counselling and Psychotherapy/Revue canadienne de counselling et de psychothérapie* 48 (3): 171–77.

Audet, C., S. Collins, M. Jay, K. Irvine, A. Hill-Lehr, & C. Schmolke. 2014. "Poverty, mental health, and counsellors for social justice: Reflections on an interactive workshop." *Canadian Journal of Counselling and Psychotherapy/Revue canadienne de counselling et de psychothérapie* 48 (3): 321–42.

Austin, J. 2014 "Decolonizing Ways of Knowing: Communion, Conversion and Conscientization." Retrieved December 1, 2016, from https://eprints.usq.edu.au/28348/1/Austin-Ch31-Av.pdf.

Austin, L.A. 2013. *Counselling primer*. New York: Taylor and Francis.

Azibo, D. 2015. "Can psychology help spur re-birth of African civilization? Notes on the African personality (psychological Africanity) construct: Normalcy, development, and abnormality." *Journal of Pan African Studies* 8 (1): 146–87.

Bährer-Kohler, S. 2012. *Social determinants and mental health*. New York: Nova Science Publishers.

Bailey, D., & P. Chatterjee. 2015. "Organization development and community development: True soulmates or uneasy bedfellows?" *Journal of Sociology and Social Welfare* 19 (2): 17–21.

Bailey, T., W. Williams, & B. Favors. 2014. "Internalized racial oppression in the African American community." In *Internalized oppression: The psychology of marginalized groups*, edited by E. David, 137–62. New York: Springer.

Bailey, T.K.M., Y.B. Chung, W.S. Williams, A.A. Singh, & H.K. Terrell. 2011. "Development and validation of the Internalized Racial Oppression Scale for Black individuals." *Journal of Counseling Psychology* 58 (4): 481–93.

Bajaj, M. 2011. "Human rights education: Ideology, location, and approaches." *Human Rights Quarterly* 33 (2): 481–508.

Baldwin, J.A. 1981. "Notes on an Africentric theory of Black personality." *The Western Journal of Black Studies* 5 (3): 172.

Baldwin, M., & N. Gould, eds. 2012. *Social work, critical reflection and the learning organization*. London: Ashgate.

Balfour, B., & T.R. Alter. 2016. "Mapping community innovation: Using social network analysis to map the interactional field, identify facilitators, and foster community development." *Community Development* 47 (4): 1–18.

Ball, L.C., J.L. Bazar, J. MacKay, E.N. Rodkey, A. Rutherford, & J.L. Young. 2013. "Using psychology's feminist voices in the classroom." *Psychology of Women Quarterly* 37 (2): 261–66.

Baluch, S.P., A.L. Pieterse, & M.A. Bolden. 2004. "Counselling psychology and social justice: Houston … we have a problem." *Counseling Psychologist* 32 (1): 89–98.

Banks, S., H.L. Butcher, A. Orton, & J. Robertson, eds. 2013. *Managing community practice: Principles, policies and programmes*. London: Policy Press.

Bannister, D. 2015. "The internal politics of psychotherapy." In *Psychology and Psychotherapy (Psychology Revivals): Current Trends and Issues*, edited by D. Pilgrim, 139–50. New York: Routledge.

Barden, S.M., & C.S. Cashwell. 2013. "Critical factors in cultural immersion: A synthesis of relevant literature." *International Journal for the Advancement of Counseling* 35 (4): 286–97.

Barker, C. 2013. *Marxism and social movements*. In The Wiley Blackwell Encyclopedia of Social & Political Movements. New York: Wiley.

Barlow, D.H., ed. 2014. *Clinical handbook of psychological disorders: A step-by-step treatment manual*. New York: Guilford Press.

Barnes, D.M., & I.H. Meyer. 2012. "Religious affiliation, internalized homophobia, and mental health in lesbians, gay men, and bisexuals." *American Journal of Orthopsychiatry* 82 (4): 505–15.

Barnett, W.S. 2011. "Effectiveness of early educational intervention." *Science* 333 (6045): 975–78.

Barrett, M. 2014. *Women's oppression today: The Marxist/feminist encounter*. London: Verso Books.

Barter, K. 2001. "Building community: A conceptual framework for child protection." *Child Abuse Review* 10 (4): 262–78.

Basch, C.H. 2014. "Poverty, health, and social justice: The importance of public health approaches." *International Journal of Health Promotion and Education* 52 (4): 181–87.

Baskin, C. 2011. *Strong helpers' teachings: The value of Indigenous knowledges in the helping professions*. Toronto: Canadian Scholars' Press.

Battiste, M. 2011. *Reclaiming Indigenous voice and vision*. Vancouver: UBC Press.

Beasley, S.T., I.K. Miller, & K.O. Cokley. 2015. "Exploring the impact of increasing the number of Black men in professional psychology." *Journal of Black Studies*. Published online before print. doi: 10.1177/0021934715599424

Beauboeuf-Lafontant, T. 2014. "Becoming Jane Addams: Feminist developmental theory and 'the college woman.'" *Girlhood Studies* 7 (2): 61–78.

Bedi, R.P., B.E. Haverkamp, R. Beatch, D.G. Cave, J.F. Domene, G.E. Harris, & A.M. Mikhail. 2011. "Counselling psychology in a Canadian context: Definition and description." *Canadian Psychology* 52 (2): 128–38.

Beer, A.M., L.B. Spanierman, J.C. Greene, & N.R. Todd. 2012. "Counselling psychology trainees' perceptions of training and commitments to social justice." *Journal of Counseling Psychology* 59 (1): 120–33.

Beetham, D. 2013. *The legitimation of power*. New York: Palgrave Macmillan.

Belfield, C.R., M. Nores, S. Barnett, & L. Schweinhart. 2006. "The High/Scope Perry Preschool Program: Cost–benefit analysis using data from the age-40 follow-up." *Journal of Human Resources* 41 (1): 162–90.

Bennett, S.T., & D.R. Babbage. 2014. "Cultural adaptation of CBT for aboriginal Australians." *Australian Psychologist* 49 (1): 19–21.

Bernal, G.E., & M.M. Domenech Rodríguez. 2012. *Cultural adaptations: Tools for evidence-based practice with diverse populations*. Washington, DC: American Psychological Association.

Bernal, M.E., & A.M. Padilla. 1982. "Status of minority curricula and training in clinical psychology." *American Psychologist* 37 (7): 780–87.

Betz, H.G., & S. Meret. 2009. "Revisiting Lepanto: The political mobilization against Islam in contemporary Western Europe." *Patterns of Prejudice* 43 (3–4): 313–34.

Bhatt, G., R.G. Tonks, & J.W. Berry. 2013. "Culture in the history of psychology in Canada." *Canadian Psychology* 54 (2): 115–23.

Bhullar, N., N.S. Schutte, & J.M. Malouff. 2012. "Associations of individualistic-collectivistic orientations with emotional intelligence, mental health, and satisfaction with life: A tale of two countries." *Individual Differences Research* 10 (3): 165–75.

Billing, T.K., R. Bhagat, E. Babakus, B.N. Srivastava, M. Shin, & F. Brew. 2013. "Work-family conflict in four national contexts: A closer look at the role of individualism-collectivism." *International Journal of Cross Cultural Management.* doi: 10.1177/1470595813502780

Blackorby, C., & D. Donaldson. 1980. "Ethical indices for the measurement of poverty." *Econometrica* 48 (4): 1053–60.

Blackstock, C. 2011. "The Canadian Human Rights Tribunal on First Nations child welfare: Why if Canada wins, equality and justice lose." *Children and Youth Services Review* 33 (1): 187–94.

Blakemore, K., & L. Warwick-Booth. 2013. *Social policy: An introduction.* London: McGraw-Hill.

Bonnett, A. 2013. *Radicalism, anti-racism and representation.* New York: Routledge.

Boothroyd, P. 1996. "Community development: The missing link in welfare policy." In *Ideology, Development and Social Welfare: Canadian Perspectives*, third ed., edited by Bill Kirwin. Toronto: Canadian Scholars' Press.

Boothroyd, P., & H.C. Davis. 1993. "Community economic development: Three approaches." *Journal of Planning Education and Research* 12 (3): 230–40.

Borden, S.L. 2013. "Detroit: Exploiting images of poverty." *Journal of Mass Media Ethics* 28 (2): 134–37.

Borys, D.S., & K.S. Pope. 1989. "Dual relationships between therapist and client: A national study of psychologists, psychiatrists, and social workers." *Professional Psychology, Research and Practice* 20 (5): 283–93.

Bott, E., & E.B. Spillius. 2014. *Family and social network: Roles, norms and external relationships in ordinary urban families.* New York: Routledge.

Bowles, S., & H. Gintis. 2002. "Social capital and community governance." *Economic Journal* 112 (483): F419–36.

Bowman, S.L. 2015. "Conversations and collaborations: What has really changed?" *Counseling Psychologist* 43 (1): 127–37.

Boyle, K. 2001. "The ruins of Detroit: Exploring the urban crisis in the motor city." *Michigan Historical Review* 27 (1): 109–27.

Bradshaw, C.P., S. Soifer, & L. Gutierrez. 1994. "Toward a hybrid model for effective organizing in communities of color." *Journal of Community Practice* 1 (1): 25–42.

Bradshaw, T.K. 2007. "Theories of poverty and anti-poverty programs in community development." *Community Development* 38 (1): 7–25.

Brah, A., & A. Phoenix. 2013. "Ain't I a woman? Revisiting intersectionality." *Journal of International Women's Studies* 5 (3): 75–86.

Brave Heart, M.Y.H., J. Chase, J. Elkins, & D.B. Altschul. 2011. "Historical trauma among indigenous peoples of the Americas: Concepts, research, and clinical considerations." *Journal of Psychoactive Drugs* 43 (4): 282–90.

Brennan, T. 2002. *The interpretation of the flesh: Freud and femininity.* New York: Routledge.

Brinkerhoff, R.O., D.M. Brethower, J. Nowakowski, & T. Hluchyj, eds. 2012. *Program evaluation: A practitioner's guide for trainers and educators,* vol. 2. New York: Springer Science & Business Media.

Bronfenbrenner, U. 2009. *The ecology of human development: Experiments by nature and design.* Cambridge, MA: Harvard University Press.

Brown, C.B., S. Collins, & N. Arthur. 2014. "Fostering multicultural and social justice competence through counsellor education pedagogy." *Canadian Journal of Counselling and Psychotherapy/Revue canadienne de counselling et de psychothérapie* 48 (3): 300–20.

Brueggemann, W. 2013. *The practice of macro social work.* Boston: Cengage Learning.

Bryson, J.M., M.Q. Patton, & R.A. Bowman. 2011. "Working with evaluation stakeholders: A rationale, step-wise approach and toolkit." *Evaluation and Program Planning* 34 (1): 1–12.

Bulhan, H.A. 2004. *Frantz Fanon and the psychology of oppression.* New York: Springer Science & Business Media.

Bullough, V.L. 2014. *Before Stonewall: Activists for gay and lesbian rights in historical context.* New York: Routledge.

Burton, M., & C. Kagan. 2005. "Liberation social psychology: Learning from Latin America." *Journal of Community & Applied Social Psychology* 15 (1): 63–78.

Busche, M., E. Scambor, & O. Stuve. 2012. "An intersectional perspective in social work and education." *ERIS Web Journal* 3 (1): 2–14.

Buse, K., N. Mays, & G. Walt. 2012. *Making health policy.* London: McGraw-Hill Education.

Byne, W. 2014. "Forty years after the removal of homosexuality from the DSM: Well on the way but not there yet." *LGBT Health* 1 (2): 67–69.

Cabrera, N., & F. Villarruel. 2009. *Handbook of US Latino psychology: Developmental and community-based perspectives.* London: Sage.

Cabrera, N.J., & R.H. Bradley. 2012. "Latino fathers and their children." *Child Development Perspectives* 6 (3): 232–38.

Caldwell, J.C., & E.M. Vera. 2010. "Critical incidents in counselling psychology professionals' and trainees' social justice orientation development." *Training and Education in Professional Psychology* 4 (3): 163–76.

Cameron, J.G., & P. Kerans. 1985. "Social and political action." In *An introduction to social work practice in Canada,* edited by S. Yelaja, 11–25. Toronto: Prentice Hall.

Canadian Council on Social Development. 2015. A profile of economic security in Canada. Retrieved August 10, 2015, from: http://www.ccsd.ca/factsheets/economic_security/poverty/

Canadian Museum for Human Rights. 2015. "Newsroom." Retrieved August 13, 2015, from: https://humanrights.ca

Canadian Psychological Association. 2000. *Canadian code of ethics for psychologists,* 3rd ed. Ottawa: Canadian Psychological Association.

Carr, B.B., E.B. Hagai, & E.L. Zurbriggen. 2015. "Queering Bem: Theoretical intersections between Sandra Bem's scholarship and queer theory." *Sex Roles,* 1–14. Online before print. doi: 10.1007/s11199-015-0546-1

Carriere, J., & C. Richardson. 2012. "Relationship is everything: Holistic approaches to Aboriginal child and youth mental health." *First Peoples Child & Family Review* 7 (2): 8–26.

Carroll, K.K., & D.F. Jamison. 2011. "African-centered psychology, education and the liberation of African minds: Notes on the psycho-cultural justification for reparations." *Race, Gender, & Class* 28 (1/2): 52–72.

Case, A.D., & C.D. Hunter. 2012. "Counterspaces: A unit of analysis for understanding the role of settings in marginalized individuals' adaptive responses to oppression." *American Journal of Community Psychology* 50 (1–2): 257–70.

Castellano, M.B., & L. Archibald. 2006. *Final report of the Aboriginal Healing Foundation: Promising healing practices in aboriginal communities*. Ottawa: Aboriginal Healing Foundation.

Cels, S., J. De Jong, & F. Nauta. 2012. *Agents of change: Strategy and tactics for social innovation*. Washington, DC: Brookings Institution Press.

Centers for Disease Control and Prevention. 2015. "Social determinates of health." Retrieved August 10, 2015, from: http://www.cdc.gov/nchhstp/socialdeterminants/index.html

Centre for Race and Gender. 2016. "Defining 'Islamophobia.'" Retrieved March 12, 2016, from: http://crg.berkeley.edu/content/islamophobia/defining-islamophobia

Césaire, A. 2001. *Discourse on colonialism*. New York: NYU Press.

Chaddad, F., & C. Iliopoulos. 2013. "Control rights, governance, and the costs of ownership in agricultural cooperatives." *Agribusiness* 29 (1): 3–22.

Chang, B. 2013. "Education for social change: Highlander education in the Appalachian Mountains and study circles in Sweden." *International Journal of Lifelong Eduction* 32 (6): 705–23.

Chantler, K., & S. Smailes. 2004. "Working with differences: Issues for research and counselling practice." *Counselling & Psychotherapy Research* 4 (2): 34–39.

Chapman-Hilliard, C., & V. Adams-Bass. 2015. "A conceptual framework for utilizing Black history knowledge as a path to psychological liberation for Black youth." *Journal of Black Psychology*. Online in advance of print: doi: 10.1177/0095798415597840

Chaskin, R.J., & D.M. Greenberg. 2013. "Between public and private action: Neighborhood organizations and local governance." *Nonprofit and Voluntary Sector Quarterly* 44 (2) 248–67. doi: 10.1177/0899764013510407

Chavez-Korell, S., E.A. Delgado-Romero, & R. Illes. 2012. "The National Latina/o Psychological Association like a phoenix rising." *Counseling Psychologist* 40 (5): 675–84.

Cheney, G., I. Santa Cruz, A.M. Peredo, & E. Nazareno. 2014. "Worker cooperatives as an organizational alternative: Challenges, achievements and promise in business governance and ownership." *Organization* 21 (5): 591–603.

Cherki, A., & N. Benabid. 2006. *Frantz Fanon: A portrait*. Ithaca, NY: Cornell University Press.

Cheshire, L. 2012. "Reconsidering sexual identities: Intersectionality theory and the implications for educating counsellors." *Canadian Journal of Counselling and Psychotherapy/Revue canadienne de counselling et de psychothérapie* 47 (1): 4–13.

Chess, S., K.B. Clark, & A. Thomas. 1953. "The importance of cultural evaluation in psychiatric diagnosis and treatment." *Psychiatric Quarterly* 27 (1–4): 102–14.

Choo, H., & M. Ferree. 2010. "Practicing intersectionality in sociological research: A critical analysis of inclusions, interactions, and institutions in the study of inequalities." *Theory and Society* 28 (2): 129–49.

Clark, K.B. 1988. *Prejudice and your child.* Middletown, CT: Wesleyan University Press.

Clark, K.B., & M.K. Clark. 1939. "Segregation as a factor in the racial identification of Negro pre-school children: A preliminary report." *Journal of Experimental Education* 8 (2): 161–63.

Clark, K.B., & M.K. Clark. 1940. "Skin color as a factor in racial identification of Negro preschool children." *Journal of Social Psychology* 11 (1): 159–69.

Clark, K.B., & J. Hopkins. 1969. *A relevant war against poverty: A study of community action programs and observable social change.* New York: Harper & Row.

Clark, K.B., I. Chein, & S.W. Cook. 2004. "The effects of segregation and the consequences of desegregation: A (September 1952) social science statement in the *Brown v. Board of Education of Topeka* Supreme Court case." *American Psychologist* 59 (6): 495–501.

Coady, M.M. 1939. *Masters of their own destiny: The story of the Antigonish movement of adult education through economic cooperation.* New York: Harper & Brothers.

Coady, M.M. 1942. *The Antigonish way.* St. Francis, NS: Extension Department.

Cobb-Clark, D.A., & S. Schurer. 2012. "The stability of big-five personality traits." *Economics Letters* 115 (1): 11–15.

Coben, D. 2013. *Radical heroes: Gramsci, Freire and the politics of adult education,* vol. 1006. New York: Routledge.

Coburn, D. 2004. "Beyond the income inequality hypothesis: Class, neo-liberalism, and health inequalities." *Social Science & Medicine* 58 (1): 41–56.

Cochran, B.N., & J.S. Robohm. 2015. "Integrating LGBT competencies into the multicultural curriculum of graduate psychology training programs: Expounding and expanding upon hope and Chappell's choice points: Commentary on 'Extending training in multicultural competencies to include individuals identifying as lesbian, gay, and bisexual: Key choice points for clinical psychology training programs.'" *Clinical Psychology: Science and Practice* 22 (2): 119–26.

Cohen, A.P. 2013. *Symbolic construction of community.* New York: Routledge.

Cohen, S., B.H. Gottlieb, & L.G. Underwood, eds. 2000. "Social relationships and health." In *Social support measurement and intervention: A guide for health and social scientists,* 1–25. New York: Oxford University Press.

Cokley, K., O. Awosogba, & D. Taylor. 2014. "A 12-year content analysis of the Journal of Black Psychology (2000–2011): Implications for the field of Black psychology." *Journal of Black Psychology* 40 (3): 215–38.

Cole, E., E.D. Rothblum, & P. Chesler. 2014. *Feminist foremothers in women's studies, psychology, and mental health.* New York: Routledge.

Collins, S., & N. Arthur. 2007. "A framework for enhancing multicultural counselling competence." *Canadian Journal of Counselling* 41 (1): 31–49.

Collins, S., N. Arthur, C. Brown, & B. Kennedy. 2013. "Counsellor and supervisor views of multicultural and social justice education." *Journal of Counsellogy* 1: 279–95.

Commission on Social Determinates of Health. 2008. *Closing the gap in a generation: Health equity through action on the social determinants of health. Final report of the Commission on Social Determinants of Health.* Geneva: World Health Organization.

Connelly, S., S. Markey, & M. Roseland. 2013. "We know enough: Achieving action through the convergence of sustainable community development and the social economy." In *The economy of green cities*, edited by R. Simpson & M. Zimmerman, 191–203. London: Springer.

Constantine, M.G., S.M. Hage, M.M. Kindaichi, & R.M. Bryant. 2007. "Social justice and multicultural issues: Implications for the practice and training of counselors and counseling psychologists." *Journal of Counseling and Development* 85 (1): 24–29.

Cooper, S. 2014. "A synopsis of South African psychology from apartheid to democracy." *American Psychologist* 69 (8): 837–47.

Corak, M. 2013. "Income inequality, equality of opportunity, and intergenerational mobility." *Journal of Economic Perspectives* 27 (3): 79–102.

Corey, G., M. Corey, C. Corey, & P. Callanan. 2014. *Issues and ethics in the helping professions*. Boston: Cengage Learning.

Cote, J.E., & C.G. Levine. 2014. *Identity, formation, agency, and culture: A social psychological synthesis*. New York: Psychology Press.

Cotterell, J. 2013. *Social networks in youth and adolescence*. New York: Routledge.

Coulter, K. 2012. "Solidarity in deed: Poor people's organizations, unions, and the politics of antipoverty work in Ontario." *Anthropology of Work Review* 33 (2): 101–12.

Couture, J. 1983. *Traditional Aboriginal spirituality and religious practice in federal prisons: An interim statement on policy and procedures*. Draft report. Edmonton, Alberta. http://www.publicsafety.gc.ca/cnt/rsrcs/lbrr/ctlg/dtls-en.aspx?d=PS&i=921838

Couture, J.E. 2000. "Native studies and the academy." In *Indigenous knowledges in global contexts: Multiple readings of our world*, edited by G. Sefa Dei, B. Hall, & D. Rosenberg, 157–67. Toronto: University of Toronto Press.

Crenshaw, K. 1989. "Demarginalizing the intersection of race and sex: A black feminist critique of antidiscrimination doctrine, feminist theory and antiracist politics." *University of Chicago Legal Forum*, Issue 1: Article 8. http://chicagounbound.uchicago.edu/cgi/viewcontent.cgi?article=1052&context=uclf

Creswell, J.W. 2013. *Research design: Qualitative, quantitative, and mixed methods approaches*. London: Sage.

Crosland, A. 2013. *The future of socialism: New edition with foreword by Gordon Brown*. London: Constable.

Crosland, A. 2014. *The future of socialism* (revised 50th ed.). London: Constable & Robinson.

Cross, T. L. 2008. "Cultural competence." In *The Encyclopedia of social work*, edited by T. Mizrahi & L. Davis, 487–91. Toronto: Oxford University Press.

Cross, W.E., Jr., B.O. Grant, & A. Ventuneac. 2012. "Black identity and well-being: Untangling race and ethnicity." In *African American identity: Racial and cultural dimensions of the black experience*, edited by J. Sullivan & A. Esmail, 125–46. New York: Lexington Press.

Crucil, C. 2015. "Community as client: An investigation of what helps and what hinders the integration of social justice into counselling practice." MA thesis, University of British Columbia.

Cruz, M.R., & C.C. Sonn. 2011. "(De)colonizing culture in community psychology: Reflections from critical social science." *American Journal of Community Psychology* 47 (1–2): 203–14.

Cuddy, A.J., E.B. Wolf, P. Glick, S. Crotty, J. Chong, & M.I. Norton. 2015. "Men as cultural ideals: Cultural values moderate gender stereotype content." *Journal of Personality and Social Psychology* 109 (4): 622–35.

Cullingworth, J.B., ed. 2015. *Urban and regional planning in Canada.* New Brunswick, NJ: Transaction Publishers.

Cummings, T., & C. Worley. 2014. *Organization development and change.* Boston: Cengage Learning.

Currie, E., T. Goddard, & R.R. Myers. 2014. "The Dark Ghetto revisited: Kenneth B. Clark's classic analysis as cutting edge criminology." *Theoretical Criminology* 19 (1): 5–22.

Darian-Smith, E. 2015. "The constitution of identity: New modalities of nationality, citizenship, belonging and being." RegNet Working Paper 66, Regulatory Institutions Network. Canberra, Australia.

David, E.J.R. 2013. *Internalized oppression: The psychology of marginalized groups.* New York: Springer.

Davis, B., M.B.R. Stafford, & C. Pullig. 2014. "How gay–straight alliance groups mitigate the relationship between gay-bias victimization and adolescent suicide attempts." *Journal of the American Academy of Child and Adolescent Psychiatry* 53 (12): 1271–78.

Dean, H., & L. Platt, eds. 2016. *Social advantage and disadvantage.* London: Oxford University Press.

DeFilippis, J. 2001. "The myth of social capital in community development." *Housing Policy Debate* 12 (4): 781–806.

DeFilippis, J., & S. Saegert. 2013. *The community development reader.* New York: Routledge.

Dei, G. 2012. "Reclaiming our Africanness in the diasporized context: The challenge of asserting a critical African personality." *The Journal of Pan African Studies* 4 (10): 42–57.

dela Cruz, A.M., & P. McCarthy. 2010. "Alberta Aboriginal Head Start in urban and northern communities: Longitudinal study pilot phase." *Chronic Diseases and Injuries in Canada* 30 (2): 40–45.

Delgado, M., & D. Humm-Delgado. 2013. *Asset assessments and community social work practice.* London: Oxford University Press.

Denmark, F.L., & M.A. Paludi. 2012. "Women and feminism, history of." In *Encyclopedia of the History of Psychological Theories*, edited by R. Rieber, 1201–20. New York: Springer.

Dennis, M.K. 2014. "Layers of loss, death, and grief as social determinants of Lakota Elders' behavioral health." *Best Practices in Mental Health* 10 (2): 32–47.

Denton, M., & V. Walters. 1999. "Gender differences in structural and behavioral determinants of health: An analysis of the social production of health." *Social Science & Medicine* 48 (9): 1221–35.

Devlin, B., S.E. Fienberg, D.P. Resnick, & K. Roeder, eds. 2013. *Intelligence, genes, and success: Scientists respond to the Bell Curve.* New York: Springer.

Dey, S. 2013. "Globalization and its benefits." *Critical Perspectives on International Business* 1 (1): 75–84.

Diller, J. 2014. *Cultural diversity: A primer for the human services.* Stanford, CT: Cengage Learning.

Dodaro, S., & L. Pluta. 2012. *Big picture: The Antigonish movement of Eastern Nova Scotia.* Montreal: McGill-Queen's University Press.

Dolgoff, R., & D. Feldstein. 2012. *Understanding social welfare: A search for social justice.* Toronto: Pearson Higher Education.

Domínguez, D.G., M. Bobele, J. Coppock, & E. Peña. 2015. "LGBTQ relationally based positive psychology: An inclusive and systemic framework." *Psychological Services* 12 (2): 177–85.

Donaldson, S.I. 2012. *Program theory-driven evaluation science: Strategies and applications.* New York: Routledge.

Donovan, J. 2012. *Feminist theory: The intellectual traditions.* New York: Bloomsbury.

Dorf, M.C. 2012. "Could the Occupy movement become the realization of democratic experimentalism's aspiration for pragmatic politics?" *Contemporary Pragmatism* 9 (2): 263–71.

Draguns, J.G. 2013. "Cross-cultural counselling and psychotherapy: History, issues, current status." In *Cross-Cultural Counselling and Psychotherapy*, edited by A. Marsella & P. Pedersen, 3–28. New York: Pergamon.

Dreier, P., & J.D. Hulchanski. 1993. "The role of nonprofit housing in Canada and the United States: Some comparisons." *Housing Policy Debate* 4 (1): 43–80.

Drescher, J. 2015. "Queer diagnoses revisited: The past and future of homosexuality and gender diagnoses in DSM and ICD." *International Review of Psychiatry*, 27 (5): 23–32.

Dryden, W. 2012. "Humanistic psychology: Possible ways forward." *Self & Society* 40 (1): 26–29.

Duclos, J.Y., & P. Grégoire. 2002. "Absolute and relative deprivation and the measurement of poverty." *Review of Income and Wealth* 48 (4): 471–92.

Duménil, G., & D. Lévy. 2011. *The crisis of neoliberalism.* Boston: Harvard University Press.

Duran, E., J. Firehammer, & J. Gonzalez. 2008. "Liberation psychology as the path toward healing cultural soul wounds." *Journal of Counseling and Development* 86 (3): 288–95.

Durbin, A., R. Moineddin, E. Lin, L.S. Steele, & R.H. Glazier. 2015. "Examining the relationship between neighbourhood deprivation and mental health service use of immigrants in Ontario, Canada: A cross-sectional study." *BMJ Open* 5 (3): 1–11.

Dussault, R., & G. Erasmus. 1996. *Report of the Royal Commission on Aboriginal Peoples: Looking forward, looking back.* Ottawa: Indian and Northern Affairs Canada.

Eagly, A.H., A. Eaton, S.M. Rose, S. Riger, & M.C. McHugh. 2012. "Feminism and psychology: Analysis of a half-century of research on women and gender." *American Psychologist* 67 (3): 211–30.

Edmonton Head Start Project. 2015. *Children and parents coming out ahead.* Edmonton: Edmonton Head Start Project.

Edwards, B., & J.D. McCarthy. 2004. "Resources and social movement mobilization." In *The Blackwell companion to social movements*, edited by D. Snow, S. Soule, & H. Kriesi, 116–52. Oxford: Blackwell.

Elder, J.P., T.L. Schmid, P. Dower, & S. Hedlund. 1993. "Community heart health programs: components, rationale, and strategies for effective interventions." *Journal of Public Health Policy* 14 (4): 463–79.

Emery, M., & C. Flora. 2006. "Spiraling-up: Mapping community transformation with community capitals framework." *Community Development* 37 (1): 19–35.

Engel, G.L. 1981. "The clinical application of the biopsychosocial model." *Journal of Medicine and Philosophy* 6 (2): 101–24.

Enns, C.Z., & E.N. Williams. 2012. *The Oxford handbook of feminist counselling psychology.* London: Oxford University Press.

Enns, C.Z., & M.A. Green. 2013. "Outcomes of oppression: Sociocultural influences on women's mental health." *Sex Roles* 68 (7–8): 510–13.

Enriquez, V.G. 2013. Indigenous psychology: From traditional indigenous concepts to modern psychological practice. DLSU *Dialogue: An Interdisciplinary Journal for Cultural Studies* 27 (2): 1–21.

Erasmus, G. 1977. "We the Dene." In *Dene nation: The colony within,* edited by M. Watkins, 177–81. Toronto: University of Toronto Press.

Evans-Campbell, T. 2008. "Historical trauma in American Indian/Native Alaska communities a multilevel framework for exploring impacts on individuals, families, and communities." *Journal of Interpersonal Violence* 23 (3): 316–38.

Ewen, L.A. 2015. *Corporate power and urban crisis in Detroit.* Princeton, NJ: Princeton University Press.

Family Resource Alliance. 2015. Apply for Head Start program. Retrieved August 31, 2015, from: http://www.familyresourcealliance.net/head-start-program/

Fanon, F. 1952. *Black skin, white masks: The experiences of a black man in a white world.* New York: Grove Press.

Fanon, F. 1961. *The wretched of the Earth.* New York: Grove Press.

Fawcett, S.B., A. Paine-Andrews, V.T. Francisco, J.A. Schultz, K.P. Richter, R.K. Lewis, E.L. Williams, et al. 1995. "Using empowerment theory in collaborative partnerships for community health and development." *American Journal of Community Psychology* 23 (5): 677–97.

Feit, M.D., & M. Bonds. 2014. *Race, politics, and community development funding: The siscolor of money.* New York: Routledge.

Feldman, S., & C. Johnston. 2014. "Understanding the determinants of political ideology: Implications of structural complexity." *Political Psychology* 35 (3): 337–58.

Ferdinand, L., J. Fudrow, K.S. Calhoun, & J. Wisniewski. 2013. *An introduction to research methods: Needs assessment.* Pittsburgh: Surveys, Focus Groups and Personas.

Ferguson, R.F., & W.T. Dickens, eds. 2011. *Urban problems and community development.* Washington, DC: Brookings Institution Press.

Ferrera, M.J. 2011. "The intersection of colonial mentality, family socialization, and ethnic identity formation among second generation Filipino American youth." PhD diss., University of Chicago.

Fields, D. 2015. "Contesting the financialization of urban space: Community organizations and the struggle to preserve affordable rental housing in New York City." *Journal of Urban Affairs* 37 (2): 144–65.

Fine, M. 2012. "Resuscitating critical psychology for 'revolting' times." *Journal of Social Issues* 68 (2): 416–38.

Fink, A. 2013. *Conducting research literature reviews: From the internet to paper*. New York: Sage.

Finks, P.D. 1984. *The radical vision of Saul Alinsky*. New York: Paulist Press.

Fitzgerald, P. 2013. *Therapy talk: Conversation analysis in practice*. New York: Palgrave Macmillan.

Flynn, P., & V.A. Hodgkinson, eds. 2013. *Measuring the impact of the nonprofit sector*. New York: Springer Science & Business Media.

Fodor, E. 1999. "Better not bigger: How to take control of urban growth and improve your community." *Human Ecology Review* 6 (2): 126–27.

Frankel, H., & S. Frankel. 2007. "Family therapy, family practice, and child and family poverty: Historical perspectives and recent developments." *Journal of Family Social Work* 10 (4): 43–80.

Frank-Miller, E.G., S.J. Lambert, & J.R. Henly. 2015. "Age, wage, and job placement: Older women's experiences entering the retail sector." *Journal of Women & Aging* 27 (2): 157–73.

Freire, P. 1970. *Pedagogy of the oppressed*. New York: Continuum.

Freire, P. 2014. *Pedagogy of hope: Reliving pedagogy of the oppressed*. New York: Bloomsbury.

Freire, P., & D. Macedo. 2013. *Literacy: Reading the word and the world*. New York: Routledge.

Frese, M. 2015. "Cultural practices, norms, and values." *Journal of Cross-Cultural Psychology* 46 (10): 1327–30.

Friedel, T.L., J.A. Archibald, R.B. Head, G. Martin, & M. Muñoz. 2012. "Editorial: Indigenous pedagogies: Resurgence and restoration." *Canadian Journal of Native Education* 35 (1): 1–6.

Friesen, J.W. 2014. Review of *A metaphoric mind: Selected writings of Joseph Couture*, edited by Ruth Couture and Virginia McGowan. *Aboriginal Policy Studies* 3 (1–2): 240–41.

Fuchs, C. 2014. *OccupyMedia! The Occupy movement and social media in crisis capitalism*. Croydon, UK: John Hunt Publishing.

Fulton, M. 1995. "The future of Canadian agricultural cooperatives: A property rights approach." *American Journal of Agricultural Economics* 77 (5): 1144–52.

Funnell, S.C., & P.J. Rogers. 2011. *Purposeful program theory: Effective use of theories of change and logic models*, vol. 31. New York: John Wiley & Sons.

Gada, M.Y. 2015. "The Muslims are coming! Islamophobia, extremism, and the domestic war on terror." *Arab Studies Quarterly* 37 (2): 205–08.

Galbraith, M.W. 1990. "The nature of community and adult education." In *Education through community organizations*, edited by M.W. Galbraith, 3–11. San Francisco: Jossey-Bass.

Gallardo, M.E. 2013. *Developing cultural humility*. New York: Sage.

Gamson, W.A., & M.L. Sifry. 2013. "The #Occupy movement: An introduction." *Sociological Quarterly* 54 (2): 159–63.

Ganesh, S., & H.M. Zoller. 2012. "Dialogue, activism, and democratic social change." *Communication Theory* 22 (1): 66–91.

Gelé, K., S. McNamara, S.H. Phillips, R.D. Shelby, G. Grossman, S.C. Vaughan, & R. Roughton. 2012. "Emerging views on gender and sexuality celebrating twenty years of new perspectives on lesbian, gay, bisexual, and trans people." *Journal of the American Psychoanalytic Association* 60 (5): 949–67.

Gentzoglanis, A. 1997. "Ten economic and financial performance of cooperatives and investor-owned firms: An empirical study." In *Strategies and structures in the agro-food industries*, edited by J. Nillson & G. van Dyjk, 171. Assen, The Netherlands: Van Gorcum, 1997.

Gergen, M.M., & S.N. Davis. 2013. *Toward a new psychology of gender: A reader*. New York: Routledge.

Geven, S., M. Kalmijn, & F. van Tubergen. 2016. "The ethnic composition of schools and students' problem behavior in four European countries: The role of friends." *Journal of Ethnic and Migration Studies*. doi: 10.1080/1369183X.2015.1121806

Gibson, M.F. 2012. "Opening up: Therapist self-disclosure in theory, research, and practice." *Clinical Social Work Journal* 40 (3): 287–96.

Gibson, N.C. 2003. *Fanon: The postcolonial imagination*. Cambridge: Polity Press.

Giger, N., J. Rosset, & J. Bernauer. 2012. "The poor political representation of the poor in a comparative perspective." *Representation* 48 (1): 47–61.

Gil, D.G. 2013. *Confronting injustice and oppression: Concepts and strategies for social workers*. New York: Columbia University Press.

Gill, K. 2014. "Oppression, intersectionality and privilege theory." *Irish Marxist Review* 3 (9): 62–68.

Gills, B.K., & K. Gray. 2012. "People power in the era of global crisis: Rebellion, resistance, and liberation." *Third World Quarterly* 33 (2): 205–24.

Gitlin, T. 2012. *Occupy nation: The roots, the spirit, and the promise of Occupy Wall Street*. New York: Harper Collins.

Glassgold, J.M., & J. Drescher, eds. 2014. *Activism and LGBT psychology*. New York: Routledge.

Goddard, J., D. McKillop, & J.O. Wilson. 2014. "US credit unions: Survival, consolidation, and growth." *Economic Inquiry* 52 (1): 304–19.

Gohmann, S.F., B.K. Hobbs, & M. McCrickard. 2008. "Economic freedom and service industry growth in the United States." *Entrepreneurship Theory and Practice* 32 (5): 855–74.

Goldstein, B.E. 2012. *Collaborative resilience: Moving through crisis to opportunity*. Cambridge, MA: MIT Press.

Goldstein, S. 2015. *Cross-cultural explorations: Activities in culture and psychology*. New York: Routledge.

Gone, J.P. 2013a. "A community-based treatment for Native American historical trauma: Prospects for evidence-based practice." *Spirituality in Clinical Practice* 1 (S): 78–94. doi.org/10.1037/2326-4500.1.S.78

Gone, J.P. 2013b. "Redressing First Nations historical trauma: Theorizing mechanisms for indigenous culture as mental health treatment." *Transcultural Psychiatry* 50 (5): 683–706.

Gone, J.P., & P.E. Calf Looking. 2011. "American Indian culture as substance abuse treatment: Pursuing evidence for a local intervention." *Journal of Psychoactive Drugs* 43 (4): 291–96.

Gonzalez, J., E. Simard, T. Baker-Demaray, & C.I. Eyes. 2013. "The internalized oppression of North American Indigenous peoples." *Internalized Oppression: The Psychology of Marginalized Groups* 31: 232–63.

Gonzalez, N.A., F.C. Fabrett, & G.P. Knight. 2009. "Acculturation, enculturation, and the psychosocial adaptation of Latino youth." In *Handbook of U.S. Latino Psychology: Developmental and Community-Based Perspective*, edited by F.A. Villaruel, G. Carlo, J.M. Grau, M. Azmitia, N.J. Cabrera, & T.J. Chahin, 115–134. Thousand Oaks, CA: Sage.

Goodman, L.A., B. Liang, J.E. Helms, R.E. Latta, E. Sparks, & S.R. Weintraub. 2004. "Training counselling psychologists as social justice agents: Feminist and multicultural principles in action." *Counseling Psychologist* 32 (6): 793–836.

Goodman, R.D. 2013. "The transgenerational trauma and resilience genogram." *Counselling Psychology Quarterly* 26 (3–4): 386–405.

Goodman, R.D., J.M. Williams, R.C.Y. Chung, R.M. Talleyrand, A.M. Douglass, H.G. McMahon, & F. Bemak. 2015. "Decolonizing traditional pedagogies and practices in counselling and psychology education: A move towards social justice and action." In *Decolonizing "multicultural" counselling through social justice*, edited by D. Goodman & P. Gorski, 147–64. New York: Springer.

Gorodnichenko, Y., & G. Roland. 2012. "Understanding the individualism–collectivism cleavage and its effects: Lessons from cultural psychology." In *Institutions and comparative economic development*, edited by M. Aoki, T. Kuran, & G. Roland, 213–36. London: Palgrave.

Gough, B., M. McFadden, & M. McDonald. 2013. *Critical social psychology: An introduction*. New York: Palgrave Macmillan.

Gough, M.Z., & J. Accordino. 2013. "Public gardens as sustainable community development partners: Motivations, perceived benefits, and challenges." *Urban Affairs Review* 49 (8): 851–87.

Gray, J.S., & W.J. Rose. 2012. "Cultural adaptation for therapy with American Indians and Alaska Natives." *Journal of Multicultural Counseling and Development* 40 (2): 82–92.

Green, G.P., & A. Haines. 2015. *Asset building & community development*. New York: Sage.

Greenleaf, A.T., & R.M. Bryant. 2012. "Perpetuating oppression: Does the current counselling discourse neutralize social action." *Journal for Social Action in Counseling and Psychology* 4 (1): 18–29.

Griffiths, T., T. Connor, B. Robertson, & L. Phelan. 2013. "Is Mayfield Pool saved yet? Community assets and their contingent, discursive foundations." *Community Development Journal: An International Forum*.

Grills, C. 2013. "The context, perspective, and mission of ABPsi past and present." *Journal of Black Psychology* 39 (3): 276–83.

Grinnell, R.M., P.A. Gabor, & Y.A. Unrau. 2012. *Program evaluation for social workers: Foundations of evidence-based programs*. London: Oxford University Press.

Groffman, P.M., J. Cavender-Bares, N.D. Bettez, J.M. Grove, S.J. Hall, J.B. Heffernan, & K. Nelson. 2014. "Ecological homogenization of urban USA." *Frontiers in Ecology and the Environment* 12 (1): 74–81.

Grothaus, T., G. McAuliffe, & L. Craigen. 2012. "Infusing cultural competence and advocacy into strength-based counselling." *Journal of Humanistic Counselling* 51 (1): 51–65.

Grusec, J.E., & P.D. Hastings, eds. 2014. *Handbook of socialization: Theory and research*. New York: Guilford Publications.

Gummere, R.M. 1988. "The counselor as prophet: Frank Parsons, 1854–1908." *Journal of Counseling and Development* 66 (9): 402–05.

Gunew, S., ed. 2013. *Feminist knowledge: Critique and construct.* New York: Routledge.

Guo, J. 2015. "The legal loophole that allowed Dylann Roof to get a gun." *Washington Post,* 18 June. http://www.washingtonpost.com/blogs/govbeat/wp/2015/06/18/the-legal-loophole-that-allowed-dylann-roof-to-get-a-gun/

Gutierrez, L.M., & E.A. Lewis. 2012. "Education, participation, and capacity building in community organizing with women of color." In *Community organizing and community building for health and welfare,* edited by M. Minkler, 215–28. New Brunswick, NJ: Rutgers University Press.

Hall, I., ed. 2015. *Radicals and reactionaries in twentieth-century international thought.* New York: Palgrave Macmillan.

Hammack, P.L. 2008. "Narrative and the cultural psychology of identity." *Personality and Social Psychology Review* 12 (3): 222–47.

Hankivsky, O. 2012. "Women's health, men's health, and gender and health: Implications of intersectionality." *Social Science & Medicine* 74 (11): 1712–20.

Hanna, L., & J. Moore. 2014. "Community-driven social inclusion practice: A case study of a multicultural women's friendship group." In *Practising social inclusion,* 170–81. Abingdon, UK: Taylor & Francis.

Hardina, D. 2013. *Analytical skills for community organization practice.* New York: Columbia University Press.

Hart, M. 2002. *Seeking mino-pimatisiwin: An Aboriginal approach to helping.* Halifax: Fernwood Books.

Hartnack, C. 2015. "Presentism and difference: On the inclusion of Indigenous psychologies in the history of psychology." *Psychological Studies* 60 (1): 1–5.

Hartung, P.J., & D.L. Blustein. 2002. "Reason, intuition and social justice: Elaborating on Parson's career decision-making model." *Journal of Counseling and Development* 80 (1): 41–47.

Haslam, S.A., S.D. Reicher, & M.J. Platow. 2013. *The new psychology of leadership: Identity, influence and power.* New York: Psychology Press.

He, X., N. Sebanz, J. Sui, & G.W. Humphreys. 2014. "Individualism-collectivism and interpersonal memory guidance of attention." *Journal of Experimental Social Psychology* 54: 102–14.

Helms, J.E. 2003. "A pragmatic view of social justice." *Counseling Psychologist* 31 (3): 305–13.

Hermann, C. 2014. "Structural adjustment and neoliberal convergence in labour markets and welfare: The impact of the crisis and austerity measures on European economic and social models." *Competition & Change* 18 (2): 111–30.

Heywood, A. 2012. *Political ideologies: An introduction.* New York: Palgrave Macmillan.

Hickey, G., S. McGilloway, M. O'Brien, Y. Leckey, & M. Devlin. 2015. "A theory-based evaluation of a community-based funding scheme in a disadvantaged suburban city area." *Evaluation and Program Planning* 52: 61–69.

HighScope. 2015. "Mission and vision." Retrieved August 31, 2015, from: http://www.highscope.org/Content.asp?ContentId=6

Hill, M. 2013. *Feminist therapy as a political act.* New York: Routledge.

Hill, M., & M. Ballou. 2013. *The foundation and future of feminist therapy*. New York: Routledge.

Hipolito-Delgado, C.P., J.M. Cook, E.M. Avrus, & E.J. Bonham. 2011. "Developing counselling students' multicultural competence through the multicultural action project." *Counselor Education and Supervision* 50 (6): 402–21.

Hirst, P. 2014. "Six problems and advances in the theory of ideology." *Ideology* 11: 234–40.

Hirst, P., G. Thompson, & S. Bromley. 2015. *Globalization in question*. New York: John Wiley & Sons.

Hoener, C., W.B. Stiles, B.J. Luka, & R.A. Gordon. 2012. "Client experiences of agency in therapy." *Person-Centered and Experiential Psychotherapies* 11 (1): 64–82.

Hofer, B.K., & P.R. Pintrich. 2004. *Personal epistemology: The psychology of beliefs about knowledge and knowing*. New York: Psychology Press.

Hogg, M.A., & D.J. Terry, eds. 2014. *Social identity processes in organizational contexts*. New York: Psychology Press.

Hollifield, J., P. Martin, & P. Orrenius. 2014. *Controlling immigration: A global perspective*. Stanford, CA: Stanford University Press.

Holosko, M.J., & J.R. Barner. 2014. "Social welfare policy and institutions." In *The Routledge handbook of poverty in the United States*, edited by S. Haymes, M. Haymes, & R. Miller, 239–50. London: Routledge.

Holt, N. 2010. *Bringing the High Scope approach to your early years practice*. New York: Routledge.

Holt-Lunstad, J., T.B. Smith, M. Baker, T. Harris, & D. Stephenson. 2015. "Loneliness and social isolation as risk factors for mortality: A meta-analytic review." *Perspectives on Psychological Science* 10 (2): 227–37.

Holzemer, S.P., M. Klainberg, D.J. Murphy, K.C. Rondello, & D. Smith. 2014. "Precision and principles of community program development." In *Community health nursing: An alliance for health*, edited by S. Holzener, M. Klaimberg, D. Murphy, K. Rondello, & D. Smith, 252–67. New York: Jones & Bartlett.

Holzer, H., D. Schanzenbach, G. Duncan, & J. Ludwig. 2007. "The economic costs of poverty in the United States: Subsequent effects of children growing up poor." National Poverty Center Working Paper Series 07–09. Washington, DC: Center for American Progress.

Homan, M. 2015. *Promoting community change: Making it happen in the real world*. Belmont, CA: Brooks/Cole.

Hook, J.N., D.E. Davis, J. Owen, E.L. Worthington Jr., & S.O. Utsey. 2013. "Cultural humility: Measuring openness to culturally diverse clients." *Journal of Counseling Psychology* 60 (3): 353–66.

Horwitt, S.D. 1989. *Let them call me rebel: Saul Alinsky, his life and legacy*. New York: Alfred A. Knopf.

Hunting, G., D. Grace, & O. Hankivsky. 2015. "Taking action on stigma and discrimination: An intersectionality-informed model of social inclusion and exclusion." *Intersectionalities: A Global Journal of Social Work Analysis: Research, Polity, and Practice* 4 (2): 101–25.

Hurley, G. 2010. "Recollections of our past." Paper presented at the Canadian Counselling Psychology Conference, Montreal, QC.

Hurn, B. J., & B. Tomalin. 2013. "Multiculturalism and diversity." In *Cross-cultural communication*, edited by B. Hurn & B. Tomalin, 191–207. London: Macmillan.

Hwang, K.K. 2011. "Reification of culture in indigenous psychologies: Merit or mistake?" *Social Epistemology* 25 (2): 125–31.

Hyde, J.S. 2012. "Nation-level indicators of gender equity in psychological research: Theoretical and methodological issues." *Psychology of Women Quarterly* 36 (2): 145–48.

Ibrahim, F.A. 1984. "Cross-cultural counselling and psychotherapy: An existential-psychological approach." *International Journal for the Advancement of Counseling* 7 (3): 159–69.

Iddings, A.C.D., S.G. McCafferty, & M.L.T. Silva. 2011. "Conscientização through graffiti literacies in the streets of a São Paulo neighborhood: An ecosocial semiotic perspective." *Reading Research Quarterly* 46 (1): 5–21.

Ife, J. 2012. *Human rights and social work: Towards rights-based practice.* New York: Cambridge University Press.

Ife, J. 2013. *Community development in an uncertain world.* Cambridge: Cambridge University Press.

Israel, B.A. 1985. "Social networks and social support: Implications for natural helper and community level interventions." *Health Education & Behavior* 12 (1): 65–80.

Ivey, A.E., & N.M. Collins. 2003. "Social justice: A long-term challenge for counselling psychology." *Counseling Psychologist* 31 (3): 290–98.

Jackson, V.H. 2015. "Practitioner characteristics and organizational contexts as essential elements in the evidence-based practice versus cultural competence debate." *Transcultural Psychiatry* 52 (2): 150–73.

Jahanbakhsh, S., F. Jomehri, & A.K. Mujembari. 2015. "The comparison of women's self confidence in base of gender role." *Procedia: Social and Behavioral Sciences* 191: 2285–90.

Jasper, K. 2015. "Feminist therapy." In *The Wiley handbook of eating disorders*, edited by L. Smolak & M. Levine, 801–15. New York: Wiley.

Jitsuchon, S. 2001. "What is poverty, and how to measure it?" *TDRI Quarterly Review* 15 (3): 7–11.

Johnson, C.V., & H.L. Friedman, eds. 2014. *The Praeger handbook of social justice and psychology.* 3 vols. Santa Barbara, CA: ABC-CLIO.

Johnson, S.D. 2012. "Gay affirmative psychotherapy with lesbian, gay, and bisexual individuals: Implications for contemporary psychotherapy research." *American Journal of Orthopsychiatry* 82 (4): 516–22.

Johnston, K. 2012. "Access for all? Struggles over citizenship and social policy." *Canadian Women's Studies* 29 (3): 124–37.

Joseph, B. 2015. "History of Assembly of First Nations." Retrieved August 20, 2015, from: http://www.ictinc.ca/blog/history-of-assembly-of-first-nations

Joshanloo, M., & S. Afshari. 2011. "Big five personality traits and self-esteem as predictors of life satisfaction in Iranian Muslim University students." *Journal of Happiness Studies* 12 (1): 105–13.

Joshi, D., & R.K. O'Dell. 2013. "Global governance and development ideology: The United Nations and the World Bank on the left-right spectrum." *Global Governance: A Review of Multilateralism and International Organizations* 19 (2): 249–75.

Jost, J.T., & D.M. Amodio. 2012. "Political ideology as motivated social cognition: Behavioral and neuroscientific evidence." *Motivation and Emotion* 36 (1): 55–64.

Jost, J.T., C.M. Federico, & J.L. Napier. 2013. "Political ideologies and their social psychological functions." In *The Oxford handbook of political ideologies*, edited by M. Freeden, L. Sargent, & M. Stears, 232–50. Oxford: Oxford University Press.

Justice, B., & J. Stanley. 2016. "Teaching in the time of Trump." *Social Education* 80 (1): 36–41.

Kaiser, E.J., D.R. Godschalk, & F.S. Chapin. 1995. *Urban land use planning.* Vol. 4. Urbana: University of Illinois Press.

Kaplan, A. 1973. "On the strategy of social planning." *Policy Sciences* 4 (1): 41–61.

Kasdan, D.O. 2014. "A tale of two hatchet men: Emergency financial management in Michigan." *Administration & Society* 23: 211–23.

Katz, D., & R.L. Kahn. 1978. *The social psychology of organizations.* Oxford: Wiley.

Kearns, A., E. Whitley, C. Tannahill, & A. Ellaway. 2015. "Loneliness, social relations and health and well-being in deprived communities." *Psychology Health and Medicine* 20 (3): 332–44.

Keefe, D. 2015. "Andragogy in the Appalachians: Myles Horton, the Highlander Folk School, and education for social and economic justice." *International Journal of Adult Vocational Education and Technology* 6 (3): 16–30.

Kennedy, B.A., & N. Arthur. 2014. "Social justice and counselling psychology: Recommitment through action/Justice sociale et psychologie du counselling: engagement renouvelé dans l'action." *Canadian Journal of Counselling and Psychotherapy* 48 (3): 186–205.

Kerstetter, K. 2012. "Insider, outsider, or somewhere in between: The impact of researchers' identities on the community-based research process." *Journal of Rural Social Sciences* 27 (2): 99–117.

Kertzner, R. 2013. "In memoriam: Richard Isay (December 1934–June 2012)." *Journal of Gay & Lesbian Mental Health* 17 (1): 127–28.

Kirmayer, L. 2012. "Rethinking cultural competence." *Transcultural Psychiatry* 49 (2): 149–64.

Kirmayer, L.J., G.M. Brass, & C.L. Tait. 2000. "The mental health of Aboriginal peoples: Transformations of identity and community." *Canadian Journal of Psychiatry* 45 (7): 607–16.

Kirmayer, L.J., K. Fung, C. Rousseau, H.T. Lo, P. Menzies, J. Guzder, S. Ganesan, et al. 2012. "Guidelines for training in cultural psychiatry." *Canadian Journal of Psychiatry* 57 (3): 1–16.

Kirschenbaum, H. 2015. "Values and ethics in counselling and psychotherapy." *British Journal of Guidance & Counselling* 43 (3): 372–75.

Kiselica, M.S., & M. Robinson. 2001. "Bringing advocacy counselling to life: The history, issues, and human dramas of social justice work in counselling." *Journal of Counselling and Development: JCD* 79 (4): 387–97.

Klasnja, P., & W. Pratt. 2012. "Healthcare in the pocket: Mapping the space of mobile-phone health interventions." *Journal of Biomedical Informatics* 45 (1): 184–98.

Kloos, B., J. Hill, E. Thomas, A. Wandersman, & M. Elias. 2011. *Community psychology: Linking individuals and communities.* Toronto: Cengage Learning.

Klor, E. 2012. "A primer for teen parent services: Issues, program development, and advocacy." *Young Adult Library Services* 11 (1): 19–26.

Knowles, M.S., E.F. Holton, III, & R.A. Swanson. 2014. *The adult learner: The definitive classic in adult education and human resource development.* New York: Routledge.

Kohl, J., & M. Horton. 1988. *The long haul: An autobiography.* New York: Columbia University.

Kubik, W., C. Bourassa, & M. Hampton. 2009. "Stolen sisters, second class citizens, poor health: The legacy of colonization in Canada." *Humanity & Society* 33 (1–2): 18–34.

Kunst, J.R., D.L. Sam, & P. Ulleberg. 2013. "Perceived Islamophobia: Scale development and validation." *International Journal of Intercultural Relations* 37 (2): 225–37.

Kunst, J.R., H. Tajamal, D.L. Sam, & P. Ulleberg. 2012. "Coping with Islamophobia: The effects of religious stigma on Muslim minorities' identity formation." *International Journal of Intercultural Relations* 36 (4): 518–32.

Kuperminc, G.P., N.J. Wilkins, G.J. Jurkovic, & J.L. Perilla. 2013. "Filial responsibility, perceived fairness, and psychological functioning of Latino youth from immigrant families." *Journal of Family Psychology* 27 (2): 173–82.

Lantz, P.M., J.W. Lynch, J.S. House, J.M. Lepkowski, R.P. Mero, M.A. Musick, & D.R. Williams. 2001. "Socioeconomic disparities in health change in a longitudinal study of US adults: The role of health-risk behaviors." *Social Science & Medicine* 53 (1): 29–40.

Larrain, J. 2013. *Ideology and cultural identity: Modernity and the third world presence.* New York: John Wiley & Sons.

Larsen, G., & R. Lawson. 2013. "Consumer rights: A co-optation of the contemporary consumer movement." *Journal of Historical Research in Marketing* 5 (1): 97–114.

Larsson, T. 2001. *The race to the top: The real story of globalization.* Washington, DC: Cato Institute.

Laska, S.B., & D. Spain, eds. 2013. *Back to the city: Issues in neighborhood renovation.* New York: Pergamon.

Lasswell, H.D., & A. Kaplan. 2013. *Power and society: A framework for political inquiry.* New York: Transaction Publishers.

Lau, J., & K.M. Ng. 2014. "Conceptualizing the counselling training environment using Bronfenbrenner's ecological theory." *International Journal for the Advancement of Counseling* 36 (4): 423–39.

Lavallee, L.F., & J.M. Poole. 2010. "Beyond recovery: Colonization, health and healing for Indigenous people in Canada." *International Journal of Mental Health and Addiction* 8 (2): 271–81.

Laverack, G. 2012. "Where are the champions of global health promotion?" *Global Health Promotion* 19 (2): 63–65.

Leach, J. 2014. *Improving mental health through social support: Building positive and empowering relationships.* New York: Jessica Kingsley Publishers.

Ledwith, M. 2011. *Community development: A critical approach.* London: Policy Press.

Ledwith, M. 2015. *Community development in action: Putting Freire into practice.* London: Policy Press.

Lee, B. 1986. *Pragmatics of community organization.* Mississauga, ON: Common Act Press.

Lee, D. 1984. "Counselling and culture: Some issues." *Personnel and Guidance Journal* 62 (10): 592–97.

Lee, H., M. Andrew, A. Gebremariam, J.C. Lumeng, & J.M. Lee. 2014. "Longitudinal associations between poverty and obesity from birth through adolescence." *American Journal of Public Health* 104 (5): e70–76.

Lee, S.A., C.A. Reid, S.D. Short, J.A. Gibbons, R. Yeh, & M.L. Campbell. 2013. "Fear of Muslims: Psychometric evaluation of the Islamophobia scale." *Psychology of Religion and Spirituality* 5 (3): 157–71.

Lefebvre, R.C., & J.A. Flora. 1988. "Social marketing and public health intervention." *Health Education & Behavior* 15 (3): 299–315.

LeFebvre, R., & V. Franke. 2013. "Culture matters: Individualism vs. collectivism in conflict decision-making." *Societies (Basel, Switzerland)* 3 (1): 128–46.

Leutner, F., G. Ahmetoglu, R. Akhtar, & T. Chamorro-Premuzic. 2014. "The relationship between the entrepreneurial personality and the big five personality traits." *Personality and Individual Differences* 63: 58–63.

Levy, D., H. Itzhaky, L. Zanbar, & C. Schwartz. 2012. "Sense of cohesion among community activists engaging in volunteer activity." *Journal of Community Psychology* 40 (6): 735–46.

Liang, C.T., J. Salcedo, A.L. Rivera, & M.J. Lopez. 2009. "A content and methodological analysis of 35 years of Latino/a-focused research." *Counseling Psychologist* 37 (8): 1116–46.

Liben, L.S., & R.S. Bigler. 2015. "Understanding and undermining the development of gender dichotomies: The legacy of Sandra Lipsitz Bem." *Sex Roles*. Online in advance of print: doi:10.1007/s11199-015-0519-4

Lightfoot, E., J.S. McCleary, & T. Lum. 2014. "Asset mapping as a research tool for community-based participatory research in social work." *Social Work Research* 38 (1): 59–64.

Lin, N. 1999. "Building a network theory of social capital." *Connections* 22 (1): 28–51.

Lindsey, L., & C.E. Wilson. 1994. "Spurring a dialogue to place the African European experience within the context of an Afrocentric philosophy." *Journal of Black Studies* 25 (1): 41–61.

Liu, J.H., K. Lawson-Te Aho, & A. Rata. 2014. "Constructing identity spaces for First Nations people towards an Indigenous psychology of self-determination and cultural healing." *Psychology and Developing Societies* 26 (2): 143–53.

Loder-Jackson, T. 2013. "Myles Horton." In *A Critical Pedagogy of Resistance*, 77–80. Amsterdam: Sense Publishers.

Loewen, G., P. Cates, & P. Chorney. 2003. Maintaining Momentum–CD/CED Gathering, 26 November, Winnipeg, MB.

Loewenthal, D. 2013. "Future of talk therapy." In *Handbook of counselling and psychotherapy in an international context*, edited by R. Moodley, U. Gielen, & R. Wu, 348–58. New York: Routledge.

Loppie Reading, C., & F. Wien. 2009. *Health inequities and social determinates of Aboriginal peoples' health*. Ottawa: National Coordinating Centre for Aboriginal Health.

Lor, M., P. Xiong, L. Park, R.J. Schwei, & E.A. Jacobs. 2016. "Western or traditional healers? Understanding decision making in the Hmong population." *Western Journal of Nursing Research*. Online before print: doi: 10.1177/0193945916636484

Lovett, T., C. Clarke, & A. Kilmurray. 1983. *Adult education and community action*. London: Croom Helm.

Loxley, J. 2003. "Financing community economic development in Winnipeg." *Economie et Solidarités* 34 (1): 82–104.

Lucero, J., N. Wallerstein, B. Duran, M. Alegria, E. Greene-Moton, B. Israel, S. Kastelic, et al. 2016. "Development of a mixed methods investigation of process and outcomes of community-based participatory research." *Journal of Mixed Methods Research* 1. doi: 10.1177/1558689816633309

Lynam, M.J., & S. Cowley. 2007. "Understanding marginalization as a social determinant of health." *Critical Public Health* 17 (2): 137–49.

Lynch, J., & G.D. Smith. 2002. "Commentary: Income inequality and health: The end of the story?" *International Journal of Epidemiology* 31 (3): 549–51.

Lynch, J.W., G.D. Smith, G.A. Kaplan, & J.S. House. 2000. "Income inequality and mortality: Importance to health of individual income, psychosocial environment, or material conditions." *BMJ: British Medical Journal* 320 (7243): 1200–04.

MacDonald, D. 2015. "Creative ways of talking: A narrative literature review concerning emotional support for adults with mild or moderate learning difficulties." *British Journal of Learning Disabilities* 44 (3): 233–39.

MacDonald, D.B., & G. Hudson. 2012. "The genocide question and Indian residential schools in Canada." *Canadian Journal of Political Science* 45 (2): 427–49.

MacPherson, I. 2010. "Credit unions." In *International encyclopedia of civil society*, edited by H. K. Anheier and S. Toepler, 592–96. London: Springer.

Maillé, C. 2015. "Feminist interventions in political representation in the United States and Canada: Training programs and legal quotas." *European Journal of American Studies* 10 (1): 2–15.

Marcus, J., & H. Le. 2013. "Interactive effects of levels of individualism-collectivism on cooperation: A meta-analysis." *Journal of Organizational Behavior* 34 (6): 813–34.

Markowitz, G., & D. Rosner. 2013. *Children, race, and power: Kenneth and Mamie Clark's Northside Center.* New York: Routledge.

Marmot, M., & R.G. Wilkinson. 2001. "Psychosocial and material pathways in the relation between income and health: A response to Lynch et al." *BMJ: British Medical Journal* 322 (7296): 1233–36.

Marmot, M., & R.G. Wilkinson, eds. 2005. *Social determinants of health.* London: Oxford University Press.

Marranci, G. 2004. "Multiculturalism, Islam and the clash of civilisations theory: Rethinking Islamophobia." *Culture and Religion* 5 (1): 105–17.

Marsella, A. 2012. "Psychology and globalization: Understanding a complex relationship." *Journal of Social Issues* 68 (3): 454–72.

Martell, C.R. 2014. "The hybrid case study of 'Adam': Perspectives from behavioral activation and the influence of heteronormativity on LGB-affirmative therapy." *Pragmatic Case Studies in Psychotherapy* 10 (2): 106–16.

Martín-Baró, I., A. Aron, & S. Corne. 1994. *Writings for a liberation psychology.* Cambridge, MA: Harvard University Press.

Martinez, J.L., Jr., & R.H. Mendoza, eds. 2013. *Chicano psychology.* Chicago: Academic Press.

Mathews, G., G.L. Ribeiro, and C.A. Vega, eds. 2012. *Globalization from below: The world's other economy.* New York: Routledge.

Mathie, A., & G. Cunningham. 2005. "Who is driving development? Reflections on the transformative potential of asset-based community development." *Canadian Journal of Development Studies* 26 (1): 175–86.

Maton, K.I. 2008. "Empowering community settings: Agents of individual development, community betterment, and positive social change." *American Journal of Community Psychology* 41 (1–2): 4–21.

Mattern, M., & N.S. Love. 2013. "Activist arts, community development, and democracy." In *Doing democracy: Activist art and cultural politics*, edited by N. S. Love and M. Matern, 339–66. Albany, NY: SUNY Press.

Matthews, C.R., & E.M. Adams. 2009. "Using a social justice approach to prevent the mental health consequences of heterosexism." *Journal of Primary Prevention* 30 (1): 11–26.

Matthews, T., A. Danese, J. Wertz, C.L. Odgers, A. Ambler, T.E. Moffitt, & L. Arseneault. 2016. "Social isolation, loneliness and depression in young adulthood: A behavioural genetic analysis." *Social Psychiatry and Psychiatric Epidemiology* 51: 339–48.

Mawhiney, A., & H. Nabigon. 2011. "Aboriginal theory: A Cree medicine wheel guide for healing First Nations." In *Social work treatment: Interlocking theoretical approaches*, edited by Francis J. Turner, 15–29. New York: Oxford University Press.

Mayo, J.B., Jr. 2015. "Youth work in gay straight alliances: Curriculum, pedagogy, and activist development." *Child and Youth Services* 36 (1): 79–93.

Mays, V.M., S.D. Cochran, & N.W. Barnes. 2007. "Race, race-based discrimination, and health outcomes among African Americans." *Annual Review of Psychology* 58: 201–25.

Mazzula, S.L. 2009. *Bicultural competence: The role of acculturation, enculturation, collective self-esteem, and racial identity.* New York: Columbia University Press.

Mbiti, J.S. 2015. *Introduction to African religion.* Long Grove, IL: Waveland Press.

McIntyre, L., P.B. Patterson, L.C. Anderson, & C.L. Mah. 2016. "Household food insecurity in Canada: Problem definition and potential solutions in the public policy domain." *Canadian Public Policy* 42 (1): 83–93.

McKenna, S.A., & D.S. Main. 2013. "The role and influence of key informants in community-engaged research: A critical perspective." *Action Research* 11 (2): 113–24.

McLeod, J. 2013. *An introduction to counselling.* London: McGraw-Hill Education.

McMahon, M., N. Arthur, & S. Collins. 2008. "Social justice and career development: Looking back, looking forward." *Australian Journal of Career Development* 17 (2): 21–29.

McManus, K. 2013. "The Antigonish movement: Moses Coady and adult education today." *Canadian Journal of University Continuing Education* 24 (1): 15–22.

McMichael, A.J. 2013. "Globalization, climate change, and human health." *New England Journal of Medicine* 368 (14): 1335–43.

McMurtry, J.J., & F. Brouard. 2015. "Social enterprises in Canada: An introduction." *Canadian Journal of Nonprofit and Social Economy Research* 6 (1): 6.

McNay, L. 2013. *Foucault and feminism: Power, gender and the self.* New York: John Wiley & Sons.

Mehra, A., M. Kilduff, & D.J. Brass. 1998. "At the margins: A distinctiveness approach to the social identity and social networks of underrepresented groups." *Academy of Management Journal* 41 (4): 441–52.

Mentinis, M. 2014. "Friendship: Towards a radical grammar of relating." *Theory & Psychology* 25 (1): 63–79.

Merriam, S.B., & R.G. Brockett. 2011. *The profession and practice of adult education: An introduction.* New York: John Wiley & Sons.

Michaelides, M., & J. Benus. 2012. "Are self-employment training programs effective? Evidence from Project GATE." *Labour Economics* 19 (5): 695–705.

Migliore, L.A. 2011. "Relation between big five personality traits and Hofstede's cultural dimensions: Samples from the USA and India." *Cross Cultural Management: An International Journal* 18 (1): 38–54.

Mignone, J., & J. O'Neil. 2005. "Social capital and youth suicide risk factors in First Nations communities." *Canadian Journal of Public Health* 96 (Suppl 1): S51–54.

Miller, M.J., & K. Sendrowitz. 2011. "Counselling psychology trainees' social justice interest and commitment." *Journal of Counseling Psychology* 58 (2): 159–69.

Minkler, M., ed. 2012. *Community organizing and community building for health and welfare.* New Brunswick, NJ: Rutgers University Press.

Minkler, M., & N. Wallerstein, eds. 2011. *Community-based participatory research for health: From process to outcomes.* New York: John Wiley & Sons.

Minkov, M., & G. Hofstede. 2011. "The evolution of Hofstede's doctrine." *Cross Cultural Management: An International Journal* 18 (1): 10–20.

Mirowsky, J. 2013. "Analyzing associations between mental health and social circumstances." In *Handbook of the sociology of mental health,* edited by C. Aneshensel, C. Phelan, & J. Bierman, 143–65. London: Springer Netherlands.

Moane, G. 1994. "A psychological analysis of colonialism in an Irish context." *Irish Journal of Psychology* 15 (2–3): 250–65.

Moane, G. 2014. "Liberation psychology, feminism, and social justice psychology." In *The Praeger handbook of social justice and psychology,* edited by C. Johnson & H. Friedman, 115–30. Santa Barbara, CA: Praeger.

Mohatt, N.V., C.C.T. Fok, R. Burket, D. Henry, & J. Allen. 2011. "Assessment of awareness of connectedness as a culturally-based protective factor for Alaska native youth." *Cultural Diversity & Ethnic Minority Psychology* 17 (4): 444–55.

Montgomery, S.A., & A.J. Stewart. 2012. "Privileged allies in lesbian and gay rights activism: Gender, generation, and resistance to heteronormativity." *Journal of Social Issues* 68 (1): 162–77.

Moodley, R., & B. Kinha. 2015. "Therapy without borders: Bridging counselling and psychotherapy across cultures." In *International counselling case studies handbook,* edited by R. Moodley, M. Lengyell, R. Wu, & U. Gielen, 277–92. Alexandra, VA: American Counselling Association.

Moodley, R., & S. Palmer. 2014. *Race, culture and psychotherapy: Critical perspectives in multicultural practice.* New York: Routledge.

Moodley, R., S.L. Stewart, & C. Choudhury. 2011. "Special issue: Integrating traditional healing practices into health promotion and education." *International Journal of Health Promotion and Education* 49 (3): 72–73.

Morel, N., B. Palier, & J. Palme. 2012. *Towards a social investment welfare state? Ideas, policies and challenges.* New York: Policy Press.

Morrissette, V., B. McKenzie, & L. Morrissette. 1993. "Towards an Aboriginal model of social work practice: Cultural knowledge and traditional practices." *Canadian Social Work Review/Revue canadienne de service social* 10 (1): 91–108.

Mosley, E.A., C.K. Bouse, & K. Stidham Hall. 2015. "Water, human rights, and reproductive justice: Implications for women in Detroit and Monrovia." *Environmental Justice* 8 (3): 78–85.

Mukuka, R. 2012. "Afrocentric psychology: Conceptual perspectives from Bemba authors." *International Journal of Psychology* 47: 460–80.

Munn-Giddings, C., & R. Winter. 2013. *A handbook for action research in health and social care.* New York: Routledge.

Muntaner, C., E. Ng, C. Vanroelen, S. Christ, & W.W. Eaton. 2013. "Social stratification, social closure, and social class as determinants of mental health disparities." In *Handbook of the sociology of mental health*, edited by C. Aneshensel, C. Phelan, & J. Bierman, 205–27. London: Springer Netherlands.

Murayama, H., Y. Fujiwara, & I. Kawachi. 2012. "Social capital and health: a review of prospective multilevel studies." *Journal of Epidemiology* 22 (3): 179–87.

Naples, N., ed. 2012. *Community activism and feminist politics: Organizing across race, class, and gender.* New York: Routledge.

Naples, N.A., & K. Bojar. 2013. *Teaching feminist activism: Strategies from the field.* New York: Routledge.

Neto, L.M., & H.Á. Marujo. 2014. "Positive community psychology and positive community development: Research and intervention as transformative-appreciative actions." In *Positive Nations and Communities*, edited by Helena Águeda Marujo & Luís Miguel Neto, 209–30. London: Springer.

Nettles, R., & R. Balter. 2011. *Multiple minority identities: Applications for practice, research, and training.* New York: Springer Publishing.

Neuman, S.B., & D. Celano. 2012. *Giving our children a fighting chance: Poverty, literacy, and the development of information capital.* New York: Teachers College Press.

Neuman, W.L. 2005. *Social research methods: Quantitative and qualitative approaches*, vol. 13, 26–28. Boston: Allyn and Bacon.

Neville, H.A., B. Viard, & L. Turner. 2015. "Race and recognition pathways to an affirmative black identity." *Journal of Black Psychology* 41 (3): 247–71.

Newman, J.A., & M. Lovell. 1993. "A description of a supervisory group for group counselors." *Counselor Education and Supervision* 33 (1): 22–31.

Nilsson, J., G.L. Svendsen, & G.T. Svendsen. 2012. "Are large and complex agricultural cooperatives losing their social capital?" *Agribusiness* 28 (2): 187–204.

Nobles, W.W. 2013. "Fundamental task and challenge of Black psychology." *Journal of Black Psychology* 39 (3): 292–99.

Nobles, W.W., & S. Cooper. 2013. "Bridging forward to African/Black psychology." *Journal of Black Psychology* 39 (3): 345–49.

Nores, M., C.R. Belfield, W.S. Barnett, & L. Schweinhart. 2005. "Updating the economic impacts of the High/Scope Perry Preschool program." *Educational Evaluation and Policy Analysis* 27 (3): 245–61.

Northern Star. 2016. "About us." Retrieved March 30, 2016, from: https://northernstarblankets.wordpress.com

Northouse, P.G. 2015. *Leadership: Theory and practice.* Los Angeles: Sage.

Nortje, G., B. Oladeji, O. Gureje, & S. Seedat. 2016. "Effectiveness of traditional healers in treating mental disorders: A systematic review." *Lancet Psychiatry* 3 (2): 154–70.

Nutbeam, D. 2008. "What would the Ottawa Charter look like if it were written today?" *Critical Public Health* 18 (4): 435–41.

O'Donovan, A., W.K. Halford, & B. Walters. 2011. "Towards best practice supervision of clinical psychology trainees." *Australian Psychologist* 46 (2): 101–12.

O'Hara, P. 2006. *Social inclusion health indicators: A framework for addressing the social determinants of health: A policy and practice paper.* Edmonton: Edmonton Social Planning Council.

O'Neill, R.E., R.W. Albin, K. Storey, R.H. Horner, & J.R. Sprague. 2014. *Functional assessment and program development.* Boston: Cengage Learning.

O'Shaughnessy, T., & A.R. Spokane. 2013. "Lesbian and gay affirmative therapy competency, self-efficacy, and personality in psychology trainees." *Counseling Psychologist* 41 (6): 825–56.

Obasi, E.M., S.L. Speight, D.M. Rowe, & L. Turner-Essel. 2012. "The Association of Black Psychologists: An organization dedicated to social justice." *Counseling Psychologist* 40 (5): 656–74.

Oden, S., L.J. Schweinhart, D.P. Weikart, S.M. Marcus, & Y. Xie. 2000. *Into adulthood: A study of the effects of Head Start.* Ypsilanti, MI: High/Scope Press.

Olson-Buchanan, J.B., L.L.K. Bryan, & L.F. Thompson, eds. 2013. *Using industrial-organizational psychology for the greater good: Helping those who help others.* New York: Routledge.

Omoto, A.M., ed. 2014. *Processes of community change and social action.* New York: Psychology Press.

Orozco, M., & R. Rouse. 2013. "Migrant hometown associations and opportunities for development." In *The community development reader,* edited by J. DeFillips & S. Saegert, 280–85. New York: Routledge.

Ortmann, G.F., & R.P. King. 2007. "Agricultural cooperatives I: History, theory and problems." *Agrekon* 46 (1): 18–46.

Ostrander, S.A. 2013. "Agency and initiative by community associations in relations of shared governance: between civil society and local state." *Community Development Journal: An International Forum* 48 (4): 511–24.

Owe, E., V.L. Vignoles, M. Becker, R. Brown, P.B. Smith, S.W. Lee, M. Eastbrook, et al. 2013. "Contextualism as an important facet of individualism–collectivism personhood beliefs across 37 national groups." *Journal of Cross-Cultural Psychology* 44 (1): 24–45.

Oyserman, D., H.M. Coon, & M. Kemmelmeier. 2002. "Rethinking individualism and collectivism: Evaluation of theoretical assumptions and meta-analyses." *Psychological Bulletin* 128 (1): 3–72.

Padilla, A.M., & E. Olmedo. 2009. "Synopsis of key persons, events, and associations in the history of Latino psychology." *Cultural Diversity & Ethnic Minority Psychology* 15 (4): 363–73.

Padilla, A.M., & R.A. Ruiz. 1973. *Latino mental health: A review of literature.* Rockville, MD: National Institute of Mental Health.

Palmer, A., & J. Parish. 2008. "Social justice and counselling psychology: Situating the role of graduate student research, education, and training." *Canadian Journal of Counselling* 42 (4): 278–92.

Paludi, M.A., & S. Haley. 2014. "Scientific racism." In *Encyclopedia of critical psychology*, edited by Thomas Teo, 1697–700. New York: Springer.

Paniagua, F.A. 2013. *Assessing and treating culturally diverse clients: A practical guide.* Los Angeles: Sage.

Parham, T.A., A. Ajamu, & J.L. White. 2015. *Psychology of Blacks: Centering our perspectives in the African consciousness.* New York: Psychology Press.

Parra-Cardona, J.R., K. Holtrop, & D. Cordova. 2005. "'We are clinicians committed to cultural diversity and social justice': Good intentions that can wane over time." *Guidance & Counselling* 21 (1): 36–46.

Parsons, F. 1909. *Choosing a vocation.* Boston: Houghton Mifflin.

Passmore, K. 2014. *Fascism: A very short introduction.* Oxford: Oxford University Press.

Pedersen, P., & W. Lonner, eds. 2015. *Counselling across cultures.* 7th ed. New York: Sage.

Peel, E., & D. Riggs. 2014. *Introducing lesbian, gay, bisexual, trans and queer psychology.* University of Worcester. Retrieved September 4, 2016, from: http://eprints.worc.ac.uk/3456/

Peffer, R.G. 2014. *Marxism, morality, and social justice.* Princeton, NJ: Princeton University Press.

Pehrson, S., & C.W. Leach. 2012. "Beyond 'old' and 'new': For a social psychology of racism." In *Beyond prejudice: Extending the social psychology of conflict, inequality and social change*, edited by J. Dixon and M. Levine, 120–38. New York: Cambridge University Press.

Penfold, G., L. Rethoret, & T. MacDonald. 2016. "Non-profit and co-operative organizations and the provision of social housing." *Scaling up: The convergence of social economy and sustainability*, edited by M. Gismondi, S. Connelly, M. Beckie, S. Markey, & M. Roseland, 169–92. Edmonton: Athabasca University Press.

Pereira, H., & P.A. Costa. 2013. "1st international conference on LGBT psychology and related fields." *Psychology, Community & Health* 2 (2): 55–57.

Perlman, B., & E.A. Hartman. 1987. "Psychologist administrators in community mental health organizations." *Professional Psychology, Research and Practice* 18 (1): 36–41.

Perlman, D., A.G. Hunter, & A.J. Stewart. 2015. "Psychology, history, and social justice: Concluding reflections." *Journal of Social Issues* 71 (2): 402–13.

Phillimore, J., & A. McCabe. 2015. "Small-scale civil society and social policy: The importance of experiential learning, insider knowledge and diverse motivations in shaping community action." *Voluntary Sector Review* 6 (2): 135–51.

Phillips, R. 2015. "Building community well-being across sectors with 'for benefit' community business." In *Community well-being and community development*, edited by S. Lee, Y. Kim, & R. Phillips, 25–37. London: Springer International Publishing.

Phillips, R., & R. Pittman. 2014. *An introduction to community development.* New York: Routledge.

Philp, M., S. Egan, & R. Kane. 2012. "Perfectionism, over commitment to work, and burnout in employees seeking workplace counselling." *Australian Journal of Psychology* 64 (2): 68–74.

Pickler, N. 2015. "Obama: 'Racism, we are not cured of it. And it's not just a matter of it not being polite to say n—— in public.'" Retrieved June 22, 2015, from:

http://news.nationalpost.com/news/world/obama-racism-we-are-not-cured-of-it-and-its-not-just-a-matter-of-it-not-being-polite-to-say-n-in-public

Pierro, A., B.H. Raven, C. Amato, & J.J. Bélanger. 2013. "Bases of social power, leadership styles, and organizational commitment." *International Journal of Psychology* 48 (6): 1122–34.

Pieterse, A.L., S.A. Evans, A. Risner-Butner, N.M. Collins, & L.B. Mason. 2009. "Multicultural competence and social justice training in counselling psychology and counselor education a review and analysis of a sample of multicultural course syllabi." *Counseling Psychologist* 37 (1): 93–115.

Pilisuk, M., J. McAllister, & J. Rothman. 1996. "Coming together for action: The challenge of contemporary grassroots community organizing." *Journal of Social Issues* 52 (1): 15–37.

Pomfret, R. 2013. *The economic development of Canada.* Toronto: Routledge.

Poonwassie, A., & A. Charter. 2001. "An Aboriginal worldview of helping: Empowering approaches." *Canadian Journal of Counselling* 35 (1): 63–73.

Poortinga, W. 2012. "Community resilience and health: The role of bonding, bridging, and linking aspects of social capital." *Health & Place* 18 (2): 286–95.

Porter, J. 2015. *Vertical mosaic: An analysis of social class and power in Canada.* Toronto: University of Toronto Press.

Portes, A., & E. Vickstrom. 2015. "Diversity, social capital, and cohesion." In *Migration: Economic change, social challenge*, edited by C. Dustmann, 161–86. Oxford: Oxford University Press.

Poteat, V.P. 2015. "Individual psychological factors and complex interpersonal conditions that predict LGBT-affirming behavior." *Journal of Youth and Adolescence* 44 (8): 1494–507.

Potvin, L., & C.M. Jones. 2011. "Twenty-five years after the Ottawa Charter: The critical role of health promotion for public health." *Canadian Journal of Public Health* 102 (4): 244–48.

Presbey, G.M. 2015. "Globalization and the crisis in Detroit." *Perspectives on Global Development and Technology* 14 (1–2): 261–77.

Prilleltensky, I. 1989. "Psychology and the status quo." *American Psychologist* 44 (5): 795–802.

Prilleltensky, I. 1997. "Values, assumptions, and practices: Assessing the moral implications of psychological discourse and action." *American Psychologist* 52 (5): 517–35.

Prilleltensky, I. 2001. "Value-based praxis in community psychology: Moving toward social justice and social action." *American Journal of Community Psychology* 29 (5): 747–78.

Prilleltensky, I. 2008. "The role of power in wellness, oppression, and liberation: The promise of psychopolitical validity." *Journal of Community Psychology* 36 (2): 116–36.

Prilleltensky, I. 2012. "Wellness as fairness." *American Journal of Community Psychology* 49 (1–2): 1–21.

Prilleltensky, I. 2013. "Wellness without fairness: The missing link in psychology." *South African Journal of Psychology* 43 (2): 147–55.

Public Health Agency of Canada. 2015. "Community action plan for children." Retrieved August 31, 2015, from: http://www.phac-aspc.gc.ca/hp-ps/dca-dea/prog-ini/capc-pace/index-eng.php

Punch, K.F. 2013. *Introduction to social research: Quantitative and qualitative approaches.* Atlanta: Sage.

Purcell, M. 2014. "Public participation in new local governance spaces: The case for community development in local strategic partnerships." In *The European Conference on Politics, Economics and Law 2014: Official conference proceedings,* edited by M. Purcell, 143–59. Huddersfield, UK: International Academic Forum.

Putnam, R.D. 1993. "The prosperous community." *American Prospect* 4 (13): 35–42.

Pyles, L. 2013. *Progressive community organizing: Reflective practice in a globalizing world.* New York: Routledge.

Rabaka, R. 2010. *Forms of Fanonism: Frantz Fanon's critical theory and the dialectics of decolonization.* New York: Lexington Books.

Rahilly, E.P. 2015. "The gender binary meets the gender-variant child: Parents' negotiations with childhood gender variance." *Gender & Society* 29 (3): 338–61.

Ramser, P. 1996. *Review of ethics for psychologists: A commentary on the APA ethics code.* Washington, DC: American Psychological Association.

Raphael, D. 2006. "Social determinants of health: Present status, unanswered questions, and future directions." *International Journal of Health Services* 36 (4): 651–77.

Raphael, D. 2009. *Social determinants of health: Canadian perspectives.* Toronto: Canadian Scholars' Press.

Ratner, C. 2012. "Macro cultural psychology." In *The Oxford handbook of culture and psychology,* edited by J. Valsiner, 207–37. London: Oxford.

Ratner, C. 2014. "Psychology of oppression." In *Encyclopedia of critical psychology,* edited by T. Teo, 1557–70. New York: Springer.

Ratts, M.J., & P.B. Pedersen. 2014. *Counselling for multiculturalism and social justice: Integration, theory, and application.* New York: John Wiley & Sons.

Rauch, A., J.S. Deker, & A.G. Woodside. 2015. "Consuming alone: Broadening Putnam's 'bowling alone' thesis." *Psychology & Marketing* 32 (9): 967–76.

Realo, A., & M. Beilmann. 2012. "Individualism–collectivism and social capital at the individual level." *Trames* 16 (3): 205–17.

Reamer, F.G. 2012. *Boundary issues and dual relationships in the human services.* New York: Columbia University Press.

Reed, R., & L. Smith. 2014. "A social justice perspective on counselling and poverty." In *Counselling for multiculturalism and social justice: Integration, theory, and application,* edited by M. Ratts & P. Pedersen, 259–74. Alexandra, VA: American Counseling Association.

Reeve, D. 2000. "Oppression within the counselling room." *Disability & Society* 15 (4): 669–82.

Reeves, A., & S.L. Stewart. 2015. "Exploring the integration of Indigenous healing and Western psychotherapy for sexual trauma survivors who use mental health services at Anishnawbe Health Toronto." *Canadian Journal of Counselling and Psychotherapy* 49 (1): 57–78.

Rein, M. 1969. "Social planning: The search for legitimacy." *Journal of the American Institute of Planners* 35 (4): 233–44.

Reisch, M., & J. Andrews. 2014. *The road not taken: A history of radical social work in the United States.* New York: Routledge.

Reutter, L., W. Sword, D. Meagher-Stewart, & E. Rideout. 2004. "Nursing students' beliefs about poverty and health." *Journal of Advanced Nursing* 48 (3): 299–309.

Richards, P.S., & A.E. Bergin. 2005. *A spiritual strategy for counselling and psychotherapy.* Washington, DC: American Psychological Association.

Richardson, B. 1989. *Drumbeat: Anger and renewal in Indian country.* Toronto: Summerhill Press.

Rivlin, A.M. 2015. *Systematic thinking for social action.* Washington, DC: Brookings Institution Press.

Roberts, H. 1979. *Community development: Learning and action.* Toronto: University of Toronto Press.

Robinson, B., & M.G. Hanna. 1994. "Lessons for academics for grassroots community organizing: A case study—the Industrial Areas Foundation." *Journal of Community Practice* 1 (4): 63–94.

Robinson, L. 2012. *Psychology for social workers: Black perspectives on human development and behaviour.* New York: Routledge.

Roehr, B. 2012. Obituary: Richard Isay. *The British Medical Journal.* Retrieved September 4, 2016, from: http://www.bmj.com/content/345/bmj.e5609.full

Roopnarine, J., & J.E. Johnson. 2013. *Approaches to early childhood education.* Columbus, OH: Merrill/Prentice Hall.

Root, M.P., & L. Brown. 2014. *Diversity and complexity in feminist therapy.* New York: Routledge.

Roseland, M. 2000. "Sustainable community development: Integrating environmental, economic, and social objectives." *Progress in Planning* 54 (2): 73–132.

Rothblum, E.D., & M. Hill. 2016. *Learning from our mistakes: Difficulties and failures in feminist therapy.* New York: Routledge.

Rothman, J. 1996. "The interweaving of community intervention approaches." *Journal of Community Practice* 3 (3–4): 69–99.

Roughley, R.A., & T.G. Morrison. 2013. "Introduction to the special issue on sexual orientation and gender identity in counselling psychology." *Canadian Journal of Counselling and Psychotherapy/Revue canadienne de counselling et de psychothérapie* 47 (1): 1–3.

Rowbotham, S. 2013. *Women in movement (Routledge revivals): Feminism and social action.* New York: Routledge.

Royse, D., B. Thyer, & D. Padgett. 2015. *Program evaluation: An introduction to an evidence-based approach.* Boston: Cengage.

Rubin, A., & E. Babbie. 2013. *Research methods for social work.* Boston: Cengage Learning.

Rubin, H., & I. Rubin. 1988. *Community organizing and development.* New York: Allyn and Bacon.

Rubin, J., & I.S. Rubin. 2008. *Community organizing and development.* 4th ed. New York: Pearson.

Rubington, E., & M. Weinberg. 2010. *The study of social problems: Seven perspectives.* 7th ed. London: Oxford University Press.

Runnymeade Trust. 1997. "Islamophobia." Retrieved March 2016 from: http://www.runnymedetrust.org/uploads/publications/pdfs/islamophobia.pdf

Russell, P.H. 2014. "Royal Commission on Aboriginal Peoples: An exercise in policy education." *Commissions of Inquiry and Policy Change: A Comparative Analysis* 154: 22–25.

Salmond, C., P. Crampton, P. King, & C. Waldegrave. 2006. "NZiDep: A New Zealand index of socioeconomic deprivation for individuals." *Social Science & Medicine* 62 (6): 1474–85.

Sarlo, C.A. 2009. *The economic well-being of Canadians: Is there a growing gap?* Vancouver: The Fraser Institute.

Savaya, R., & F. Gardner. 2012. "Critical reflection to identify gaps between espoused theory and theory-in-use." *Social Work* 37: 387–95.

Savickas, M.L. 2007. "Internationalisation of counselling psychology: Constructing cross-national consensus and collaboration." *Applied Psychology* 56 (1): 182–88.

Scanlon, E., & K. Devine. 2001. "Residential mobility and youth well-being: Research, policy, and practice issues." *Journal of Sociology and Social Welfare* 28 (1): 119–38.

Schalock, R.L., & C.V. Thornton, eds. 2013. *Program evaluation: A field guide for administrators.* New York: Springer Science & Business Media.

Scharrer, E., & S. Ramasubramanian. 2015. "Intervening in the media's influence on stereotypes of race and ethnicity: The role of media literacy education." *Journal of Social Issues* 71 (1): 171–85.

Schriner, K.F., & S.B. Fawcett. 1988. "Development and validation of a community concerns report method." *Journal of Community Psychology* 16 (3): 306–16.

Schweinhart, L.J., & D.P. Weikart. 1993. "Success by empowerment: The High/Scope Perry preschool study through age 27." *Young Children* 49 (1): 54–58.

Schweinhart, L.J., & D.P. Weikart. 1997. "The High/Scope preschool curriculum comparison study through age 23." *Early Childhood Research Quarterly* 12 (2): 117–43.

Schwenk, C.R. 1988. *The essence of strategic decision making.* Lexington, MA: Lexington Books.

Scott, J. 2012. *Social network analysis.* Atlanta: Sage.

Seitz, J., & P. O'Neill. 1996. "Ethical decision-making and the code of ethics of the Canadian Psychological Association." *Canadian Psychology* 37 (1): 23–30.

Selsky, J.W., & A.E. Smith. 1994. "Community entrepreneurship: A framework for social change leadership." *Leadership Quarterly* 5 (3–4): 277–96.

Shakil, M. 2015. "Social work with community organization: A method of community development." *Journal for Studies in Management and Planning* 1 (4): 196–204.

Shalukoma, C., P. Duez, J. Bigirimana, J. Bogaert, C. Stévigny, C. Pongombo, & M. Visser. 2016. "Characterization of traditional healers in the mountain forest region of Kahuzi-Biega, South-Kivu, DR Congo." *Biotechnologie, Agronomie, Société et Environnement* 20 (1): 25–41.

Shapiro, T., T. Meschede, & S. Osoro. 2013. *The roots of the widening racial wealth gap: Explaining the black-white economic divide.* Waltham, MA: Institute on Assets and Social Policy.

Sharf, R. 2015. *Theories of psychotherapy & counselling: Concepts and cases.* New York: Cengage Learning.

Sue, D.W., R.T. Carter, M.T. Casas, N.A. Fouad, A.E. Ivey, M. Jensen, T. LaFromboise, et al. 1998. *Multicultural counselling competencies: Individual and organizational development.* Thousand Oaks, CA: Sage.

Sugrue, T.J. 2014. *The origins of the urban crisis: Race and inequality in postwar Detroit.* Princeton, NJ: Princeton University Press.

Sullivan, M.J., K.M. McNamara, M. Ybarra, & E.Q. Bulatao. 1995. "Psychologists as state legislators: Introduction to the special section." *Professional Psychology, Research and Practice* 26 (5): 445–48.

Sullivan, T.J. 2012. *Introduction to social problems.* Toronto: Pearson.

Suresha, R., ed. 2016. *Bisexual perspectives on the life and work of Alfred C. Kinsey.* New York: Routledge.

Sutherland, N., C. Land, & S. Böhm. 2013. "Anti-leaders (hip) in social movement organizations: The case of autonomous grassroots groups." *Organization* 21 (6): 759–61.

Sutphen, M.P., & B. Andrews, eds. 2003. *Medicine and colonial identity.* London: Routledge.

Swanepoel, H., & F. De Beer. 2012. *Community development: Breaking the cycle of poverty.* Claremont, South Africa: Juta and Company.

Swank, E., & B. Fahs. 2012. "Resources, social networks, and collective action frames of college students who join the gay and lesbian rights movement." *Journal of Homosexuality* 59 (1): 67–89.

Tamasese, K., C. Peteru, C. Waldegrave, & A. Bush. 2005. "Ole Taeao Afua, the new morning: A qualitative investigation into Samoan perspectives on mental health and culturally appropriate services." *Australian and New Zealand Journal of Psychiatry* 39 (4): 300–09.

Tamasese, T., & C. Waldgrave. 2012. "Belonging, sacredness and liberation." Paper presented at Therapeutic Conversations X Conference, Vancouver, BC.

Tamburro, A., & P.R. Tamburro. 2014. "Social services and Indigenous peoples of North America: Pre-colonial to contemporary times." In *Social issues in contemporary Native America: Reflections from Turtle Island*, edited by H. Weaver, 45–58. New York: Routledge.

Tate, K.A., E.T. Rivera, & L.M. Edwards. 2015. "Colonialism and multicultural counselling competence research: A liberatory analysis." In *Decolonizing "multicultural" counselling through social justice*, edited by K. Tate, E. Torres Rivera, & L. Edwards, 41–54. New York: Springer.

Tennant, M., M. O'Brien, & J. Sanders. 2008. *The history of the non-profit sector in New Zealand.* Wellington, NZ: Office for the Community and Voluntary Sector.

The Family Centre. 2015. Publications. Retrieved August 22, 2015, from: http://www.familycentre.org.nz/Publications/index.html

Thomas, R. 2016. *Planning Canada: A case study approach.* London: Oxford University Press.

Thoreson, R.R. 2014. *Transnational LGBT activism.* Minneapolis: University of Minnesota Press.

Thornicroft, G., & S. Maingay. 2002. "The global response to mental illness: An enormous health burden is increasingly being recognised." *British Medical Journal* 325 (7365): 608–10.

Tilly, C. 2014. "Disintegrating democracy at work: Labor unions and the future of good jobs in the service economy." *Contemporary Sociology: A Journal of Reviews* 43 (1): 77–79.

Tong, R. 2013. *Feminist thought: A comprehensive introduction.* New York: Routledge.

Tonnies, F. 1957. *Community and society.* East Lansing: Michigan State University Press.

Toomey, R.B., & S.T. Russell. 2013. "Gay-straight alliances, social justice involvement, and school victimization of lesbian, gay, bisexual, and queer youth implications for school well-being and plans to vote." *Youth & Society* 45 (4): 500–22.

Tracy, E.M., & J.K. Whittaker. 1990. "The social network map: Assessing social support in clinical practice." *Families in Society* 71 (8): 461–470.

Tracy, E.M., & N. Abell. 1994. "Social network map." *Social Work Research* 18 (1): 56–60.

Triandis, H.C., & M.J. Gelfland. 1998. "Converging measurement of horizontal and vertical individualism and collectivism." *Journal of Personality and Social Psychology* 74: 118–28.

Trierweiler, S.J., & G. Stricker. 2013. *The scientific practice of professional psychology.* New York: Springer Science & Business Media.

Trompenaars, F. 2012. "Foreward." In *Building cultural competence: Innovative activities and models,* edited by K. Berardo & D.K. Deardorff. Sterling, VA: Stylus Publishing.

Truth and Reconciliation Commission of Canada. 2015. *Calls to action.* Ottawa: Truth and Reconciliation Commission of Canada.

Tseng, W.S., G. Bartocci, G. Rovera, V. Infante, & V. De Luca. 2014. "The future of cultural psychiatry." *World Cultural Psychiatry Research Review* 9: 27–39.

Turcotte, M. 2015. *Trends in social capital in Canada.* Ottawa: Statistics Canada.

Turtle Island Native Network. 2007. "In passing—Cree Elder, Dr. Joseph Couture." Retrieved September 4, 2016, from: http://www.turtleisland.org/discussion/viewtopic.php?f=22&t=5483

Tyler, T.R. 2000. "Social justice: Outcome and procedure." *International Journal of Psychology* 35 (2): 117–25.

Ubpin, B. 2011. "The 147 companies that control everything." *Forbes.* Retrieved August 14, 2015, from: http://www.forbes.com/sites/bruceupbin/2011/10/22/the-147-companies-that-control-everything/

Umaña-Taylor, A.J., & K.A. Updegraff. 2013. "Latino families in the United States." In *Handbook of marriage and the family,* edited by M. Sussman & S. Steinmetz, 723–47. New York: Springer.

United Nations. 2015. "Detroit: Disconnecting water from people who cannot pay—an affront to human rights." Retrieved August 22, 2015, from: http://www.ohchr.org/EN/NewsEvents/Pages/DisplayNews.aspx?NewsID=14777#sthash.DbfiCAB8.dpuf

Valencia-Garcia, D., J.M. Simoni, M. Alegría, & D.T. Takeuchi. 2012. "Social capital, acculturation, mental health, and perceived access to services among Mexican American women." *Journal of Consulting and Clinical Psychology* 80 (2): 177–85.

Van Stekelenburg, J. 2012. "The Occupy movement: Product of this time." *Development* 55 (2): 224–31.

Vargas, J.H., & M. Kemmelmeier. 2013. "Ethnicity and contemporary American culture: A meta-analytic investigation of horizontal-vertical individualism-collectivism." *Journal of Cross-Cultural Psychology* 44 (2): 195–222.

Vasquez, M.J. 2012. "Psychology and social justice: Why we do what we do." *American Psychologist* 67 (5): 337–46.

Veenstra, G., & A.C. Patterson. 2016. "Black-white health inequalities in Canada." *Journal of Immigrant and Minority Health* 18 (1): 51–57.

Velez, B.L., B. Moradi, & C. DeBlaere. 2014. "Multiple oppressions and the mental health of sexual minority Latina/o individuals." *Counseling Psychologist* 27: 222–29.

Vera, E.M., & S.L. Speight. 2003. "Multicultural competence, social justice, and counselling psychology: Expanding our roles." *Counseling Psychologist* 31 (3): 253–72.

Verbos, A.K., & M. Humphries. 2014. "A Native American relational ethic: An Indigenous perspective on teaching human responsibility." *Journal of Business Ethics* 123 (1): 1–9.

Verkuyten, M. 2004. *The social psychology of ethnic identity*. New York: Psychology Press.

Vodde, R., & J.P. Gallant. 2002. "Bridging the gap between micro and macro practice: Large scale change and a unified model of narrative-deconstructive practice." *Journal of Social Work Education* 38 (3): 439–58.

Vontress, C.E. 1988. "An existential approach to cross-cultural counselling." *Journal of Multicultural Counseling and Development* 16 (2): 73–83.

Voydanoff, P. 2014. *Work, family, and community: Exploring interconnections*. New York: Psychology Press.

Wahowiak, L. 2014. "Access to water surfaces as human rights issue as poor in Detroit lose services: Sanitation at risk." *Nation's Health* 44 (8): 1–20.

Waldegrave, C. 2005. "'Just therapy' with families on low incomes." *Child Welfare* 84 (2): 265–76.

Waldegrave, C. 2009. "Cultural, gender, and socioeconomic contexts in therapeutic and social policy work." *Family Process* 48 (1): 85–101.

Wallace, B.A., & S.L. Shapiro. 2006. "Mental balance and well-being: Building bridges between Buddhism and Western psychology." *American Psychologist* 61 (7): 690–701.

Walrond-Skinner, S. 2014. *Family therapy (psychology revivals): The treatment of natural systems*. New York: Routledge.

Walsh, W.B. 2003. "Person-environment psychology and well-being." In *Counselling psychology and optimal human functioning: Contemporary topics in vocational psychology*, edited by W.B. Walsh, 93–121. Mahwah, NJ: Lawrence Erlbaum.

Walsh, W.B., K.H. Craik, & R.H. Price, eds. 1992. *Person-environment psychology: New directions and perspectives*. New York: Routledge.

Walsh, W.B., K.H. Craik, & R.H. Price, eds. 2000. *Person-environment psychology: New directions and perspectives*. New York: Routledge.

Warburton, D. 2013. *Community and sustainable development: Participation in the future*. New York: Routledge.

Ward, C., & L. Kus. 2012. "Back to and beyond Berry's basics: The conceptualization, operationalization and classification of acculturation." *International Journal of Intercultural Relations* 36 (4): 472–85.

Warren, R., & L. Lyon, eds. 1988. *New perspectives on the American community*. 5th ed. Chicago: Dorsey.

Waters, A., & L. Asbill. 2013. "Reflections on cultural humility." *American Psychological Association*.

Watts, R.J. 2004. "Integrating social justice and psychology." *Counseling Psychologist* 32 (6): 855–65.

Watts, R.J., & I. Serrano-García. 2003. "The quest for a liberating community psychology: An overview." *American Journal of Community Psychology* 31 (1): 73–78.

Watts, S. 2015. "The conscience of a nation: The social work of Jane Addams in Chicago's immigrant communities." *Saber and Scroll* 3 (2): 5–10.

Weaver, H.N. 2014. *Social issues in contemporary Native America: Reflections from Turtle Island.* London: Ashgate.

Webber, H.S. 2015. "A case study in community development." *The university as urban developer: Case studies and analysis,* edited by D. Perry & W. Weiwel, 65. Cambridge, MA: Lincoln Institute of Land Policy.

Weikart, D.P., J.T. Bond, & J.T. McNeil. 1978. *The Ypsilanti Perry Preschool Project: Preschool years and longitudinal results through fourth grade (No. 3).* Ypsilanti, MI: High/ Scope Foundation.

Weil, M. 2014. *Community practice: Conceptual models.* New York: Routledge.

Weil, M., M.S. Reisch, & M.L. Ohmer, eds. 2012. *The handbook of community practice.* New York: Sage.

Weinberg, M., & C. Campbell. 2014. "From codes to contextual collaborations: Shifting the thinking about ethics in social work." *Journal of Progressive Human Services* 25 (1): 37–49.

Wesley-Esquimaux, C.C. 2007. "The intergenerational transmission of historic trauma and grief." *Indigenous Affairs* 4: 6–11.

Whiteside, N. 2014. "The Beveridge Report and its implementation: A revolutionary project?" *Histoire@ Politique* 24 (3): 24–37.

Whitman, J.S., & C.J. Boyd. 2013. *The therapist's notebook for lesbian, gay, and bisexual clients: Homework, handouts, and activities for use in psychotherapy.* New York: Routledge.

Winter, L.A. 2015. "The presence of social justice principles within professional and ethical guidelines in international psychology." *Psychotherapy and Politics International* 13 (1): 55–66.

Winter, L.A., & T. Hanley. 2015. "'Unless everyone's covert guerrilla-like social justice practitioners …': A preliminary study exploring social justice in UK counselling psychology." *Counselling Psychology Review* 30 (2): 33–46.

Wong, P.T., L.C. Wong, & C. Scott. 2006. "Beyond stress and coping: The positive psychology of transformation." In *Handbook of multicultural perspectives on stress and coping,* edited by P. Wong & L. Wong, 1–26. New York: Springer.

Woolford, A. 2009. "Ontological destruction: Genocide and Canadian Aboriginal peoples." *Genocide Studies and Prevention* 4 (1): 81–97.

World Health Organization. 2008. *Human development report 2007/2008.* New York: Macmillan.

World Health Organization. 2013. *Global and regional estimates of violence against women: Prevalence and health effects of intimate partner violence and non-partner sexual violence.* New York: World Health Organization.

World Health Organization. 2014. "Mental health: A state of well-being." Retrieved September 14, 2016, from: http://www.who.int/features/factfiles/mental_health/en/

World Health Organization. 2015. "Social determinats of health." Retrieved August 10, 2015, from: http://www.who.int/social_determinants/en/

Wrong, D.H. 1968. "Some problems in defining social power." *American Journal of Sociology* 73 (6): 673–81.

Wyer, R.S., C.Y. Chiu, & Y.Y. Hong, eds. 2013. *Understanding culture: Theory, research, and application*. New York: Psychology Press.

Yang, K.S. 2012. "Indigenous psychology, Westernized psychology, and indigenized psychology: A non-Western psychologist's view." *Chang Gung Journal of Humanities and Social Sciences* 5 (1): 1–32.

Yang, L.Q., P.E. Spector, J.I. Sanchez, T.D. Allen, S. Poelmans, C.L. Cooper, L. Lapierre, et al. 2012. "Individualism–collectivism as a moderator of the work demands-strains relationship: A cross-level and cross-national examination." *Journal of International Business Studies* 43 (4): 424–43.

Yarbrough, E. 2012. "A conversation with Robert Cabaj, MD." *Journal of Gay & Lesbian Mental Health* 16 (3): 279–88.

Young, R.A., & J.J. Nicol. 2007. "Counselling psychology in Canada: Advancing psychology for all." *Applied Psychology* 56 (1): 20–32.

Zeldin, S., B.D. Christens, & J.L. Powers. 2013. "The psychology and practice of youth-adult partnership: Bridging generations for youth development and community change." *American Journal of Community Psychology* 51 (3–4): 385–97.

Zigler, E., & S.J. Styfco. 2004. *The Head Start debates*. Baltimore: Brookes Publishing Company.

INDEX